ROOTS OF RED CLYDESIDE 1910 – 1914?

LABOUR UNREST AND INDUSTRIAL RELATIONS IN WEST SCOTLAND

Edited by
WILLIAM KENEFICK
and
ARTHUR McIVOR

JOHN DONALD PUBLISHERS LTD
EDINBURGH

ISBN 0 85976 434 6

British Library Cataloguing in Publication Data
A catalogue record for this book is available from the British Library

Phototypeset by WestKey Limited, Falmouth, Cornwall
Printed and bound in Great Britain by Bell & Bain Limited, Glasgow

Acknowledgements

This book emerges from the work undertaken by the Glasgow Labour History Workshop – a research collective operating since 1987 – on the 1910–14 period of 'labour unrest'. We would like to duly express our thanks to all those who have given papers and who have contributed to the Workshop over the past few years. We have benefitted substantially from these debates and discussions, both formally and over a convivial drink in Buzbys or the Press Bar. Those responsible for the individual presentations during the 1994–5 series of Workshop seminars which have evolved into chapters in this volume merit a special thanks. Without their participation this book could not, of course, have been produced. Support for the Workshop over the years has come from the History Department, University of Strathclyde and from the Scottish Labour History Society. Various regional archivists and librarians helped with sources and information, but we would like to single out the indefatigable Audrey Canning, at the William Gallacher Library, Scottish Trades Union Congress, for particular thanks. We would also like to acknowledge our thanks to the Modern History Department, University of Dundee and the History Department, University of Strathclyde for providing administrative, secretarial and financial assistance to aid this publication. Finally, our thanks go to our partners and our families for their encouragement, support and forbearance during the preparation of this book.

W.K.
A.McI.

Contributors

Helen Corr

Lecturer in Sociology in the Department of Government, University of Strathclyde. Her interests lie in gender, teachers and education in the field of historical sociology. She has published extensively in these areas and on biographies of political activists in the Scottish labour movement in W. Knox, *Scottish Labour Leaders, 1918–1939* and in the forthcoming *New Dictionary of National Biography*.

Ricky Devlin

Part-time lecturer in Human Resource Management, University of Strathclyde (1992–6), and final year doctoral research student at the University of Paisley researching Scottish Trade Unionism 1885–1914: Federal Trade Unionism, Union Democracy and Class Formation. Member of the Glasgow Labour History Workshop.

Glasgow Labour History Workshop

A research collective, operating since 1987, based at the University of Strathclyde. Those involved in chapter 1 comprised I. Ballantyne, L. Christie, R. Devlin, W. Kenefick, I. Maver, A. McIvor, H. Paterson, and L. Tuach. Those involved in chapter 9 comprised I. Ballantyne, C. Collins, L. Forster, H. Maguiness, A. McIvor, H. Savage and L. Tuach.

William Kenefick

Lecturer in Modern Scottish History, Dept of Modern History, University of Dundee. Main research interests lie in the history of docks and waterside labour. Publications include *Ardrossan: the Key to the Clyde* (1993). Currently working on a book on the social history of Clydeside dockers. Member Glasgow Labour History Workshop.

William Knox

Lecturer in Scottish History, University of St Andrews. Research interests lie in Scottish social and labour history in the nineteenth and twentieth centuries. Has published extensively in these areas, including

Hanging by a Thread: The Scottish Cotton Industry, c.1850–1914 (Carnegie, 1995); *James Maxton* (Manchester University Press, 1987) and *Scottish Labour Leaders, 1918–1939* (Mainstream, 1984).

Irene Maver

Lecturer, Scottish History Department, University of Glasgow. Co-editor (with W Hamish Fraser) of the *History of Glasgow, volume II, 1833–1912* (Manchester University Press, 1996). Has contributed a number of articles on Glasgow's municipal politics between the eighteenth and twentieth centuries. Currently writing a single-volume history of Glasgow.

Arthur McIvor

Lecturer in History, University of Strathclyde. Research interests lie in employers, labour management and occupational health, c1850–1950. Publications include *Organised Capital: Employers' Associations and Industrial Relations in Northern England, 1880–1939* (Cambridge University Press, 1996) and (co-edited with Rob Duncan), *Militant Workers* (John Donald, 1992).

Alan McKinlay

Professor of Corporate Strategy, University of Stirling. Currently researching British business in Europe and the social history of industrial relations. Publications include *Strategy and the Human Resource* (Blackwell, 1993) and (with R.J. Morris), *The ILP on Clydeside, 1893–1932* (Manchester University Press, 1991).

George Rawlinson

Officer with Scottish Asian Action Committee. Previously a part-time history tutor\lecturer at Salford University and Glasgow Caledonian University. Member of the Glasgow Labour History Workshop. Publications and main research interests lie in the history of unemployment.

Alexander Renfrew

History postgraduate, University of Strathclyde. Currently writing up his doctorate on Mechanisation and Industrial Relations in Scottish Coalmining, c1880–1939. Member of the Glasgow Labour History Workshop.

Anna Robinson

History graduate, University of Strathclyde. Member of the Glasgow Labour History Workshop with particular interest in the history of women workers before First World War.

James Smyth

Lecturer in History, University of Stirling. Main interests lie in the history of women in politics, the Independent Labour Party and employment in local communities. Published extensively on these topics, including contributions to E. Breitenbach and E. Gordon (eds), *The World is Ill-Divided* (Edinburgh University Press, 1990) and *Out of Bounds* (Edinburgh University Press, 1992).

Contents

INTRODUCTION

Roots of Red Clydeside, c. 1910–1914?

Arthur McIvor and William Kenefick

Scottish labour history has developed significantly over the past thirty years or so, and with this proliferation of research has come a more detached, objective and scientific approach. But major weaknesses persist and coverage remains thin in many areas of working-class experience. Attention has been unduly focused upon the lives of male, skilled, protestant workers and on the classic period of 1914–1922, associated with the resurgence of class consciousness and the process of radicalisation, conventionally labelled 'Red Clydeside'.[1] This has generated lively and fruitful debates on skilled work culture and politics and on the impact of the First World War upon the nature of class relations. What we aim to do in this book is to shed some light into a neglected period within Scottish labour history – the Edwardian years – concentrating upon the experience of workers and their relationships with employers in the industrial region of Clydeside over the immediate pre-war years, c1910–14.

This was a period of unparalleled industrial unrest, with a major strike wave disrupting relatively peaceful social relations. There is little published material on this phenomenon in Scotland – and this is the basic *raison d'etre* for this collection of essays, which explore the causes, patterns, characteristics and implications of the labour unrest of c1910–14 on Clydeside.[2] One key objective is to push back the parameters of the Red Clydeside debate before 1914 and analyse the formative period for those participating in the well-known wartime and post-war protests against capital, landlords and the state. We hope this book will go some way towards challenging the orthodox interpretation which focuses on the First World War as the cause of the heightened class consciousness and militancy in the region. At the very least, we aim to suggest some revision and stimulate some debate. Needless to say, the contributors have differing views on this issue! If the volume generates

1

further thinking, discussion and research on this topic it will have achieved its primary purpose.

The historiography of the 1910–14 labour unrest

Whilst the Scottish dimension has been neglected, within British labour historiography the 'labour unrest' of 1910–14 has generated considerable commentary and much controversy. Contemporary opinion, whilst divided and diffuse, tended to stress the deep-rooted crisis that afflicted Edwardian society, the instability of political institutions and industrial relations. The mainstream press, including the *Glasgow Herald*, played its part in cultivating a sense of malaise through journalistic cliche and wildly sensationalist reporting of strikes and protests. Syndicalist, industrial unionist and socialist ideas were held up as primary agents in this dissolution of social stability:

> . . . Glasgow has felt the surge of a movement that has swept the great centres of population throughout the country. To us the most deplorable feature of the troubles into which the country has plunged is the utter indiscipline of the forces which agitation has set in motion. . . . The restraints imposed by the older and more respectable type of trade unionism are flouted by workers who have come under the spell of incendiary advisers like those who made the Confederation of Labour a menace to the structure of French society. . . . The present situation is the gravest that has been known for a century. . . .[3]

Such views were fuelled by alarmist prognoses from the government's conciliation department and from employers. The 1914 Annual Report of the Association of Chambers of Commerce warned: 'Syndicalism is one of the worst forms of tyranny which the world has ever seen'.[4] A sense of escalating crisis is encapsulated in George Dangerfield's classic treatise, *The Strange Death of Liberal England* (first published in 1935). Writing in the mid-1970s, Bob Holton argued that syndicalist ideas diffused widely within the working class and played a major role in the pre-war strike wave.[5] These years were characterised, Holton posits, by a 'proto-syndicalist mood of revolt' – characterised by spontaneous and unofficial action and a broad commitment within the working class to the notion of direct action to achieve reform. Moreover, there evolved in Britain a syndicalist

2

movement – an organisational structure with a distinctive political ideology and strategy – as important as that of France. Other writers have broadly accepted Holton's interpretation. Richard Price, for example, supporting the notion of social crisis between 1910–14 and claiming that syndicalist ideas permeated, to some degree or other, almost all trade unions during this period.[6] Raymond Challinor and Michael Haynes develop similar perspectives.[7]

Increasingly, however, such views have been challenged by historians who have argued that there was no 'crisis' in Edwardian society – continuity and stability were more notable than dramatic change – and that there is little solid evidence of syndicalist influence within unions and during the strikes of 1910–14.[8] This critique has come from the right and the left. Henry Pelling and Hugh Clegg have argued that there was negligible syndicalist influence within either the trade unions or the major industrial strikes between 1910–14.[9] Only a handful of dual unions were created, no large unions were imbued with revolutionary aims from within (though there was a shift to the left), the Triple Industrial Alliance was a failure in practice, and in only two of the fourteen main strikes in Britain over 1910–14 was there any significant syndicalist influence. To Hinton, Burgess, Van Gore and White these years witnessed a surge in class consciousness and a fracturing of relatively peaceful industrial relations, but there were clear limits to this challenge of labour: capitalism was not threatened and, significantly, syndicalist ideas played little part in this process.[10] Levels of industrial militancy, moreover, have been artificially distorted in an upward direction by inclusion of figures from coal mining, as Church has demonstrated.[11] In one of the most recent overviews of trade union history Laybourn affirms such interpretations, arguing that:

> . . . it is difficult, if not impossible, to believe that syndicalism was in any sense pervasive among the British working class . . . in essence, then, the impact of syndicalism has been exaggerated. There was little threat to the industrial status quo before 1914. . . .[12]

Similarly, E.H. Hunt notes that there was little support for syndicalism outside South Wales,[13] and even where there was an active syndicalist leadership, as could be seen along the South Wales waterfront – one Alf Cox being known locally as 'Tom Mann the

Second' – the rank and file 'were more concerned with gaining higher wages than overthrowing capital'.[14]

The movement away from 'labour' and towards social and 'working-class' history has also been important in putting the events of these years in perspective. John Benson's work, for example, has persuasively demonstrated just how little most workers were affected by trade unions, labour politics or strike action before World War One.[15] For the majority of workers, collective organisation and action were just not a significant part of their everyday experience. The problems of eking out a daily existence in a period of deep poverty and wide social inequalities was as likely to have a constraining as a radicalising impact.

What also appears evident from the literature, however, are marked regional variations in social relations prior to the First World War. In reality, it may well be that we have a rich mosaic of experience across Britain and that as a consequence generalisations are difficult, perhaps even impossible. Reid has argued this case persuasively.[16] There were marked geographical variations before First World War in levels of collective organisation, wage rates, strike propensity and in the ways in which employers responded to strikes.[17] The evidence indicates that syndicalism struck a chord in Liverpool, South Wales and London, particularly amongst transport workers, miners and building workers respectively.[18] One way to progress the debate on 1910–14 is to open up new, detailed, in-depth regional case studies and to encourage inter-regional analysis. The heavily industrialised and proletarianised region of west central Scotland provides as good a case study as any. Moreover, this region has particular significance because of the evidence of heightened class consciousness and a radical challenge to state and capital on 'Red Clydeside' during the 1914–18 war. If anywhere, surely we should expect to find evidence of sharpened class antagonisms and radical socialist and syndicalist ideologies on the Clyde before 1914. Is this the case? Was this area affected by the 'labour unrest' of 1910–14 and to what degree? Did the unrest destabilise Scottish capitalism and threaten the stability of pre-war Scottish society? How can the strike wave in west Scotland be explained? What was the role of Clydeside employers and management – frequently characterised within the literature as notoriously anti-union and authoritarian? And, what were the immediate effects and broader ramifications of this intense phase of industrial conflict?

Capital and labour relations on Clydeside, c. 1910–14

Within the more limited and fragmentary historiography of Scottish labour the experience of workers in the Edwardian period has been seriously neglected. This has been partly because the dynamics of change and crisis during the First World War and immediate post war years, embracing the debate on 'Red Clydeside', has acted as a magnet for Scottish labour historians, especially, though not exclusively, of the left.[19] Whilst the work of Knox, Gordon, Melling and Smith, amongst others, provides comprehensive and sensitive analyses of social relations on Clydeside from the mid-Victorian years, there has been no systematic treatment of the labour unrest of 1910–14 on Clydeside.[20] General social histories of Scotland simply ignore it.[21] What exists in Scotland is little more than a shadowy reflection of the debate on the 'labour unrest'. In Marwick's classic history of labour Scottish involvement in the main national strikes of these years is noted, with a short, narrative commentary which implies nothing distinctive occured north of the border.[22] In contrast to this assumption of convergence, James Young emphasises the spontaneous character of Scottish strike activity and the 'eruption of class consciousness' over 1910–14, but concludes that the labour unrest was less 'intense' than in England.[23] This seems a very dubious proposition and finds little support in the contributions to this volume.[24]

Where ideology and the role of syndicalism has been the focal point, as in the work of Challinor, Kendall and Vernon there has been a tendency to exaggerate the importance of syndicalist and industrial unionist ideology on the Clyde.[25] Here, the importance of the syndicalist- orientated Socialist Labour Party (SLP), the syndicalist-influenced British Socialist Party and the Marxist education classes of John MacLean (which started around 1908) in incubating class consciousness has been stressed. They all helped provide cadres of activists (notably miners and engineers) who stirred up discontent in the pre-war years. The SLP had its base on the Clyde and had created a dual union, the Industrial Workers of Great Britain (with a major foothold in the Singer Corporation, Clydebank in 1910–11). In his memoirs, Harry McShane commented on how syndicalist ideas permeated deep within the ranks of revolutionary socialists after 1910, generating an intense debate on the respective merits of industrial and political action as strategies to achieve social transformation.[26] To McShane, the socialist movement on the Clyde was enervated through political agitation, the Home Rule issue, and in the forge of industrial unrest and confrontation over 1910–14.

In contrast, Knox, Smith, Morris and McKinlay have argued that the revolutionary left – including the SLP and MacLean – had little influence in pre-war Clydeside labour politics, which was dominated by a commitment to parliamentarianism, labourism and 'respectable' protest.[27] Liberalism maintained its popularity on the Clyde up to 1914, and increasingly it was the crusading evangelism of the Independent Labour Party which attracted politically conscious workers, rather than syndicalist or Marxist ideas. Class consciousness on pre-war Clydeside was fractured, still in the process of composition, and whilst these were turbulent years, this was not a society in crisis. No hard evidence exists to support the notion of the working class on Clydeside defecting wholesale to socialist, never mind revolutionary socialist ideas on the eve of First World War.

The role of women workers also features quite prominently in the Scottish literature on the unrest of 1910–14. In the most detailed studies to date of pre-war industrial action in Scotland, Gordon has demonstrated that syndicalist influence was insignificant in the numerous strikes involving women workers.[28] Such struggles were a reaction against domineering employers, to gain tangible improvements in wages and working conditions and to obtain recognition and bargaining rights for trade unions as a mechanism to protect concessions and improvements over the long term. Gordon's work does, however, demonstrate the politicising impact of industrial action. She also definitively challenges the notion of female quiescence and docility in industrial relations before the First World War.

The contributions to this volume engage with various aspects of these questions and areas of debate. One issue has been the basic one of measuring levels of activity. It has been demonstrated through the quantitative research of the Glasgow Labour History Workshop (chapter 1) and the work of Devlin (chapter 3) that official figures tend to drastically under-record strikes, and that Clydeside workers were as involved in industrial action as other comparable industrial regions over these years. As in England, strike propensity was concentrated in the mining, shipbuilding, engineering, metals, textiles and transport sectors. However, unlike England there was no noticeable tailing off in the strike rate. Industrial militancy on the Clyde was sustained through to the outbreak of war in 1914. Moreover, chapters in this volume by Knox and Corr on cotton mill workers (ch 5), Rawlinson and Robinson on the United Turkey Red strike of 1911 (ch. 8) and the GLHW on the Singer strike (ch. 9) all provide some further support for Gordon's thesis that female workers were actively engaged in industrial militancy and protest. Thus, Young's dismissive under- statement of levels of conflict in Scotland in contrast to England appears to us to be untenable.[29] However, it is important to keep this in perspective and to recognise that the prevailing situation hardly constituted a paralysis of industry capable of destabilising capitalism or threatening the stability of society in west Scotland over 1910–14. Whilst the strike wave across the Clyde had breadth as well as depth, there were still whole sectors which were not affected and where labour relations remained stable and workers quiescent, including the professions, agriculture and fishing, clothing, domestic service and shopwork. The turbulence of these years, therefore, needs to be qualified. Indeed, even taking a generous estimate (based on comparing strike statistics in chapter 1 against total employment – see table on p. 8, on average Clyde workers lost less than 2 per cent of their annual working time over 1910–14 through engagement in strike action.

Explaining the pre-war strike wave on Clydeside has proven difficult, not least because each dispute was unique and the product of a conjuncture of different circumstances and contingencies. However, there are some common threads running through the constituent chapters of this volume which coagulate into a significant contribution to pivotal debates on the labour unrest of 1910–14. Four themes merit highlighting here: firstly, the issue of syndicalism and the role of ideology in the Clyde strikes; secondly, the economic factors linked to labour markets and wages; thirdly, the role of employers and labour management; and, fourthly, the alienating effects of changes in work organisation and the labour process commonly summarised in the notion of 'work intensification'.

Whilst syndicalist and industrial unionist ideas were present and under widespread discussion, the evidence from the contributors to this volume indicates that syndicalist organisations (notably the SLP) attracted little support and that syndicalist ideas had only a very marginal

Main sectors of employment in the Clydeside region, 1911

	male	female	total
transport and communications	88,441	7,033	95,474
miscellaneous services	25,427	68,228	93,655
distribution	52,611	32,086	84,697
mining and quarrying	82,406	1,048	83,453
textiles	20,052	45,082	65,134
mechanical engineering	58,774	1,916	60,690
construction	52,682	67	52,749
clothing	15,597	36,894	52,491
metal manufacture	48,748	150	48,898
shipbuilding and marine engineering	45,314	268	45,582
agriculture, fishing and forestry	31,672	7,625	39,297
professional and scientific	17,388	16,497	33,885
other metal manufacture	25,784	1,462	27,246
food, drink and tobacco	13,678	8,775	22,453
Total Employed	716,239	262,505	978,744
Total Population	1,116,379	1,142,463	2,258,842

Source: C.H. Lee, *British Regional Employment Statistics, 1841–1971* (1979). The Clydside region is defined as comprising the counties of Dumbarton, Lanark, Renfrew, Ayr, Argyll and Bute.

influence upon the labour unrest on Clydeside prior to 1914. Syndicalists such as Tom Mann and Madame Sorgue addressed meetings in Scotland and there is evidence of public debates on the merits and drawbacks of industrial unionism (see chapters 6 and 8). Victor Grayson toured Scotland during the 1912 miners' strike, expressing sympathy for syndicalism and empathy with Mann's ideas, including his inflammatory recommendation to soldiers not to shoot on strikers. Anarcho-syndicalism also had a foothold in Clydeside, with a presence significant enough to produce a monthly paper, *The Herald of Revolt*.[31] James Larkin received widespread rank-and-file support during well-attended mass meetings in Glasgow and Edinburgh in December 1913, in marked contrast to TUC opposition to calls for a general strike in sympathy with the locked-out Dublin transport workers.[32] However, in only one strike – at Singer, Clydebank in 1911 – is there clear evidence of direct syndicalist involvement (see chapter 9). Here the SLP penetrated the plant, successfully developed the tactic of sympathy action and achieved, briefly, mass membership of its industrial union, the sewing machine branch of the IWGB. However, SLP involvement did not constitute domination. The ILP was as much in evidence during the Singer strike, and the 200 strong strike committee was composed of workers from a broad range of political views.[33]

Moreover, the recurrent demands for trade union recognition across a broad swathe of strikes on the Clyde over 1910–14 (especially those of women and unskilled labourers) – noted by almost all the contributors – clearly demonstrates a commitment to (rather than alienation from) trade-union structures and collective bargaining, which cuts against the grain of syndicalist criticisms of the mechanism of conciliation between capital and labour. In the mining towns in Lanarkshire, Renfrew has identified only a very shadowy syndicalist presence: MacLean's Marxist economics classes appear to have had more influence (chapter 7). Neither McKinlay (shipbuilding, metal working and engineering: chapter 4), Knox and Corr (the cotton thread sector: chapter 5), Maver (tramwaymen: chapter 10), Kenefick (docks: chapter 6) nor Rawlinson and Robinson (United Turkey Red: chapter 8) find signs of any tangible syndicalist presence at an organisational level during the industrial disputes of this period.

Accounting for the relative failure of syndicalism either to sink deep organisational roots or significantly to influence strike activity on the Clyde is difficult. However, part of the explanation may well lie in the more localised, independent, federalised and activist-led trade-union movement in Scotland, where the trades councils played a much more important role than in England.[34] Within this structure, Scottish workers did not have such a sense of distance from their union officials. The space occupied by the ILP may well have also stole some of the thunder of the syndicalists.[35] Joan Smith has also argued that the relative absence of sectarianism on the Clyde, in contrast to Liverpool, contributed to support for the ILP and a weakened syndicalist presence on Clydeside:

> The labour movement in Glasgow did not face a hostile protestant working class. In Liverpool protestant sectarianism more or less dictated a syndicalist approach to organisation; socialist trade unions pinned their hopes on the idea that one big strike wave would sweep aside both religious sectarianism and the political basis for Tory Democracy and Catholic Nationalism.[36]

Finally, the extreme dogmatism and sectarianism of the DeLeonite SLP-IWGB strand of syndicalism dominant on the Clyde alienated much potential support.[37] Dual unionism lacked applicability where (unlike in the USA) a matrix of unions were already in existence.

There is, however, much evidence to suggest that Holton's notion of a 'proto-syndicalist mood of revolt' has some resonance on the Clyde over 1910–14. Sectionalism and conservatism were still clearly evident within the crafts, as McKinlay has demonstrated in chapter 4. However, much of the militancy of 1910–14 in west Scotland (as elsewhere) was spontaneous and unofficial and involved sympathy action and heavy organised picketing and mass rallies, often in a carnival atmosphere. The more widespread diffusion of syndicalist (and socialist) ideas was undoubtedly enhanced by the sacking of those most active in the Singer strike of 1911 and their subsequent dispersal across the length and breadth of the Clyde (see chapter 9). However, in the absence of corroborative material, and examples of syndicalist organisation and activity in other strikes on the Clyde over 1910–14, the conclusion must be that syndicalist ideology played only a very limited role in the industrial discontent of these years.

Economic factors undoubtedly played an important role in generating industrial conflict on the Clyde over 1910–14, as the GLHW have argued in chapter 1. The erosion of real wage levels and bitter experience of poverty and deprivation on the Clyde during the depressions of 1904–5 and 1908–9 constituted the preconditions for industrial militancy. Tightening labour markets during the economic boom years of 1910–14 provided workers with the capacity to organise and the confidence to undertake and sustain industrial action (Paisley and Neilston excepted: see Knox and Corr; chapter 5). This was especially the case amongst female workers and the unskilled where trade union membership increased dramatically, workers flooding especially into the National Federation of Women Workers and the Workers' Union. On the other hand, such a scenario eroded employers bargaining power, not least by impacting adversely upon their capability to utilise the time-honoured tactic of exploiting the overstocked Clydeside labour market to recruit replacement and blackleg labour. Successful strike action had something of a domino effect, demonstrating the utility of direct action and encouraging other groups to break with tradition and try such tactics. Knox and Corr, Rawlinson and Robinson and the GLHW (in chapter 9) all provide examples of previously acquiescent and deferential groups of workers becoming radicalised by the force of events over c1910–14.

Several chapters suggest that employers' strategies and labour management tactics were critical factors which incubated discontent, raising the tempo of strike action on Clydeside over 1910–14. This casts further light into a relatively neglected dimension of the labour unrest debate, noted, though not developed, by Hugh Clegg.[38] The evidence for 1910–14 largely confirms prevailing interpretations of pre-war Clydeside industrialists as authoritarian anti-unionists with a deep-rooted antipathy to collective bargaining. Devlin's innovative computer-based quantitative inter-regional comparison of strike activity and employer responses to strikes provides much substantive evidence to corroborate the notion of despotic control exercised by Clydeside employers (see chapter 3). Within a cruder, archaic industrial relations system, managerial authoritarianism prevailed; trade unions were numerically weaker and strikes were less successful than elsewhere. Despotic paternalism characterised United Turkey Red, the thread manufacturers in Paisley and Neilston, and the Glasgow tramways, under the virtual dictatorship of the general manager, James Dalrymple (chapters 5, 8 and 10). However, McIvor (in chapter 2) and McKinlay (in chapter 4) suggest some caveats to this thesis, emphasising the range of employer attitudes and strategies. McKinlay notes the contrasting managerial styles between shipbuilding, engineering and steel manufacture. In the latter industry, little attempt was made before 1914 to extend managerial control over the labour process, subcontracting craftworkers being left with virtual autonomy over the way work was organised and performed. McIvor discusses the role of employers' organisations (both as strikebreakers and mediators), the range of management policies and emphasises the tactical manoeuvring taking place over the period 1910 to 1914. These were years when union recognition and collective bargaining rights were spreading steadily on Clydeside, partly due to pressure from the Labour Department of the Board of Trade. Nevertheless, heavy-handed and draconian management policies, at both the collective and company levels, continued to be much in evidence and to alienate Clydeside workers. Such intransigence significantly cranked up levels of discontent and prolonged disputes as workers increasingly insisted on union recognition as a prerequisite for returning to work.

Product market developments, notably the cumulative impact of increased competition and squeezed profit margins, helped to crystallise managerial attempts to cut labour costs. This pressure on profits intensified employer intolerance of trade unions and precipitated a drive to extend control over the labour process and intensify work-loads. Richard Price has been the foremost proponent of the idea that 1910–14 witnessed a particularly bitter phase of a long struggle over control and authority at work.[39] Almost all the contributions refer to this phenomenon, which must be considered, in the light of so much evidence, to be a major causal factor in the strike wave on Clydeside over 1910–14. Kenefick argues that attempts to speed-up work and cut labour costs through reduction of squad sizes generated a bitter struggle for control over the labour process in the Glasgow docks (chapter 6). Renfrew identifies work intensification as a major cause of discontent in the Lanarkshire coalfield and notes a positive correlation between mechanisation and strike propensity (chapter 7). Fatigue caused by long working hours on the trams was an important causal factor in the 1911 tramwaymen's strike (Maver; chapter 10). Similarly, work intensification was a pivotal issue in the Singer, United Turkey Red and the Paisley and Neilston thread industry strikes (see chapters 5, 8 and 9).

1910–14: Roots of Red Clydeside?

To what extent then can the roots of Red Clydeside be located in the years c1910–14? On the one hand, there is no denying the massive transformations in the labour market, working conditions, state controls, and levels of class consciousness that took place as a result of the First World War. McKinlay has argued in chapter 4 that class consciousness was severely fractured within the engineering, shipbuilding and metal working trades on the Clyde pre-1914 and that it took the radically different circumstances of the 1914–18 war to erode craft sectionalism and radicalise metal working artisans. Neither Knox and Corr nor Kenefick find much evidence for their groups of workers (cotton mill workers and dockers respectively) being actively engaged in wartime industrial militancy: they were not part of the constituency of Red Clydeside. The same might be said for the tramway workers. Jim Smyth (in chapter 11) and Knox have posited that labour-process developments, work intensification and industrial unrest over 1910–14 did not necessarily translate into political awareness.[40] The political wing of the labour movement on Clydeside, whilst diverse, virtually ignored women and the unskilled, and, increasingly over 1910–14, became divorced from the industrial struggle and even hostile to it (chapter 11).[41] This dualism within the labour movement, between the separate roles of trade unions and political groups, undermined worker resistance and eroded class consciousness.

On the other hand, industrial relations in the pre-war period of unrest undoubtedly had some influence upon workers and activists. For many – such as Harry McShane – these were formative years in which political ideas and class consciousness were incubated. Moreover, the tight labour markets of the pre-war years facilitated labour mobility and aided the process whereby ideas were diffused across the Clyde. The mass sacking of activists in the spring and summer of 1911 from the one plant on the Clyde (Singer) where syndicalism had a significant presence was also influential. Clydeside workers were becoming more aware of exploitative working (and housing) conditions and here the increasingly sophisticated information networks of the growing trade-union movement, combined with the socialist press (especially the ILP paper *Forward*) played a key role. In many of the case studies in this book, the industrial action undertaken had the effect of politicising workers. This is indicated at one level in the surge in union membership: STUC affiliated membership almost doubled over 1909–1914, which represented a higher proportionate rise than over the war years (Smyth: chapter 11).

There is also evidence of sharpening awareness of class divisions, and an increasing commitment to political organisations on the left. The contributions here suggest that two other (interrelated) factors are of prime importance in accounting for this. The outburst of industrial militancy and the heightened levels of class consciousness that ensued represented a spontaneous and embittered reaction against the draconian attitudes of authoritarian Clydeside employers and managers and, more importantly, against the pervasive tendency, in a more hostile economic environment, to intensify workloads and adversely shift the wage-for-effort exchange in favour of capital. This critically fractured the fragile balance of reciprocal rights and obligations, deference and paternalist responsibility that had maintained relatively peaceful relations between capital and labour on the Clyde in the second half of the nineteenth century.

The alienating impact of a range of other social factors operating on Clydeside in the years leading up to the First World War is also of importance. There was a mounting housing crisis in the city. Over-crowding was substantially higher in Glasgow – where in 1902 almost 60 per cent of the population lived in dwellings averaging more than two persons per room – than comparable Scottish and English cities.[42] Moreover, the overcrowding problem was getting worse during the first decade of the twentieth century and was exacerbated by a deteri-oration in real wage levels as prices escalated and by the characteristic insecurity and volatility of the Clydeside labour market.[43] Melling, Morris and others have demonstrated how such conditions generated a growing subterranean class struggle between landlords and tenants over rents, arrears, sequestrations and evictions over the period c1900–1914.[44] Court proceedings over evictions in Glasgow increasingly degenerated, Melling has noted, 'into a melodrama of class confrontation'.[45]

Thus the years immediately before First World War saw class conflict reach unprecedented heights on Clydeside. Class conscious-ness was to be further forged and class identities sharpened in the pressures wrought by the wartime emergency and the struggles over dilution, speed-up, profiteering, rents and draconian state controls over the period 1915–20. Nevertheless, it was upon firm foundations that the 'Red' Clydeside of the First World War and immediate post-war years was constructed. It remains highly significant that industrial unrest in the Clydeside region, against the national trend, was sustained right up to the outbreak of war. This escalating workers' challenge to the autocratic and unilateral control of Clydeside employers led one engineering employer, in an oft-quoted statement, to comment,

> . . . inroads on the powers of management in the shops had become so serious that, had war not intervened, the autumn of 1914 would probably have seen an industrial disturbance of the first magnitude. . . .[46]

There is a danger, as McKinlay points out in chapter 4, of reading history backwards. Nevertheless, there does appear to us to be ample evidence to suggest that even without the cataclysm of the First World War, there would have been a Red Clydeside. However, this is certainly no definitive statement on the matter. There are conflicts of interpretation amongst the contributors to this volume which we as editors have encouraged. Hopefully, the range of opinions expressed here will stimulate further thought and reflection on the 'pre-history' of Red Clydeside, perhaps generate additional discussion and debate, and, with luck, will stimulate more empirical research and theoretical perspectives in an attempt to sustain hypotheses and extend our understanding of capital-labour relations in the immediate pre-First World War period. We look forward with anticipation to the unfolding of that process.

NOTES

We are grateful for W. Hamish Fraser for reading and commenting on a draft of this introduction.

1. Fischer, C. and Knox, W., 'Shedding the Blinkers: German and Scottish Labour Historiography from c1960 to the Present', *Scottish Labour History Society Journal*, no. 26, 1991, pp. 32–33.

2. The idea for such a volume emerged from the Glasgow Labour History Workshop (GLHW), a research collective (in which the editors and several of the contributors are involved) which has been concentrating attention upon the 1910–14 period. See GLHW, *The Singer Strike, Clydebank, 1911* (Glasgow, 1989); GLHW, 'Roots of Red Clydeside', in Duncan, R. and McIvor, A.(eds), *Militant Workers* (1992).

3. *Glasgow Herald*, 15 August 1911.

4. Cited in Holton, B., *British Syndicalism, 1900–1914* (1976), p. 133.

5. Holton, *British Syndicalism*, p. 269. See also Holton's reappraisal in W. Mommsen and H-G. Husung (eds), *The Development of Trade Unionism in GB and Germany, 1880–1914* (1985). To a large extent, Holton's views echo those of G.D.H. Cole, writing in the 1930s. See for example, Cole, G.D.H., *The World of Labour* (1915).

6. Price, R., *Labour in British Society* (1986); Price, R., *Masters, Unions and Men* (1980), pp. 236–267.

7. Challinor, R., *The Origins of British Bolshevism* (1977); Haynes, M., 'The British Working Class in Revolt, 1910–14', *International Socialism*, no. 22 (winter, 1984)

8. For an overview see O'Day, A., *The Edwardian Age: Conflict and Stability, 1900–1914* (1979).

9. Pelling, H., *A History of British Trade Unionism* (1st pub. 1963); Clegg, H., *A History of British Trade Unionism, vol II, 1911–1933* (1985)

10. Hinton, J., *Labour and Socialism* (1983); Burgess, K., *The Challenge of Labour* (1980); Gore, V., 'Rank-and-File Dissent', in C.J. Wrigley (ed), *A History of British Industrial Relations, 1875–1914* (1982); White, J., '1910–1914 Reconsidered', in J.E. Cronin and J. Schneer (eds), *Social Conflict and the Political Order in Modern Britain* (1982).

11. Church, R., 'Edwardian Labour Unrest and Coalfield Militancy, 1890–1914', *Historical Journal*, 30, 4 (1987)

12. Laybourn, K., *A History of British Trade Unionism, c1770–1990* (1992), pp. 104, 119.

13. Hunt, E.H., *British Labour History* (1981), p 329.

14. Leng, P.J., *The Welsh Dockers* (1981), p 51; see also Kenefick, W., 'The Impact of the Past Upon the Present: The Experience of the Clydeside Dock Labour Force c.1850–1914, with Particular Reference to the Port of Glasgow (unpublished Ph.D. Thesis, University of Strathclyde, 1995), pp. 28–32, for analysis of the influence of syndicalism of Clydeside.

15. Benson, J., *The Working Class in Britain, 1850–1939* (1989), pp. 174–206.

16. Reid, A., *Social Classes and Social Relations in Britain, 1850–1914 (1992)*, pp 60–1.

17. Southall, L., in Langton, J., and Morris, R.J., (eds), *Atlas of Industrialising Britain, 1780–1914* (1986), p. 193; Hunt, E.H., *Regional Wage Variations in Britain, 1850–1914* (1973); Church, 'Edwardian Labour Unrest'; Laybourn, *A History*, pp. 107–8; See also Devlin and Renfrew in this volume (chapters 3 and 7).

18. Holton, *British Syndicalism*, pp. 77–88; 97–103; 19–21; 127–9; 167–9.

19. For a recent overview of the historiography of 'Red Clydeside' see Brotherstone, T. 'Does Red Clydeside Really Matter', in Duncan, R., and McIvor, A., (eds), *Militant Workers* (Edinburgh, 1992)

20. Knox, W., 'The Political and Workplace Culture of the Scottish Working Class, 1832–1914', in Fraser, W.H., and Morris, R.J., (eds), *People and Society in Scotland, vol 2, 1830–1914* (Edinburgh, 1990); Gordon, E., *Women and the Labour Movement 1850–1914* (1991); Melling, J., 'Scottish Industrialists and the Changing Character of Class Relations in the Clyde Region, c1880–1918', in T. Dickson (ed), *Capital and Class in Scotland* (Edinburgh, 1982); Smith, J., 'Taking the Leadership of the Labour Movement', in McKinlay, A., and Morris, R.J., (eds), *The Independent Labour Party on Clydeside, 1893–1932* (1991), pp. 56–82.

21. For example, Smout, T.C., *A Century of the Scottish People, 1830–1950* (1986); Cage R.A.(ed), *The Working Class in Glasgow, 1750–1914* (1987). This neglect could be justified if the 1910–14 unrest was unimportant in Scotland, but we would argue that this was not the case.

22. Marwick, W.H., *A Short History of Labour in Scotland* (1967)

23. Young, J.D., *The Rousing of the Scottish Working Class* (1979)

24. See especially chapters 1 and 3.

25. Challinor, *Origins*; Kendall, W., *The Revolutionary Movement in Britain, 1900–21* (1969); Vernon, H.R., 'The Socialist Labour Party and the Working Class Movement on the Clyde, 1903–21' (unpublished M.Phil thesis, Leeds University, 1967). See also Unger, D., The Roots of Red Clydeside (unpublished Ph.D thesis University of Texas 1979).

26. McShane, H. and Smith, J., *No Mean Fighter* (1978), pp. 48, 59.

27. Knox, 'Political and Workplace Culture', pp. 159–61; Smith, 'Taking the Leadership'.

28. Gordon, *Women and the Labour Movement*, pp. 258–9.

29. See footnote 18.

30. Holton, *British Syndicalism*, p. 117.

31. Holton, *British Syndicalism*, p. 143.

32. Holton, *British Syndicalism*, pp. 195–6.

33. See GLHW, *The Singer Strike,* and chapter 9 in this volume.

34. On the prominent role of the trades councils in Scotland see Hatvany, D., The

Trades Councils in Scotland, 1897–1939' (unpublished Ph.D. thesis, University of Strathclyde 1992).
35. Melling, 'Scottish Industrialists', pp. 103–4.
36. Smith, 'Taking the Leadership', pp. 76–7.
37. Holton, *British Syndicalism*, pp. 42–3; McShane and Smith, *No Mean Fighter*, pp. 36, 52–3.
38. Clegg, H.A., *A History of British Trade Unions Since 1889, vol 2, 1911–33* (1985), pp. 71–3. Clegg identifies the coalowners and railway companies as having a particularly poor cost position and hence a more intransigent stance towards workers 'not unreasonable demands'. See also McIvor, A., *Organised Capital* (1996), pp.132–43.
39. Price, *Masters*, pp. 240–41; 245–6.
40. Knox, 'Political and Workplace Cultures', p. 162.
41. See also Gordon, E.,'Women and Working Class Politics in Scotland, 1900–14', in Jamieson, L., and Corr, H., (eds), *State, Private Life and Political Change* (1990)
42. We are grateful to W. Hamish Fraser for this information and for scrutiny of the relevant material in the forthcoming History of Glasgow, vol 2.
43. For more detail see chapter 1.
44. Melling, J.,'Clydeside Rent Struggles and the Making of Labour Politics in Scotland, 1900–39', in Rodger, R., (ed), *Scottish Housing in the Twentieth Century* (1989), pp. 54–65; Morris, R.J., 'Urbanisation and Scotland', in Fraser and Morris, (eds), *People and Society in Scotland, vol 2*, pp. 83–7.
45. Melling, 'Clydeside Rent Struggles', p. 60.
46. Richmond, J.R., cited in full in chapter 4, note 58.

CHAPTER 1

The Labour Unrest in West Scotland 1910–14

Glasgow Labour History Workshop[1]

> . . . The times we are living in are so stirring and full of change that it is
> not impossible to believe that we are in the rapids of revolution. . . .
> *John MacLean to the Renfrewshire Cooperative Conference, 25 November 1911*

Whilst MacLean's prognosis of events is undoubtedly exaggerated, the period 1910 to 1914 was one of unprecedented industrial militancy in Britain. It was characterised not only by a series of major all-out battles between capital and labour in transport and mining, but also by a multiplicity of minor confrontations and skirmishes. In short, insurgency on a very broad front. This developed into a major push by labour against what has been called 'the frontier of control' between management and workers.[2] At one level, this was a struggle by previously unorganised, lesser skilled, poorer paid workers – labourers, dockers, female textile workers, apprentices, carters – to obtain recognition of workers' trade unions and a collective bargaining dialogue as the mechanism through which working conditions could be improved and wages could keep pace with inflation. The artisans and stronger unions pressed further into the terrain of managerial prerogatives, challenging the right of engineering employers to operate their machinery as they saw fit, and in boilermaking and mining, the prerogative of capital to employ non-unionists. More alarming, perhaps, alternative socialist, industrial unionist and syndicalist ideologies were gaining support and were beginning to fracture the hegemony of capitalist ideas. Through newspapers like *Forward, Justice, Clarion* and the *Socialist* the brutality and degradation of life and work under the laissez-faire, competitive market system was being exposed.

This chapter investigates the patterns and causes of industrial conflict in West Scotland over 1910–14. It will be argued, after James Cronin, that a cluster of factors coagulated to precipitate the pre-war strike wave, having an aggregate effect – a snowballing of accumulated grievances.[3] Firstly, however, we need to consider the nature and general structure of trade unions in Scotland before attempting to outline the dimensions of pre-war industrial conflict in West Scotland.

Structure of Scottish trade unionism

A number of contradictory explanations of the nature of Scottish trade unionism exist. Hamish Fraser categorised the structure of Scottish trade unionism as being largely localist and federal in organisation throughout the nineteenth century. What this meant was that individual unions, or, indeed, individual branches, could exercise a high degree of autonomy, even if their actions were still co-ordinated through other outside agencies.[4] From this standpoint, and within the general model of British trade unionism, based largely on the philosophy of the skilled unions, developments in Scotland were viewed as backward because small trade unions appeared to be unwilling to move towards larger centralised national unions. Knox stresses the sectionalism, sectarianism and 'organisational weakness' of Scottish trade unionism pre-1914 – the density of union membership in Scotland was considerably lower in the late 19th century than in England and Wales.[5] To McLean the pre-war years were characterised by the continuation of older models of unionism, particularly the further development of craft-based conservatism on Clydeside[6]. Scottish trade unionism recast itself somewhat from the late 1870s, but, in essence, implantation of collective organisation was weak and, in contrast to England, delayed. Much of the opinion surrounding developments in Scottish trade unionism, therefore, stems from this belief that an inherent weakness in Scottish union organisation existed due to the lack of bureaucratic control, strong central authority, and a general lack of financial security.

This notion of intrinsic weakness may well have been overplayed. Devlin has recently argued that the early and persistent concentration on small-scale and independent trade union development in Scotland was a strength which led to a growing sense of solidarity and the formalisation of independent political strategies. Arguably, the nature and character of Scottish trade unionism should be defined in terms of their actions, leadership and their campaigns, rather than the notion of bureaucratic efficiency. So, in order to evaluate the strengths and weaknesses of Scottish trade unionism such organisational developments should be viewed within the more intimate Scottish perspective rather than the much broader and widely differentiated British model of organisational efficiency. Fundamentally it is true to say that trade unionism in Scotland – as elsewhere – was regionally distinctive and that it reflected the structure of capital.[7]

Independent Scottish trade unions remained an important component of the movement up to World War One. As late as 1905 over 120 independent trade unions existed in Scotland.[8] Registrar of Friendly Societies records illustrate that 38 registered organisations in Scotland had a combined membership 63,422 in 1900 and even by 1913 – despite increasing pressure to amalgamate – there still existed 33 distinct Scottish unions with a combined membership of 89,049.[9] Scottish trade union membership as a proportion of Scottish Trade Union Congress (STUC) membership was 62.6 percent in 1900 and, although falling by 1913 to 45.5 percent, was still a significant proportion overall.[10] The so-called new unions of dockers, for example, successfully organised on a national basis in Scotland from 1911, still favoured the traditional local and de-centralised structures of combination and control.[11] It is also the case that many more trade unions affiliated to their local trades council than they did to the STUC. For example, in 1913 total membership of Scottish trades councils was 230,000, compared to a total STUC membership of 196,217. By contrast, trades council membership never accounted for more than 54 percent of TUC membership at any time between 1900 and 1914.[12]

Thus, events in Scotland assume a uniqueness more clearly and identifiably 'Scottish'. The small-scale trade unions (with an optimal membership base of between 1,000 and 5,000[13]), allowed for both a more activist-led trade union movement and a far greater degree of democracy. At another level there could also be seen a greater demand for localised decision-making and democracy in the west of Scotland. James Hinton, for example, notes the important precedents of localist orientations – even among supposedly centralised unions such as the Amalgamated Engineering Union – between 1897–8 and again in 1903 when there was a serious challenge mounted against executive authority by unofficial workplace organisations in the west of Scotland.

District rather than national officials held real authority. Activists, such as Gallacher, claimed extensive discussion and promotion of ideas during work, while Tom Bell noted the extent of workplace democracy with the demand for full quarterly executive reports to the membership.[14] From this standpoint, therefore, the importance of activist networks cannot be too strongly stressed. K. Middlemass argued that Glasgow Trades Council was the most powerful in the United Kingdom at that juncture; over 400 delegates met weekly, from all trades in the Clyde area, to discuss local and national affairs.[15]

J.D. Young suggests that this process of strong independent trade union growth, and its enhanced development towards the later decades of the nineteenth century, is due to the distinctive experience of Scotland and its particular and peculiar phase of industrial development when compared to that of England. Scotland was in many ways catching up with industrial developments in England and because this phase of industrialisation was occuring at a later stage, and was more concentrated within a shorter time span, it produced a different response from both the forces of capital and labour. Young posits that from this situation came the emergence of industrial relations strategies based on conflict and coercion, rather than the more conciliatory developments generally apparent in England at this time.[16] Morris and McKinlay illustrate the solidarity of the Clydeside workforce during this period, arguing that hostile, anti-unionist managerial strategies intended to create sectionalism and the segmentation of the workforce largely failed. Their analysis also indicates a reason for this in so far as artisan earnings, workplace control and general living standards were less favourable than those enjoyed by other skilled workers outside Clydeside in particular and Britain in general.[17] Thus local conditions militated against further sectionalism and helped draw the skilled and the less skilled into closer union. Even before 1914, therefore, very conscious efforts were being made within both skilled and unskilled trade union organisations in Scotland to maintain and even extend the traditional model of independent trade unionism within the more localised and federal Scottish structure. Rather than a weakness, this localist and activist-led trade union structure could be interpreted as a strength.

Strike activity in West Scotland

Between 1910 and 1914 British capitalism was convulsed by a series of major labour disputes which saw strike activity and working days lost multiply to four times the level recorded in the previous decade. Scottish workers participated fully in this strike wave, both through individual company strikes and through active participation in nation-wide conflicts of railwaymen, seamen, dockers and miners. Over 1911–13, the annual average strike rate in Scotland ran at six times the rate of the previous decade, 1900–10. In the heavy industrialised region of West Scotland, strike activity occured across a broad spectrum of industries, with a notable concentration of unrest in mining, ship-building, engineering, metal working, transport and textiles. Major sectors of employment on Clydeside not participating in strike activity to any significant extent included retail distribution, domestic service, clothing, agriculture, fishing and the professions. A comprehensive

Table 1.1. Strike Activity in the West of Scotland, 1910–1914.

	1910	1911	1912	1913	1914	Total	%
Mining	3	16	8	15	11	53	20.3
Shipbuilding & Engineering	3	10	13	11	16	53	20.3
Transport	6	20	9	6	7	48	18.4
Textiles	1	6	12	2	7	28	10.7
Metals	1	2	12	3	8	26	10.0
Construction	–	–	5	6	1	12	4.6
Printing	1	1	–	2	3	7	2.7
Chemicals	–	1	2	3	–	6	2.3
Timber & Furniture	–	2	2	2	–	6	2.3
Glass & Pottery	1	1	3	–	–	5	1.9
Municipal	–	1	1	2	1	5	1.9
Food	1	1	2	–	–	4	1.5
Retail	–	–	–	3	–	3	1.2
Miscellaneous	–	–	1	3	1	5	1.9
Number of strikes recorded.	17	61	70	58	55	261	

Source: Glasgow Herald and *Forward* 1910 to 1914. Strikes enumerated within the geographical region comprising Renfrewshire, Dumbartonshire, Lanarkshire and Ayrshire. Industrial classification is that adopted by C.H.Lee, *British Regional Employment Statistics, 1841–1971* (1979). Note: figures for 1914 cover January to July only.

Table 1.2. *Principal Industrial Disputes in Scotland, 1910–1914*

group/date	no.firms	workers	days lost
*Coalminers, Scotland, Feb – April 1912.	gen.	143,000	4,400,000
Juteworkers, Dundee, Feb – April 1912.	40	28,000	1,064,000
Dockers, Leith, June – Aug 1913.	25	4,000	172,000
Sewing Machine Workers, Clydebank, Mar – Apr 1911.	1	9,400	141,000
Ironmoulders, Falkirk, May – June 1912.	22	6,500	143,000
*Seamen and Dockers, Scotland June – Aug 1911.	gen.	13,000	113,000
Ironworkers, Falkirk, May – July 1913.	gen.	3,085	104,890
Carters, Glasgow, Jan – Feb 1913.	80–100	3,500	101,500
Dockers and Seamen, Glasgow Jan – Feb 1912.	123	7,000	84,000
Miners, Motherwell, Apr 1911 – Apr 1912.	1	265	83,210
Quarryworkers, Aberdeen, Apr – May 1913.	73	1,542	72,474
Miners, Dreghorn, July – Dec 1912.	1	450	58,050
Miners, Kilwinning, Feb – May 1910.	1	645	55,470
*Railwaymen, Scotland, August 1911.	gen.	16,000	54,000
Fishing Net Makers, Kilbirnie Apr – Sept 1913.	6	390	50,700

Notes: *These are approximate figures for numbers of Scottish workers involved in British disputes based on aggregate figures provided in H.Clegg, *A History of British Trade Unionism, Vol 2, 1911–33* and census data providing the ratio of numbers employed in Scotland compared to G.B. in C.H. Lee, *British Regional Employment Statistics, 1841–1971.*

Source: Board of Trade, *Annual Report on Strikes and Lock-Outs*; Supplemented with the Board of Trade, *Labour Gazette*; 1910–1914.

trawl of two newspapers, *Glasgow Herald* and *Forward*, from 1 January 1910 to the outbreak of World War One, provides a detailed breakdown in industrial action.

Table 1.1 indicates that strike activity was sustained in West Scotland right through to the outbreak of war, which is somewhat at odds with the generally accepted U.K. model of industrial activity which, while registering continued unrest, indicates a tailing off of activity over 1913–14. Contrary to Pelling's indications of a 'successful stemming of the tide of successful strikes' from 1912 the levels of unrest and militancy of workers was not generally weakened: at least within our geographical remit.[18] However, in 1913–4 a strike was more likely to be unofficial, and shorter in duration, and the workers most likely to be unskilled, than in 1911–12. A point not evident from these tables is also worth highlighting. Women played, as Gordon has demonstrated, an integral part in the strike activity of this period.[19] Female strike propensity was high, and women did not hesitate to fight against exploitation and struggle for better wages and conditions in the workplace, like many of their male counterparts in the lesser skilled trades, during the period under investigation. Their central demand was for trade union recognition. The dismissal of a member of the NFWW intensified a strike in the Kirktonfield Bleachworks, Neilston 1910, and is but one of many examples which show women's determination to achieve trade union recognition.[20] Such examples go someway to dispel the myth that women workers were docile and reluctant to take industrial action.

One of the major problems has been the inaccurate picture obtained from reliance on the Board of Trade strike statistics for this period. Our findings from a systematic newspaper trawl (tabulated in table 1.3 below) suggest that such 'official' figures seriously under-represented

Table 1.3. *Comparison between Board of Trade and Glasgow Labour History Workshop figures for strike incidence, 1910 and 1914*

	Board of Trade	Glasgow Labour History Workshop
1910	11	17
1911	24	43
1912	41	70
1913	49	58
1914	6★	55

Note: Board of Trade figures are for the whole of Scotland, the GLHW figures are for the West Central belt only, comprising Ayrshire, Dumbartonshire, Lanarkshire and Renfrewshire. ★These figures are quoted from the *Board of Trade Gazette* for 1914, as Board of Trade *Annual Reports* ended in 1913.

the level of strike activity at this time because of deliberate underestimation (excluding strikes which lasted less than one day and involved fewer than ten workers) and under-recording, not least by employers. For example, an official strike at Ardrossan harbour in 1912, which lasted 10 weeks and involved several hundred dockers, did not become a Board of Trade statistic as the directors of the Ardrossan Harbour Company – who controlled the port – decided not to complete or return the form sent to them by the board, commenting: 'no information should be sent unless the company was compelled to do so by statute.'[21] This was probably not an isolated case.

The economics of unrest

There is little doubt that central to the question what caused the labour unrest of 1910–1914, were the problems associated with rising prices and stagnating real wages. A Board of Trade enquiry published in 1913 estimated that from the late 1890s until 1912, basic food prices had risen by up to 25 per cent, whilst wages failed to keep pace in real terms.[22] The *Industrialist* noted a similar trend and found that on average workers wages had been 'reduced between two shillings and three shillings in the pound', or in real terms between 10 and 15 per cent.[23] Another Board of Trade investigation reported that the value of the sovereign had decreased by almost 20 per cent between 1895 and 1912, falling from a real value of 20 shillings to around 16 shillings and three pence over that period.[24] Fuel prices rose particularly rapidly. Coal prices in Glasgow had risen by 31 per cent between 1905 and 1912, and 'the average increase in rent, fuel and food together may be about 10 per cent.'[25] In September 1912 *Forward* reported on the findings of a Glasgow Trades Council investigation into the cost of living, highlighting the rapid rise in wholesale prices of twelve food items (table 1.4.) Such statistics emphasize the decreasing value of real spending power in Scotland. An S.T.U.C. report of January 1913, to the Parliamentary Committee in the House of Commons, had little doubt that the root cause of the unrest was economic:

> . . . For the past two years, labour has been clamorous and insurgent. For a decade wages have been almost stationary and the cost of living has rapidly increased . . . The nation now realises that the basic cause of the labour unrest is poverty . . . Poverty cannot be cured by conflict, but conflict indicates the seriousness of the complaint . . .[26]

Such contemporaneous reports indicate ample evidence, as Eric Hobsbawm argues, of the chief reason for the unrest being the

Table 1.4. *Wholesale Food Prices, Glasgow 1906 to 1912.*

Items	1906	1912	% increase
Butter (per cwt)	94/	115/–	22%
Bacon	40/–	65/–	65%
Sugar	16/	21/–	31%
Oatmeal	11/6d	15/6d	35%
Marmalade	14/6d	19/6d	34%
Jam	13/3d	18/3d	38%
Split peas	5/6d	8/11d	62%
Cheddar Cheese	54/–	76/–	41%
Salt	2/1d	3/3d	56%
Flour (per bag)	25/6d	33/–	29%
Tea (per 100/Ib)	95/–	116/8d	23%
Raisins (per Ib)	6d	91/2d	46%

Source: *Forward,* 21 September 1912.

perceptible stagnation or even decline in real wages.[27] In Scotland (and in Glasgow in particular) the problem was most definitely acute. There is considerable debate about Scottish wages rates in comparison to England. On the one hand there are those, including Campbell and Hunt, who see West Scotland as a relatively high wage area on the eve of World War One.[28] This interpretation, however, has been contested by Morris and McKinlay, Price and Rodger, among others.[29] The latter have demonstrated quite convincingly that real wages on Clydeside remained lower than comparable industrial regions in England. Significant factors in the industrial unrest of 1910–14 on Clydeside were discontent over both declining real wage levels and adverse regional wage differentials (for example at the docks and textile finishing).

The spontaneous explosion of worker militancy over 1910–14 was thus intimately linked to the bitter experience of many groups of workers during what Jim Treble has recently described as a 'crisis' period for Clydeside labour between 1903 and 1910.[30] Those years were punctuated by two sharp economic recessions, as table 1.5. shows, which hit the staple metal working trades on the Clyde very severely.

Into this equation comes such considerations as bad housing, overcrowding and the concomitant factors of anxiety, disease and suffering, factors which combined to create considerable discontent within working class communities. Such conditions led to a subterranean struggle over rents and the legal aspects of landlordism.[31]

Table 1.5. *Unemployment and Sequestrations for Non-Payment of Rent, 1910–14.*

	I	II	III	IV
1900	2.5			10,818
1901	3.3			10,878
1902	4.0			11,409
1903	4.7	6.5	11.4	13,092
1904	6.0	9.3	16.0	14,517
1905	5.0	7.2	11.4	15,020
1906	3.6	4.0	7.5	14,528
1907	3.7	5.0	9.0	15,602
1908	7.8	19.8	24.2	20,858
1909	7.7	17.9	22.1	21,517
1910	4.7	6.3	14.7	19,556
1911	3.0	3.4	1.8	16,450
1912	3.2	4.2	2.1	11,239
1913	2.1	2.2	1.0	4,522
1914	3.3			3,660

Legend:-
I Percentage unemployed in Britain.
II Percentage unemployed in Clyde engineering.
III Percentage unemployed in Clyde shipyards.
IV Sequestration for rent arrears, Glasgow.
Sources. Column I. J.E.Cronin, *Industrial Conflict in Modern Britain* (1979).
Columns II–IV. J.H. Treble, 'Unemployment in Glasgow 1903–1910: Anatomy of a Crisis', *Scottish Labour History Society Journal.* no.25, 1990, p39.

If stagnating real wages and living standards provided an underlying grievance, changing product and labour market circumstances gave workers the opportunity to move on to the offensive against capital. In general, full order books and tight labour markets characterised the period 1911–14. This scenario, in turn, stimulated trade union membership, particularly within the unskilled sector, and significantly raised workers collective bargaining power. Successful strike action further begot increased growth in trade unionism and raised workers confidence in united action. The first agricultural labourers' union was formed in Scotland during this period and STUC membership rose from 129,000 in 1909 to 230,000 in 1914. It would be overly reductionist, however, to base the whole analysis of unrest simply on the economic model. H.A.Clegg's own study into the period stresses such caution. He notes that earlier periods of similar unrest, in 1871–3 and 1889–90, did not follow periods of falling real wages.[32] Cronin also feels that the economic model is too narrow to explain outbreaks of labour unrest.[33] This theory thus takes little account of an independent will of labour, or, for that matter, of capital.

Capitalist strategies: work intensification, discipline and control mechanisms

There were other alienating tendencies at work during the 1900s and early 1910s which worked to fuel worker antagonism, bitterness and resistance on the Clyde. A significant worker grievance emerged in many sectors over attempts by management to speed-up and intensify work. In crude terms this meant increased workloads; a quickening pace of production; the continual division of labour; breaking with the 'customs and practices' of the past, which arguably became welded into an accumulated sense of general discontent. From the late 1890s onward, states Cronin, 'almost all workers perceived some deterioration and intensification in their work . . . industrial concentration and management strategy were working to their disadvantage'.[34]

Work intensification was in part a result of increased competition between employers and from abroad. As a consequence, management sought to maintain their profit margins and sustain or expand their share of the market by attempting to change wage payment rates or introduce new work methods. Some of the more advanced employers experimented with the American inspired 'scientific method', or the 'Taylorist method' – as at Singer, Clydebank in 1911.[35] Pressure at the point of production and work intensification was often identified in a less sophisticated manner. As often as not, 'stretch-out' took place within the parameters of existing technology and the traditional division of labour. At Weir's of Cathcart in 1914, a strike prompted this reaction from John MacLean:

> . . . This policy of rushing the men to get the work done more quickly not only supports our contention that articles tend to sell according to the time taken to make them, but shows that in the process the men are nagged until any excuse is seized to come out on strike. This clearly explains the strike . . .[36]

Elsewhere, more intrusive supervision, cuts in the piece work rates or longer hours, served to further antagonise workers. On the waterfront, while rationalisation was literally non-existent, there was a considerable effort to alter customary, time-honoured work methods. The reduction of squad sizes would be a classic example. The practice of cutting piece rates was widespread across many sectors of the economy – including shipbuilding and mining.[37] Many women workers, already low paid, also had to contend with such methods. One example of this can be seen in the Caledonia Bakery strike in Glasgow in 1911 where attempts were made to cut wages by between three and five shillings per week.[38] Indeed, in some cases even while employers were not attempting to cut wages, wages were not generally improved – as could be seen at Glasgow docks and with the networkers at Kilbirnie.[39] Furthermore, it may be suggested that in those strikes where workers came out to force their 'supervisors and foremen' into the unions, for example the strike of around 7000 dockers on the Clyde in Jan-Feb. 1911, an attempt was being made to lessen employers control at the point on production, by influencing supervision through the offices of the union. Indeed, this strike went further and demanded that clerks, measurers, watchmen and tallymen, as well as the foremen, all join the union.[40]

Workers were also fighting unrealistic bonus systems imposed to speed up production. Many had to contend with favouritism, where some workers were paid extra so as to cause divisions within the workforce and provide an incentive for people to work harder. Such concerns surfaced in a wide range of strikes in this period. A strike of coachmakers and bodybuilders at the Argyll Motor Works, Alexandria was over an increase in workload without a reciprocal increase in wages.[41] At the Stewart and Lloyd Ironworks, Dalmarnock, 120 labourers went on strike because of the introduction of a bonus scheme which they maintained was impossible to meet, while at Bayne and Duckett's, Glasgow, in 1912, the introduction of machinery cut 'making time' by a third, simultaneously halving the piece rates.[42] Often the issue of work intensification is not easily identifiable as a cause of labour disquiet, but appears significant upon closer investigation. One good example would be the engineering and shipbuilding apprentices' strike of 1912. On the surface, this was a spontaneous revolt of poorly paid apprentices against the new financial burden laid upon them by the passage of the National Insurance Act. This necessitated a weekly contribution of six and a half pence by apprentices.

However, William Knox has indicated how pressure on apprentices was the underlying cause of the dispute:

> . . . the action taken by the apprentices was less a conservative response to progressive welfare measures, but more a result of changing work patterns and increasing exploitation. Under conditions of rapid technological advance the productivity of the apprentice was rising, but his wages remained almost static . . . [43]

As an accompaniment to such methods, some employers increased their use of cheaper female labour – paid on average half the wage of their male counterparts. For example, the result of the 'ruthless rationalisation and shut down' programme adopted by the textile dyeing and printing companies in the Vale of Leven, was that 'only a minority of the male wage earners in the Vale were employed in the industry',[44] which, of course drastically reduced the overall wage bill. In the textile industry – an industry differentiated by skill and gender – the better paid work was the prerogative of men. As in other industries, women – by virtue of their gender – were excluded from the most skilled and supervisory occupations. Indeed, the hostile attitude of many trade unionists towards the employment of women tended to reinforce women's subordinate position in the labour market. Struggles over rates of pay were based on the concept of the 'family wage'. This meant that men were considered the breadwinners, needing to earn enough to keep a wife and family. Many single working women had to maintain a family, yet were not paid a family wage, while single men earned the same as their married male counterparts.[45]

However, like the economic factor, work intensification may be better classified as adding fuel to the fire, rather than acting directly, as a singular cause of the unrest. Whilst managerial driving and pressure at the point of production embittered many Clydeside workers in the pre-war years, the mechanisms utilised by capital in direct response to worker grievances, demands and actions served, in many instances, to further antagonise industrial relations and provoke renewed resistance and conflict. Capital was no monolithic, cohesive group and responses to labour initiatives varied considerably between employers and industries. Nevertheless, certain broad patterns in labour management strategies over this period are discernible.

Clydeside employers initially met the growing crop of disputes and strikes with force, coercion and intransigence. Importing non-unionist labour, blacklisting strikers, exploiting the full force of the law and threatening lockouts were the staple fare of the period. The propensity among Clydeside employers to introduce blackleg labour during strikes appears to have been particularly high, especially during the first phase. In the three years 1910 to 1912 we have positively identified blackleg importation in 29 out of 74 Clydeside strikes, or two in every five disputes. This is more than double the rate of labour replacement in England during the labour unrest.[46] This may confirm a dogged and deep-rooted mistrust of unions and collective action amongst Clydeside employers.[47]

In many cases managers and foremen used their own devices and contacts to recruit replacements during strikes, as in the Caledonian bakery in 1911, the Bonnybridge Co-op and during the refuse workers strikes at Glasgow, Port Glasgow and Greenock in 1911. Similarly, the manager of the Hallside Steel Works in Newton obtained replacements for almost 100 builders' labourers in the summer of 1912, feeding and sleeping these men in the works to avoid problems with pickets. The correspondent in *Forward* gleefully noted that the Newton blacklegs were sleeping 'inside railway arches inside the works which for years have been used by the men as occasional free and easy lavatories'.[48] To a degree, the ability of employers to substitute workers during strikes was enhanced by the creation of labour exchanges, introduced from 1909. In addition, in providing police protection for blackleg labour during strikes, the state made a further contribution to employers' dispute-busting machinery.

Where employers were organised, the strikebreaking services of their employers' association could be drawn upon. The Paisley Contractors' Association provided such services during the carters' strike in March 1911, whilst at Ardrossan harbour, the Ardrossan Harbour Company actively sought the assistance of the Shipping Federation and the National Association of Free Labour to aid their attempt to create an 'open shop' in a Clyde port.[49] The services of an established network of Free Labour organisations and agencies were also exploited by other Clydeside employers. The North British Bottle Manufacturing Company, for example, responded to a strike at their works in Shettleston in May 1910 by obtaining youths through the Salvation Army and paying a well known international 'free labour' agent, based in London (Peter Lamberti), to provide blacklegs from Germany, Russia and Holland. Needless to say none of these imported migrants were informed that there was a dispute in progress until their arrival at the works.[50]

Many other forms of labour discipline were exploited over these years. Police brutality, threatened evictions from employer-owned homes and the heavy handed use of troops (as in the 1912 miners strike) were allied with such devices as the lockout and legal action designed to intimidate the workforce. Legal actions against pickets appear with monotonous regularity during this period. Such tactics served only to further provoke workers by more clearly defining class inequalities and exposing the explicit integration of interests between state and capital.

Ideology and solidarity

Cronin and Holton argue that ideology played a significant role in the pre-war labour unrest, while others, like Hunt and Clegg place less emphasis on it.[51] Nevertheless, some analysis of the developing socialist, industrial unionist and syndicalist movements is a necessary prerequisite to the study of this period. This area of investigation is also important as it raises the problem of assessing 'consciousness' and labour's ability, or lack of it, to organise itself into strong industrial and political organisations. Although Hunt rejects the notion that ideology played a significant role in the period, pointing to the lack of support for syndicalism outside South Wales, others, including Dangerfield, believe that there was an upsurge in political activity and unrest in the workplace which 'was stemmed only by the firing of some bullets at Sarajevo'.[52]

Clegg notes the 'significant' role played by syndicalists, or men who 'sympathised' with syndicalist ideas, in his own analysis of the period, but he is cautious not to over-emphasize the role of ideology. For all the solidarity shown by workers and the commitment by labour leaders, the role of ideology is not necessarily the 'cause of the unrest. Rather it was one of its manifestations'.[53] In contrast, other commentators accord greater importance to the role of ideology. Syndicalism, according to Richard Price, 'had made deep inroads into virtually every major union by 1914' and was by no means of 'negligible importance', as some suggest. It spread the notion of workers' control, making it 'widespread currency in the period 1912–22 and . . . a serious alternative to nationalisation' as the main form of socialisation.[54]

Syndicalism was also a convinced critic of 'labourism', the Labour Party and of Parliamentary politics. Indeed, syndicalism was also critical of trade unionism, primarily when viewed as bureaucratic, unaccountable to its membership, and sectional in outlook. The fact that many of the strikes during the 'labour' unrest were unofficial, including examples of action which directly rejected union leaders' recommendations, is seen as evidence that the rank and file were questioning the role of the traditional labour leadership. A situation like this could arguably have proved fertile ground indeed for the fermentation of syndicalist or revolutionary socialist ideas, even as a proof of 'ideology in action'. The rejection of 'labourism' may have also helped matters. Could this have been the case in Scotland? The *Glasgow Herald* wrote as follows:-

> . . . It is evident that labour, to an extent that its accredited leaders would not have deemed possible, has got out of hand or has submitted itself to the guidance of men whose ability to release the forces of anarchy is no index of their power to undo the mischief they have done . . .[55]

In a later article this theme was continued when they criticised the orthodox leadership for bowing in docility to the 'leadership of the rank and file'. What seems to be implicit in these accounts is the recognition that labour was capable of exhibiting an independent will, possibly even a consciousness, through the rejection of orthodoxy.[56]

Another model used in analysing strike causation is the political-organisational one. Cronin offers this model as a credible foundation for the analysis of industrial unrest. The workers ability to act collectively depends on their organisational strength: the stronger their organisation the greater their strength and the greater their ability to translate 'oppression into protest . . . grievance into strike'. Our evidence suggests, that this could have been the case in West Central Scotland in the period 1910–1914. It may be argued that no single element was the 'root cause' of the unrest, but rather various causes became welded together to form 'aggregates of discontent'. Cronin's analysis attempts to explain the labour unrest in this fashion, but does so in class terms: conflict arising from the contradictions between capital and labour. Given Cronin's 'favourable economic and political conjuncture' these 'aggregates of discontent' are translated into strike action, such as in 1910–1914.[57]

Using Cronin's analysis, it may be argued that with a tight labour market and the growing organisational strength of labour, the economic conjuncture was favourable. In addition, with the wealth of alternative intellectual and ideological leadership and their repudiation of the traditional labour leadership and the growing reaction against the Liberal Government's social welfare legislation, it may be argued that the political climate was favourable. Thus accumulated grievances were united and expressed in strike action. High prices, lower real wages, work intensification or coercive employer strategies, persistent unemployment, the continual presence of underemployment, and class conscious leadership came together to consolidate discontent. The resultant outburst may not have been the simple translation of discontent 'over specific evils and localised enemies, but on the performance of the entire system'.[58]

In his study of British syndicalism Bob Holton notes that many contemporaries perceived 'a syndicalist mood of revolt'. Having a sympathy with this syndicalist mood of the time, Ben Tillett noted a spirit of revolt which 'had seized even those of whom we had least hope'.[59] For Bob Holton, this translates into what he defines as 'proto syndicalistic behaviour . . . a form of action that lies between vague revolt and clear cut revolutionary action'.[60] This was apparent in many of the disputes that took place in Scotland. Emmanuel Shinwell in 1911, reporting after the success of the seamens' strike of that year, noted that:

> . . . there was now recognition that sympathetic strike was an effective weapon . . . the seeds of revolution sown on Clydeside over the past few weeks are bound to have a far reaching result. Socialism has been rarely mentioned, but its principles and ideas have been expressed at every turn . . . one more link has been forged in the chain that binds labour together in an actual and living solidarity . . .[61]

There seems little doubt that much contemporary opinion viewed labour as indeed united and that ideology played its part in that unification process, even if today this is still a subject of heated debate among historians. Not only did intellectuals such as H.G. Wells and G.D.H. Cole perceive this, and labour leaders such as Tillett and Shinwell, but also many members and officers of the establishment. George Askwith of the Board of Trade; David Shackleton of the Home Office; the Association of the Chambers of Commerce: the Employers' Parliamentary Council and many others expressed their fears and concerns over the rising tide of militancy shown by labour through sympathy, and direct action.[62] To such commentators, the labour unrest was real.

Lines of communication were also tightening, aided by political propaganda and the process of organising labour. Not only did workers strike because they had seen the rewards such actions had gained other sections of the labour force, but also because they were more aware of levels of pay and working conditions experienced by other workers. In a strike of dockers at Ardrossan in 1912, the workforce exhibited an acute awareness of the wages structures of other dockers, not only at nearby ports, but in England and Wales also.[63] In the strike at the United Turkey Red works in the Vale of Leven in 1911 workers not only showed a remarkable awareness of contemporary wage rates in English textile areas, but also the terms and conditions of employment – especially the fact that female workers in Scotland were doing the direct equivalent of male workers in England, but were paid only one third their wages.[64]

Our evidence suggests that wage disputes constituted 54.2 percent of all strikes by women workers in the West of Scotland between 1910 to 1914. However, while wage and conditions disputes were apparently the main cause of strike action at this time, trade union recognition almost always became a central issue too. Most female workers in Scotland at the beginning of the 20th century were non-unionised. However, between 1910 and 1914 this situation changed considerably, particularly in the textile industry. This was mostly due to the work of the National Federation of Women Workers. Disputes often escalated into much more than their humble origins suggest. One example of this type of escalation can be seen in the so called 'mill girls' demonstration at Kilwinning in 1910, where, according to the *Glasgow Herald*, 'all the local people' were behind them, with local miners promising sympathetic support for 'their sisters'.[65] This type of solidarity was to be seen to a greater degree in another strike at Kilbirnie in 1913. Female networkers there struck for over twenty weeks – the longest strike of any group of female workers in the West of Scotland during this period – engendering substantial sympathy action and virtually the complete support of the people of that town. The strike was eventually resolved in favour of the women, but its real significance may lie in the sympathy support the strike gained. The *Ardrossan and Saltcoats Herald* noted that there was considerable class solidarity shown by the miners, steel-workers and others who took part in the dispute.[66] Indeed, according to Eleanor Gordon, this strike 'contributed significantly to the mobilisation of labour in the area, on a class wide basis rather than a purely sectional one'.[67] Scottish women workers, Gordon argues, played an active and innovative role in what she terms 'the explosion of militancy' over 1910–1914.[68]

When industrial action was initiated it often developed a momentum of it's own, where the action itself aided solidarity and heightened political awareness. Such case studies, it may be suggested, can fit well into Cronin's model which attempts to explain the causes of unrest. Furthermore, there is little doubt that the ongoing industrial strike activity inextricably accompanied a great deal of political activity and propaganda. The strike leaders in Scotland, such as Joseph Houghton (of the Dockers Union, who led the Ardrossan dispute, among many at this time), Emanuel Shinwell (of the Seamens Union) or Kate Mclean (of the National Federation of Women Workers, involved in the agitations at Kilwinning, Kilbirnie and the Vale of Leven), or the SLP leaders involved in the 1911 Singer strike no doubt had a deep rooted ideological strain to their trade union and organisational activities. Indeed it may be difficult to separate their political aims and identity from their industrial aims. This is not to say that the ideological commitment of Houghton, Shinwell or Mclean was a syndicalist one, but there is little doubting their socialist commitment in particular and their political commitment in general. As can be seen in their many speeches during this period, all had an acute awareness of what constituted class divisions in their society. This industrial, ideological and social solidarity, owed something to the structure of trade unionism in Scotland – which had evolved, as noted previously, along rather different lines from the rest of the U.K. A stronger reliance on a federal system of organisation in Scotland had resulted in trade unions becoming collections of small autonomous societies and semi-autonomous branches with decisions being made generally at a local level. More-over, as late as 1892, according to the Webbs, two thirds of all Scottish trade unionists resided in the Glasgow area.[69] Even by 1914 over 58 percent of all delegates to the STUC general congress came from this area.[70] Therefore, Scottish trade unionism was highly federalised, geographically concentrated and more directly activist led.

Conclusion

Scottish labour historians have tended to neglect the labour unrest of 1910–14. Our research has shown that Clydeside was convulsed by a strike wave of at least similar dimensions to that of comparable industrial regions in England and Wales, whilst it has been demonstrated that official statistics seriously under-estimate levels of industrial militancy in this region. The main industries involved were also similar: strike activity being focused in mining, shipbuilding, engineering, metals, transport and textiles. The causes of this unrest were multi-faceted; different factors affected different industries. However, Cronin's argument for an accumulation of grievances adequately summarises the experience of Clydeside. A combination of real wage erosion and high levels of underemployment and insecurity in the 1900s, with tightening labour market conditions from c1910 and an all-pervasive process of work intensification generated increased levels of discontent. Dissatisfaction was further exacerbated by draconian employer responses to legitimate grievances and demands.

The achievements of the pre-war strike wave in the West of Scotland merit separate and detailed consideration. Lack of space precludes such an analysis here. Suffice to say, perhaps, that Clydeside labour encroached significantly into managerial terrain, pressing forward the inalienable rights of ordinary workers. One indication of the erosion of managerial prerogatives and the undermining of employer authority in the pre-war period was the growing failure of employers to maintain the 'open shop' principle.[71] Our evidence suggests that the ability of employers in West Central Scotland to successfully resist the challenge of labour during the period 1910–1914 was seriously diluted. Powerful employers' associations – such as those in coal, engineering and shipbuilding – found the unions they faced able to match them in organisation and often exceed them in solidarity. The evidence implies that at this juncture employers in West Scotland may seriously have underestimated the power of the labour force, not only of organised labour, but the degree of support within many working class communities too. Evidently, the years of unilateral and autocratic capitalism in the West Central region of Scotland were numbered.

NOTES

1. The reseach collective involved in this project comprised Ishbel Ballantyne, Louise S Christie, Ricky Devlin, William Kenefick, Arthur McIvor, Hugh Paterson, Irene Sweeney, Liz Tuach. We would also like to thank Rob Duncan for his helpful comments on earlier drafts of this paper, Audrey Canning at the Willie Gallagher Library (STUC) for her generous guidance to relevant source material and all who made contributions of one sort or another through the Glasgow Labour History Workshop to this project.

2. Goodrich, C., *The Frontier of Control* (1920).

3. Cronin, J.E., *Industrial Conflict in Modern Britain* (1979).

4. Fraser, W.H., 'Trades Councils in the Labour Movement in the Nineteenth Century', in MacDougall I. (ed) *Essays in Scottish Labour History* (Edinburgh, 1978).

5. Knox, W., 'The Political and Workplace Culture of the Scottish Working Class, 1832–1914', in Fraser, W.H. and Morris, R.J. (eds) *People and Society in Scotland Vol II*, 1830–1914 (Edinburgh 1990), pp. 149–50. See also Melling, J., 'Scottish Industrialists and the Changing Character of Class Relations in the Clyde Region, c1880–1918' in Dickson, T., (ed), *Capital and Class in Scotland* (Edinburgh, 1982).

6. See McLean, I., *The Legend of Red Clydeside* (Edinburgh, 1983)

7. Devlin, R., 'Trade Union Structures and Strike Patterns in Scotland', Glasgow Labour History Workshop Seminar Series, University of Strathclyde, Session 1994/5 (unpublished paper).

8. *Report of the Royal Commission on Trade Disputes and Trade Combinations, BPP* 1906: Cd 2826.

9. Registrar of Friendly Societies in Scotland (Scottish Record Office)

10. Statistics generated from *Annual Reports of Friendly Societies*, 1900–1914, and STUC *Reports* 1900–1914.

11. Kenefick, W., 'The Impact of the Past upon the Present': The Experience of the Clydeside Dock Labour Force with particular reference to the Port of Glasgow' (unpublished PhD thesis, University of Strathclyde), 1995.

12. Figures drawn from current Ph.D. research project, by Ricky Devlin, Univeristy of Paisley. Calculations made from STUC *Annual Reports* 1900–14 and Clinton A., *The Trade Union Rank and File: Trades Council in Britain 1900–1940* (1972). See also Hatvany, D., 'Trades Councils in Scotland, c.1897–1939' (unpublished PhD., University of Strathclyde), 1992.

13. Compiled from *Report of the R C on Trade Disputes and Trade Combinations*, 1906, which showed that 19.4 percent of all Scottish societies were in this membership range.

14. See Hinton J., *The First Shop Stewards Movement* (1973); Gallacher W., *Revolt on the Clyde* (1936), and T Bell, *Pioneering Days* (1941).

15. Middlemass, K., *The Clydesiders; A Left Wing Struggle for Parliamentary Power* (1965). The Clyde Workers' Comittee in 1915 also epitomised the extensive nature of rank and file participation in union affairs.

16. Young, J. D., *The Rousing of the Scottish Working Class* (1983).

17. Introduction to Morris R. J. and McKinlay A., *The ILP on Clydeside*, 1893–1932 (Manchester 1991)

18. Pelling, H., *A History of British Trade Unionism* (3rd edn. 1984). p. 138.

19. Gordon, E., *Women and the Labour Movement in Scotland, 1850–1914* (1991).

20. The woman dismissed was Jeanie McKinlay; see *Forward*, 13 and 20 August 1910; 10 and 24 September 1910; 1 October 1910.

21. Kenefick, W., *Ardrossan: the Key to the Clyde – A Case Study of the Ardrossan Dock Strike 1912–1913* (Cunninghare, 1993), p 20.

22. Board of Trade, *Enquiry into the Cost of Living, Earnings and Hours (1913)*

23. *Industrialist*, October 1911, p. 4.

24. Board of Trade, *Investigation into the Changing Value of the Sovereign* (1913), cited in Tuckett A., *The Scottish Carter* (1967), p. 117. See also Challinor R., *The Origins of British Bolshevism* (1977), p. 63.

25. Board of Trade, *Investigation into the Changing Value of the Sovereign*, p. 235.

26. Kenefick, W., ' The Labour Unrest of 1910 to 1014, wth Particular Reference to the Ardrossan Dock Strike, 1912–13' (Honours Dissertation, University of Strathclyde, 1990), p. 2.

27. Hobsbawm E.H., *Industry and Empire* (1968), p. 159.

28. See Campbell, R.H., *The Rise and Fall of Scottish Industry, 1707–1939* (1980); Hunt, E.H., *Regional Wages Variations in Britain, 1850–1914* (1973).

29. See Morris, and McKinlay, *The ILP on Clydeside;* Price, S.F., 'Riveters Earnings in Clyde Shipbuilding, 1889–1913', *Scottish Economic and Social History* Vol I, 1981; Rodger, R.G., 'The Invisible Hand', in Fraser, D. and Sutcliffe, A. (eds) *The Pursuit of Urban History* (1980); Smout, T.C., *A Century of the Scottish People, 1830–1950* (1986). pp. 112–3. See also the comprehensive wages survey of railway workers in the *Glasgow Herald* 17 August 1911.

30. Treble J.H., 'Unemployment in Glasgow 1903–1910: Anatomy of a Crisis', *Scottish Labour History Society Journal*, no. 25, 1990.

31. Melling, J., 'Rent Strikes: Peoples Struggles for Housing in West Scotland, 1890–1916' (1983); Englander D., 'Landlord and Tenant in Urban Scotland', *Scottish Labour History Society Journal*, no. 15, 1981; Rodger R., 'Crisis and Confrontation in Scottish Housing, 1880–1914', in Rodger R. (ed), *Scottish Housing in the Twentieth Century* (1989)

32. Clegg H.A., *A History of British Trade Unionism Since 1889, Vol II, 1911–1933* (1985), p.24.

33. Cronin, *Industrial Conflict*, p. 29

34. Cronin, *Industrial Conflict*, p. 59. For a general discussion of work intensification in the Scottish context from the 1880s see W. Knox, 'The Political and Workplace Culture of the Scottish Working Class', in Fraser, W.H. and Morris, R.J. (eds), *People and Society in Scotland, vol II*, Glasgow, pp. 143–5.

35. See chapter 9 and The Glasgow Labour History Workshop, *The Singer Strike, Clydebank, 1911* (Glasgow, 1989)

36. Milton N., *John MacLean* (1973), pp. 73–4

37. For example, at the Meadowside Yard in Govan and the Russell and Co. Yard, Port Glasgow; see *Forward*, 19 November 1910 to 17 December 1910; *Glasgow Herald*, 16 June 1911.

38. *Forward*, 30 December 1911.

39. *Glasgow Herald*, 23 September 1913; *Forward*, 16 August 1913. See also Kenefick, 'The Impact of the Past upon the Present'.

40. *Glasgow Herald*, 4 January 1912; 5 January 1912; 17 January 1912; 22 February 1912.
41. *Glasgow Herald*, 29 November 1912; 3 December 1912.
42. *Forward*, 25 May 1912; 1 June 1912; 22 June 1912.
43. Knox W., 'Down with Lloyd George: The Apprentices Strike of 1912', *Scottish Labour History Society Journal*, 19, 1984, pp. 22.
44. Macintyre S., *Little Moscows* (1980), p. 89.
45. Gordon E., 'The Scottish Trade Union Movement, Class and Gender, 1850–1914', *Scottish Labour History Society Journal*, no. 23, 1988, pp. 30–40 for a discussion of the family wage.
46. McIvor A.J., 'Employers' Organisation and Strikebreaking in Britain, 1880–1914', *International Review of Social History*, XXIX, 1984, Part 1, pp. 11–14.
47. See chapters 2 and 3.
48. *Forward*, 3 August 1912.
49. Kenefick, 'The Labour Unrest', pp. 39–45.
50. *Forward*, 21 May; 28 May 1910; *Glasgow Herald*, 25 May 1910.
51. See Cronin, *Industrial Conflict*; Holton, *British Syndicalism 1900–1914* (1976); Clegg, *A History of British Trade Unions*, and Hunt E.H., *British Labour History*, 1815–1914 (1981).
52. Dangerfield G., *The Strange Death of Liberal England* (1961 edn), p. 351
53. Clegg, *A History of British Trade Unions*, p. 74.
54. Price R., *Labour in British Society* (1986), pp. 153–7.
55. *Glasgow Herald*, 16 August 1911.
56. *Glasgow Herald*, 28 August 1911.
57. Cronin, *Industrial Conflict*, p. 58
58. Cronin, *Industrial Conflict*, p. 99.
59. Tillett B., *The History of the London Transport Workers Strike, 1911* (1911), p. 6.
60. Holton, *British Syndicalism*, p. 76.
61. *Forward*, 12 August 1911.
62. See Askwith G., *Industrial Problems and Disputes* (1920); Wells H.G., *The Labour Unrest*, (1913); Cole G.D.H., *The World of Labour*, (1913).
63. Kenefick, 'The Labour Unrest', p. 73
64. *Glasgow Herald* 11 December 1912.
65. *Glasgow Herald*, 24 November 1910.
66. *Ardrossan and Saltcoats Herald* 20 June 1913.
67. Gordon, E., *Women and the Labour Movement*, p.254. For a full account of the strike see Gordon, pp. 247–55 and Howitt S., 'The Kilbirnie Networkers' Strike, 1913' (Unpublished Honours Dissertation; University of Strathclyde, 1988).
68. Gordon, *Women and the Labour Movement*, p. 260.
69. Webb S. and B., *History of Trade Unionism* (1950 edn), pp.425–6.
70. These figures are derived from the Scottish Trades Union Congress Annual Reports.
71. For example, the miners' strikes at Dreghorn and Bellshill; *Glasgow Herald* 5 July 1912; 18 September 1912; 1 October 1912; 30 November 1912; *Glasgow Herald*, 26 and 27 November 1913; *Forward*, 13 June 1914; For the carters strike, see *Glasgow Herald* 9 and 20 May 1914. For the dyers strike, see *Glasgow Herald*, 20, 21 and 27 May 1914, 9 June 1914. For the crane and capstanmen's strike see *Glasgow Herald* 22, 23 and 26 May 1914

CHAPTER 2

Were Clydeside Employers More Autocratic? Labour Management and the 'Labour Unrest', c.1910-1914

Arthur McIvor

Introduction

Capital-labour relations were severely fractured on Clydeside, as elsewhere, during the pre-First World War phase of industrial militancy. With the notable exception of Joseph Melling's work, the historiography of 'red Clydeside' has tended to focus much more upon the activities of workers and their workplace and political organisations than the attitudes and behaviour of employers.[1] This chapter brings employers and managers of labour back into the centre of the picture. The grounds for doing so are clear: it will be argued that the orientation and policies of employers and managers played an important role in alienating workers, generating grievances and incubating discontent over 1910-14. Hence, this chapter explores the organisational structures and the range of strategies utilised over the period c1910-1914 by Clydeside industrialists to control labour, to undermine trade unionism and to neutralise strikes. I concentrate firstly and in some detail upon one of the most neglected dimensions within the literature – collective activity – examining the role of the network of employers' organisations which emerged on the Clyde before 1914. This involves some analysis of anti-unionism and strikebreaking, followed by discussion of the transition towards union recognition and the penetration and implications of collective bargaining in the region by 1914. Most bosses, however, were not members of an employers' organisation prior to World War One, just as most workers were not members of trade unions. The final section concentrates upon labour relations activities internal to the firm, commenting upon paternalism and welfarism, supervision, and the varying company-level mechanisms of work intensification and production 'speed–up' over c1900–1914. A main aim of the chapter is to probe the validity (and suggest some revision) of a dominant hypothesis within the historiography of Clydeside industrial relations – that employers in the region were autocratic, aggressively anti-union, and implacably opposed to collective bargaining.

This chapter largely overviews existing work in this area, though it also draws upon some limited primary source research within regional newspapers and some Parliamentary Papers. Employers remain under-researched and there is much potential for further work, especially with regard to employers' relations with unskilled and female workers, at the company and organised levels.[2] My conclusions are tentative, therefore, and are aimed at contributing to the debate and generating further discussion upon employer behaviour in this period.

National distinctiveness and regional divergence

Two important themes within the historiography on employers merit particular attention at the outset. Firstly, there exists a tendency within recent historical research upon employers to stress the intrinsic weakness of British industrialists, who are portrayed as incapable of preventing the insidious rise of trade unionism, the cancer of 'restrictive practices', or of combating strikes, hence condemning the economy from late-nineteenth century to a crippling lack of competitiveness. British capitalists embraced a range of attitudes and policies towards trade unions, but emerge as being distinctively characterised by their moderation, their organisational disunity and political impotence, especially when compared with industrialists in the USA and on the European continent.[3] Phelps-Brown has argued that British employers generally associated themselves more closely with their workers and were concerned, altruistically, with 'avoidance of conflict'. Furthermore:

> . . . on an international comparison, the British employers do appear as passive in their relations with the unions, less aggressive individually than American employers, less willing to combine for defence and attack than employers in both continents. . . .[4]

In a somewhat similar vein, Jonathan Zeitlin has recently interpreted the collective activity of employers thus:

> . . . employers' associations in Britain typically lacked the internal coherance and capacity for sustained offensive action of their German, Scandinavian and American counterparts. . . . British employers were rarely willing to subordinate their individual autonomy to the demands of collective action on a long-term basis. . . .[5]

It seems to me that such a portrayal considerably understates the power of organised capital. Employers were not omnipotent, nor were they a monolithic force. Divisions and conflicts within their ranks are starkly evident from even the most cursory glance at the sources. However, one of the aims of this chapter is to sustain a rather more dynamic representation of employer behaviour in the period c1910-14 and one based on the notion of pursuit of class interests.

Whilst the national context (relatively liberal labour laws; reformist Liberal administrations from 1906; tightening labour markets; changing public opinion) provided some space for trade union implantation and strike activity, regional divergences in social relations, as Alastair Reid has suggested, undermine somewhat the notion of 'national distinctiveness'. And this is the second main theme within the historiography that I would highlight.[6] Clydeside employers have been characterised in the literature as distinctively authoritarian and anti-union, intolerant and autocratic in their dealings with the workers.[7] I would not significantly disagree with this thesis, though it remains to be corroborated through systematic empirical research. However, I would argue that as it stands it merits some reformulation because it tends to obscure the co-existence of a whole range of management strategies designed to control labour as well as a tendency over time for managerial attitudes to evolve and adapt. Within a framework that appears to have been more openly autocratic there proved, in reality, to be many ways to skin a cat. The intransigence of many Clyde employers in their dogged refusal to recognise trade unions did escalate industrial discontent. However, over the period from around the mid-1890s to 1920, there was a marked tendency on Clydeside, as elsewhere, to concede collective bargaining rights and move towards more corporatist solutions to the labour problem. This tactical concession – most marked during the decade 1910-20 – was a rational choice given quite changed labour market circumstances, where employers were faced with strong trade unions capable of sustaining long strikes. Such a transition towards procedural modes of control, moreover, had distinct advantages for industrialists. Such issues are taken up in more detail in what follows. First, however, a few comments are necessary on the Clyde economy and the institutional structure of Clydeside capitalism.

Company structure and organisational developments

By 1910–14 the Clydeside economy was quite diversified, but dominated by heavy industry, especially the export-orientated sectors of iron and steel manufacture, coal mining, engineering, shipbuilding, textiles and heavy chemicals. As competition intensified (both with England and overseas) in the late nineteenth century these industries were particularly hard-hit. Relative capital starvation – linked to the poorer state of the Scots economy and to high levels of investment abroad – only made matters worse.[8] One reaction was for companies to amalgamate and hence benefit from economies of scale. Clydeside industry was becoming increasingly concentrated into larger and larger units in the late nineteenth and early twentieth century. In textile printing and dyeing a duopoly emerged, with the formation of the United Turkey Red Co. and the Calico Printers' Association (who together controlled about 90percent of the market). Similarly, in cotton thread with the dominance of two multi-unit corporations: Coats and Clarks. Tennants (later United Alkali) was the largest chemical works in Europe, whilst other major employers of labour on Clydeside included the giant multinational Singer corporation in Clydebank, Weirs in Cathcart, the North British Locomotive works in Springburn, the big shipyards of the Upper Clyde (including John Browns, Fairfields and Yarrow) and the railway companies based in Glasgow. Heavy industry was characterised by a high level of interlocking directorships, notably between the coal companies, iron and steel, engineering and shipbuilding.[9]

Such developments should not, however, be taken out of perspective. Concentration mirrored developments south of the border; indeed, the Census of Production in 1907 indicates that the average size of Scottish firms was about the same as in England. As Melling has demonstrated, heterogeneity, fragmentation, divisions and an intensely competitive relationship characterised pre-First World War Scottish capitalism.[10] The modernised, large-scale sector co-existed with handicraft workshops, small factories and homework. The ethos of limited liability companies clashed with the more paternalist regimes of family-owned firms. There was a world of difference between the small jobbing master builder or the sweatshop tailor in Glasgow's east end, working from a rented room and employing a handful of seamstresses, and the massive corporations such as Weirs, Singer, Tennants or the North British Railway.

In another sense the classic notion of independent and individualistic entrepreneurial activity needs to be modified because increasingly in the late nineteenth and early twentieth century Clydeside employers were organising together to protect and advance their interests as a class. By 1914, an extensive matrix of 25 national employers' organisations and over 80 local associations dealing with labour matters were located in Clydeside.[11] In the building sector, over 30 local associations existed across the main Clydeside towns and their activities were coordinated through three Scottish federations; the master plasterers, master painters and the Scottish National Building Trades Federation. The coalowners were organised in county-wide associations in Ayrshire and Lanarkshire. Powerful employers' organisations existed in the Clydeside engineering and shipbuilding trades in the North-West Engineering Employers' Association and the Clyde Shipbuilders' Association. The functions of the latter were integrated to an increasing degree – they shared the same secretary (Thomas Biggart) and premises, together with the Clyde Ship Repairers' Association and Scottish associations of master brassfounders, coppersmiths and sheet metal employers. The iron and steel masters were also well-organised by 1914, in three national federations based in Glasgow. Collective organisation was also evident in the clothing industry, with two national federations based in Glasgow and four local associations in the vicinity, including separate branches in Glasgow of Jewish and non-Jewish master tailors. Amongst other industries on the Clyde where employers' organisations were active over 1910-1914 were printing and bookbinding, paper, furniture manufacture, woodworking, coopering, sailmaking, pottery, vehicle building, brickmaking, baking and brewing.[12]

Most of these organisations had antecedents in the late nineteenth century. However, the Board of Trade Directories of Industrial Associations do indicate quite clearly the steady growth of employers' associations in the region over the period 1900-1914. Almost a third of Clydeside organisations registered in 1914 were not evident in 1900. New organisations developed in transport (carting; shipping), food preparation, brewing, oil, laundries, electrical contracting, clothing and some peripheral areas of the textile trade (rope, lace and dyeing) between these years.[13] This emergence of a variegated and multi-functional matrix of powerful employers' organisations provides tangible evidence that over the two decades or so before 1914 the class identities of Scottish employers were sharpening. One powerful stimulant was the growth of trade unions and their pursuit of more aggressively militant tactics over 1910-14. Other cementing pressures were the more competitive marketplace and an increasingly interventionist, 'grandmotherly' government. In particular, the passage of social and welfare legislation over c1890-1914 constituted a powerful stimulus on employers to organise and combine, not least because this added considerably to employers' production costs.[14]

Such levels of collective organisation amongst employers on the Clyde appears quite impressive. However, again this has to be kept in perspective. Unfortunately, we have no comprehensive data on the membership of these bodies and, hence, no real idea of how representative they were of their respective constituencies. Such data remains to be painstakingly reconstructed from archival work in the surviving Clydeside associations' records.[15] However, circumstantial evidence strongly suggests that there was a considerable unorganised segment and that this was probably larger in 1914 than those affiliated and organised (with the possible exceptions of the coal, shipbuilding and engineering industries). The giant Singer corporation provides an example – it consistently stood aloof from the Engineering Employers' Federation. Internal divisions could also weaken what appeared at first sight to be powerful and monolithic bodies. The actions of most employers' organisations were undermined, by a greater or lesser degree, by in-fighting multiple interest groups, rifts between conciliators and confrontationists, hawks and doves. Divisions were based on ideological differences, or diverging product market experience or differences of company structure or on custom and practice. Competitive advantage was also a key centripetal influence, corroding solidaristic endeavours. Reid has illustrated this for Clyde shipbuilding.[16] In shipping, to give another example, there were two competing employers' associations on the Clyde before World War One and a clutch of large shipping lines (McBrayne; Cunard; White Star) that refused membership of either. Such divisions worked to undermine the power of Clyde shipping companies in their relations with their workers over 1910-14, as Paterson has demonstrated.[17] The Scottish Furniture Manufacturers' Society were weakened by a large unorganised section within the industry: 'who do not recognise trade unions, are able to employ cheaper labour and to turn out goods at less cost.'[18] There also existed in 1914 industries where employers' organisation had not established any roots on Clydeside, including agriculture, fishing, domestic service, distribution, insurance, banking and finance, most textile manufacture (including cotton and wool) and chemicals.[19] Most of these were sectors where trade unionism was insignificant and hence the vital centrifugal force bringing employers together was absent.

Organised employers' strategies: coercion and conciliation

Rejecting ideas of national culture, Howard Gospel has recently argued that the nature of markets, the structure of firms and the organisation of production were three key variables determining employer labour relations policies – or, more correctly, were factors which constrained and influenced employers' choices.[20] Employers in transport – railways, road haulage and shipping – were hemmed in by fierce competition in markets, over which they had little effective control, and this fostered a more draconian anti-unionism. Zeitlin has gone further, rejecting notions of simple economic determinism and emphasising employers' ability to make 'strategic choices' thus contributing to a variegated pattern of labour relations policies.[21] Other commentators have compared contrasting managerial styles within particular industries and sectors across and even within regions.[22] Differences in product markets, firms and production methods were important here. However, there is also the possibility that each nation state incorporated within itself many quite different forces of acculturation/socialisation. Rather than an homogeneous package this was more of a heterogeneous mosaic of influences. Clydeside provides as good a case study as any to illustrate this.

Despite divisions, the existence of an organisation proved beneficial to industrialists, strengthening the hands of individual employers in their dealings with trade unions. Such organisations played an important role in forging alliances, defending class interests and structuring industrial relations on the Clyde before World War One. Such bodies helped to undermine trade unionism, to neutralise the sectional strike weapon, to minimise the cost to employers of labour legislation (such as the Workmen's Compensation Acts), and to promote uniformity in the labour contract and labour markets, hence taking wages out of competition and removing many conflict-inducing anomalies. Employers' organisations also played a role in developing collective bargaining systems, albeit somewhat tardily in the west of Scotland.

Clydeside employers resorted to a range of underhand tactics in an attempt to undermine trade unions, neutralise strikes, intimidate workers and punish what they regarded as abhorrent behaviour or dangerous political views.[23] To openly profess left-wing views in Scotland before World War One was an extremely risky business. The Clydeside Marxist Harry McShane recalled that in periods of slack trade 'the socialists were always the first to be paid off'.[24] John MacLean (a teacher by profession) and his friend James MacDougall (a clerk at the Pollokshaws branch of the Clydesdale bank) were both sacked because of their political beliefs in this period. In MacDougall's case the employers were quite explicit in citing their fears about his agitation and wanted to nip in the bud any possibility of a branch of the Clerks' Union being created in the bank.[25] The degree and nature of job discrimination and vetting varied significantly between and within industries, and even within companies, not least because of the very high degree of autonomy which foremen exercised in such matters in this period. Selective re-employment – weeding out activists – after a dispute was common practice, as was the blacklisting of workers on strike to ensure that they were deprived of alternative employment in the region. A biased judiciary also stacked the cards further against those actively involved in strikes. Sentences for breach of the peace and other misdemenours during strikes frequently carried much heavier penalties than would normally occur.

Blackleg importation was a common employer response to strike activity on Clydeside over 1910-14, especially when strikers were unskilled or semi-skilled. Professional strikebreakers and 'free labour' agencies were on hand to provide substitute labour during disputes, as, for example, at Ardrossan in 1910-11.[26] In their survey of such tactics, the Glasgow Labour History Workshop identified labour replacement in 29 out of 74 strikes on the Clyde over 1910, 1911 and 1912. This was more than double the rate of labour replacement in the UK as a whole during the period of 'labour unrest'.[27] This suggests that Clydeside deviated somewhat from the UK trend because the period c1890-1920 witnessed a quite dramatic fall in the propensity of British employers to import blackleg labour to break strikes. This may well be the product of a seriously overstocked labour market in west Scotland.

Skilled workers (with the advantage of labour scarcity) and their unions could be treated with more respect by Clydeside employers. However, before 1914 when trade unions were still only just obtaining a foothold in most lesser skilled and female dominated sectors on the Clyde, joining a trade union and involvement in strike action could be enough to precipitate dismissal. J. P. Coats, the Paisley thread manufacturers, discriminated in this way against members of the Amalgamated Society of Dyers in the summer of 1912.[28] Jeannie McKinlay was sacked after six years service from her job at the Kirtonfield Bleachworks in 1910 because of her attempts to recruit women into the National Federation of Women Workers.[29] Elsewhere, workers were arbitrarily dismissed by autocratic employers who resented any criticism of their working conditions. In February 1911, the manager of a small clothing sweatshop on Argyle St, Glasgow (employing 20 women) sacked a worker who they suspected of providing information to the NFWW (who informed the Factory Inspector) about illegal deductions from earnings. Several years earlier this same woman had been involved in forming one of the first female unions in the Glasgow clothing trade.[30]

The railway companies, coalowners, electrical contractors, shipping lines, engineering companies and shipbuilders on Clydeside all developed sophisticated victimisation procedures before World War One, coordinated by their employers' associations. The Lanarkshire Coalmasters' Association operated what they termed 'the block' on striking miners.[31] 'The older miners', Bob Selkirk recalled, 'had a real dread of victimisation'. Selkirk and his whole section were sacked after initiating a strike at the Ormiston Coal Company when the company refused to pay extra for sorting out small coal in 1909.[32] Similarly, the Engineering Employers' Federation and the Clyde Shipbuilders' Association routinely circulated lists of striking workers to all member firms and enforced, through their rules, the use of the 'enquiry' system to vet applicants for jobs. Railway companies utilised the pretext of breaches of the health and safety 'rule book' to sack union activists, and, in some cases, even union members. Some railway workers emigrated to Australia and South America in an attempt to escape the blacklist.[33] Similarly, the Shipping Federation used medical inspections to victimise.[34] Complaints from unions, reports in the labour press, the use of aliases by victimised activists and the outpayments under victimisation pay of many unions suggest that such blacklisting activities were widespread and could be effective. However, one suspects that much depended on the state of labour markets and the extent to which individual employers within a given industry and region were organised, and hence directly involved in this formalised victimisation network.

Employers' organisations thus provided valuable practical and moral assistance during strikes. This was a particularly attractive service to medium-sized companies, where a union presence existed, but who lacked the sophisticated internal management hierarchy and the power necessary to challenge unions and defeat strikes. The revisionist interpretation of Phelps-Brown, Zeitlin et. al. downplays such utilisation of more draconian anti-labour methods that clearly represented naked pursuit of class interests. Employers' organisations facilitated the ability of individual employers to replace labour and effectively victimise strikers. Financial support and legal aid could be obtained through affiliation to organisations like the master engineers, shipbuilders and coalowners. Moreover, lock-outs occured frequently on the Clyde over 1900-1914 and some form of employers' organisation was a necessary prerequisite for the prosecution of a lock-out beyond the level of the individual firm. In this way workers could, quite literally, be starved into submission. Such heavy-handed tactics served both to intimidate and discipline workers and, as labour market conditions improved over 1910-14, to further antagonise employees and embitter capital-labour relations on the Clyde.

However, it would be wrong to just view Clydeside employers as autocratic anti-unionists. This was a diverse group and, in reality, a wide range of attitudes, responses and political orientations were evident over 1910-14. Partly because of the provocative nature of such tactics and partly in response to the rise of union power (and the increasing dissemination of alarming socialist and syndicalist ideas) some of the longer-established employers' organisations balanced the use of the stick with the carrot of collective bargaining. This was particularly the case amongst those employing skilled and well-unionised labour, including engineering, shipbuilding, coal mining, baking, building and iron and steel masters. Building craftsmen, Clydeside carpetweavers and Greenock shipwrights were among those groups of workers who bargained collectively with their employers as early as the mid-nineteenth century.[35] One of the most important functions of employers' associations across many of these craft-based industries lay in the initiatives they took to create, sustain and extend a more formalised industrial relations system – which might be theorised as an attempt to extend procedural controls and substantive norms over labour.[36] This system was based on joint, collectively agreed regulation of wages, hours and other working conditions and increasingly incorporated comprehensive disputes procedures. In engineering and shipbuilding, a jointly agreed stage-by-stage disputes procedure moving from the local to the national level had been elaborated before 1910.[37] In iron and steel manufacture, wages were regulated by joint agreement and tied automatically to a sliding scale based on the selling price of iron in the Glasgow market. Pit-level collective bargaining was also common amongst the large employers in coal mining.[38] Local collective bargaining on substantive issues had also long been a tradition in the building trades. The pre-war Glasgow carpenters' joint agreement was fairly typical, regulating hourly wage rates, working hours, overtime payments, holidays, travelling allowances, periods of notice and permissible ratios of apprentices to journeymen. Changes to the agreement were only to be made annually, subject to agreement in the joint conciliation board.[39]

However, the evidence suggests that whilst trade union recognition was growing, collective bargaining was poorly developed in West Scotland prior to World War One. Growth was upon a very low base. Through the second half of the nineteenth century Clydeside had attracted investment in heavy industry partly because of its reputation for anti-unionism. Formal union recognition and the concession of collective bargaining rights were regarded as anathema to most industrialists who refused to accept workers as equals, viewing them as a class apart, as inferior, to be governed, rather than being jointly involved in the process of management.[40] Hence the prevailing view that the provision of capital conferred the sacrosanct right to manage labour and the enterprise as employers felt fit – without any outside interference. The boilermakers' union, for example, was formally recognised for collective bargaining purposes later on the Clyde than elsewhere.[41] The weaker tradition of resolving conflict through joint bargaining is also reflected in a clear tendency within the ranks of the Clyde engineering employers to fail to agree within local and regional joint conferences under the formalised disputes procedure created by the Terms of Settlement which followed the long lock-out of 1897-8. Hence, a higher proportion of disputes than anywhere else were passed up the line to clog up Central Conference in London (table 2.1).

Table 2.1 Engineering Employers' Federation: central conferences under the disputes procedure, Jan 1910 – Aug 1914

North-West (Clydeside)	22
North-East Coast (Tyneside)	12
London	9
Manchester	6
Birmingham	5
East Scotland	7

Source: EEF, Central Conferences, 1898-1927 (EEF, 1928)

There was also an element of patriarchal control here. Eleanor Gordon has demonstrated that employer opposition to the recognition of and bargaining with female trade unions in Scotland was particularly acute.[42] This was borne out of a desire to maintain control over what was perceived as a docile and cheap segment of the labour force.

Other evidence confirms the domineering, unilateralist flavour of managerial practices on Clydeside and the deep-rooted opposition to collective bargaining prior to the First World War. Dundee, Aberdeen and 10 other English towns had general conciliation and arbitration boards by 1914, whereas Glasgow did not.[43] Nor did the city have a conciliation board for the building trades as a whole, unlike almost all other major towns and cities in the UK. In contrast to other regions, collective bargaining was insignificant in Clydeside textile manufacture and local authority employment.[44] Moreover, and most significantly, the governments official report on collective agreements in 1910 clearly exposes the paucity of collective bargaining on Clydeside. Aggregating up official figures for workpeople covered by collective agreements suggests that only around 13 per cent of workers employed on Clydeside in 1910 were directly subject to any kind of collectively agreed working conditions. If we take coal, engineering and ship-building out of this equation, less than 25,000 other Clydeside workers in 1910 were covered by collective agreements, a mere 3percent of the total number of such workers employed.[45]

It should be stressed, however, that even on the Clyde this scenario was changing over time and the years 1910 to 1914 witness some extension of bargaining rights in the area. Probably twice as many Clydeside workers were covered by collective bargaining agreements by 1914 compared to 1900.[46] This was partly prompted by the bureaucratic and corporatist tendencies of many employers' associa-tions, partly by external pressure (from public opinion and the government's conciliation department, headed by George Askwith) and partly by the counter-responses of workers who were joining unions in increasing numbers over 1900-14, initiating industrial action and forcing employers to the negotiating table. Faced with stronger and permanent trade unions, firmly implanted within a broader spec-trum of industrial labour, such a strategic transition was vitally import-ant in providing some stability to industrial relations. Elsewhere, as in Lancashire, industrialists had come to explicitly embrace such proce-dural control strategies by the end of the nineteenth century and discovered a series of advantages lying therein. Not least, the ability to contain and muzzle rank-and-file militancy by funneling disputes up a lengthy bureaucratic procedure, refusing to negotiate if formal proce-dure was breached and using union officials to police collectively agreed decisions.[47]

Such systems conceded some control over the determination of working conditions to unions and, over the long term, may have helped to fossilize Scotland's (and Britain's) characteristic structure of multi-unionism. However, collective bargaining also had the advantage to employers of enabling costs of labour to be more accurately calculated and, critically, enabled damaging, undercutting competition between employers to be more effectively controlled. Moreover, as Richard Price has demonstrated, in craft trades joint bargaining represented an encroachment by capital into the autonomous domain of unilateral artisanal regulation through trade society rules.[48] The stabilising function of collective bargaining was a key inducement persuading many employers to accept the limited dilution of managerial prerogative that was inherent in the transition to joint collective bargaining. And it should be stressed that this was *very* limited dilution of managerial rights. Collective bargaining prior to 1914 was invariably on the employers' terms, usually only upon a fairly narrow agenda of issues (wages, hours, apprentice ratios and conciliation machinery). The state of order books, moreover, usually determined wage movements, not costs of living.

By 1914 then, multi-employer bargaining dominated large sections of the Clydeside heavy industries. Moreover, some groups of semi and unskilled workers achieved bargaining rights over 1910-14, albeit severely prescribed. The list would include railway workers, seamen, dockers, engineering and some shipbuilding labourers, as well as some women workers, where recognition was achieved by the National Federation of Women Workers.[49] Clydeside employers were undoubtedly more autocratic, on the whole, than many other comparable industrial regions.[50] But the evidence indicates that much tactical maneouvring was occuring amongst industrialists over 1910-14 on the Clyde, as elsewhere. In the event, Clydeside employers failed to take the American option, ignoring opportunities to extirpate the trade unions altogether. This represented, at least in part, a strategic commitment to moderate, constitutional and economistic modes of trade unionism which could operate as a safety valve, providing a valuable bulwark against more radical alternatives (syndicalism and industrial unionism) that challenged the very basis of managerial prerogative and proprietorial control.

So, at one level joint negotiations in some sectors of the economy helped to contain industrial conflict, keeping discontent within bounds. However, the traditional antipathy amongst Clydeside capitalists towards collective bargaining did have important implications for capital-labour relations. This was a major source of conflict in the region during 1910-14 when market conditions improved. In strike after strike across Clydeside workers demands coalesced around the issue of union recognition and the concession of collective bargaining rights. One gets a sense from reading contemporary reports on strikes over 1910-14 that the achievement of formal union recognition, with bargaining rights, was considered by workers involved to be a basic prerequisite for sustaining material concessions won over the long term. Arguably, the 'labour unrest' of 1910-14 would not have achieved the depth it did had more employers and their organisations on the Clyde provided the means, through extensive networks of collective bargaining, to address grievances through formalised procedural mechanisms.

Company level labour relations strategies: welfarism, autocratic control and work intensification

Whilst the power and regulatory functions of employers' organisations were growing before First World War (and have been underestimated by many historians) still much initiative in labour relations lay at the level of the individual company. Decisions, choices, tactics and strategies at company level could and did intimately affect capital-labour relations on Clydeside and contributed significantly to the 'labour unrest' of 1910-14 in many ways. Several issues merit further investigation. Firstly, the fracturing and reformulation of the traditional control mechanisms of paternalism and welfarism. Secondly, the autocratic authority of foremen and management on the Clyde. And, finally, the all-pervasive tendency on the part of Clydeside management over c1900-1914 to intensify workloads to maintain profitability in a harsher international economic environment. These developments unleashed a reservoir of discontent across the region over 1910-14. This protest manifested itself, however, primarily in the industrial rather than the political sphere. The process of politicisation and class formation, as Knox has shown, remained incomplete prior to the war and was not just, or even primarily the product of changes in the labour process.[51] Still, to some extent, wartime 'speed-up' and draconian state control over the labour market during the First World War accentuated a process that was already underway in the preceding period.

Company paternalism, or welfarism – 'a means of fulfilling those human needs not met by the cash nexus'[52] – had long been an integral part of the repertoire of labour management strategies on Clydeside. Across many industries, including the railways, iron and steel, textiles, chemicals, coal, shipbuilding and brewing, employers provided a whole range of benefits, on an ex-gratia or systematic basis, to their workers. Such provision included company housing, pensions, sick and accident pay and company provision of social and cultural space (such as canteens, libraries, parks and company sports grounds) and activities (outings; classes and clubs). The provision of company housing was probably the most important single element of welfare policy on the Clyde before 1914. Isolated sites drew employers (especially in coal mining, shipbuilding, railways and mining) into constructing and offering company housing for the use of workers.[53] The miners rows, tenements at New Lanark and the company housing on the hill overlooking the Singer corporation in Clydebank and the North British Locomotive works in Springburn are all examples. The motivation behind such welfare provision varied, though undoubtedly some employers introduced such 'perks' out of genuine humanitarian interest (such as the Quaker employers). Systematic welfarism was costly to the employer, however, and needed to be justified by most capitalists on economic grounds. Melling has persuasively argued that the primary objects of such strategies were threefold: to regulate and improve labour supply (where industries were located in remote areas); to maximise worker efficiency (working on the maxim that healthy workers are more productive workers); and to promote labour discipline and enhance managerial control over the workforce.[54]

Scottish company paternalism has been examined in depth elsewhere.[55] In relation to our study of the labour unrest of 1910-14, several points are worth highlighting. Firstly, this matrix of benefits and 'perks' undoubtedly had the effect of inducing worker quiescence and constraining industrial militancy. In a period before the welfare state, the threat of eviction from company housing or removal of benefits or pension rights could have a salutary effect, particularly when there were so many cases of Clydeside employers actually implementing such tactics.[56] Moreover, company-financed friendly societies (which existed in the railways and some collieries) helped to inculcate loyalty to the firm and reduce reliance upon trade unions.

Secondly, evidence suggests that employer paternalism was eroding on the Clyde in the late nineteenth and early years of the twentieth century as companies grew larger, competition intensified (thus tightening resources available for welfare provision) and industrial relations became more impersonal. Keir Hardie reminisced in 1891 on the passing of paternal ties: 'In the past there was a personal relationship between the mine-owner who owned one pit and his workmen, he knew them all'.[57] This disappearance of close personal links and contraction of traditional modes of company paternalism created a space filled, to some degree, by the friendly society activities of trade unions. Such developments also generated demands for wage rises to compensate for the erosion of the non-wage benefits which characterised paternalistic work regimes.[58]

Thirdly, the prosecution of welfarist policies needs to be kept firmly in perspective. Only a small minority of firms were committed welfarists, as Melling and others have demonstrated. Few offered much in the way of job security or job tenure, basic tenets of modern systematised welfarist systems.[59] Moreover, welfare provision was deliberately selective and invariably discretionary. Managerial, salaried, clerical, supervisory and skilled workers were usually the only recipients of company largesse. Most female workers, labourers and semi-skilled workers (by far the majority of the workforce) continued to rely on their weekly wage packet, their own devices and family and neighbourhood support networks to cope with the vicious vagaries of a boom and slump economy in which competition was intensifying. Nevertheless, to some extent welfarism did sweeten the pill of exploitative capitalism, assuaging industrial conflict. However, it needs to be re-emphasised that such policies were not that common amongst Clydeside capitalists.

More typical of this pre-war period, perhaps, were traditional modes of controlling the labour force, through the iron discipline and unilateral control of employers, managers and their 'NCOs' on the shop floor – the foremen. With minimal state welfare provision, widespread victimisation and patchy protection through trade unions workers had everything to lose and little to gain by initiating and sustaining strike action. Favouritism, as Harry McShane testified, was rife on Clydeside, and was fuelled by religious sectarianism (for example in the shipyards). The discretionary power of foremen was virtually complete on the shop floor in the pre-war period on the Clyde. They practically ruled all aspects of workers lives within the factory: hiring and firing; organising production; fixing piecerates; dispensing discipline. Complaints and deepening bitterness about the draconian activities of foremen – 'the bastards in bowlers' – permeates the testimony of workers during the 1910-14 period of 'labour unrest' on the Clyde.[60]

Moreover, where companies were large and powerful strikes could be smashed without resort to external aid and the assistance of employers' associations. The strike at Singer in 1911, for example, was countered by threats of moving production to other plants, use of a postcard 'plebiscite' and mass sackings of activists. Those dismissed included the whole of the almost 200 strong Strike Committee.[61] Dalrymple's smashing of the Glasgow tramway workers strike in 1911 – amid much police brutality and large numbers of arrests – was followed by utilisation of the draconian (and somewhat outmoded) non-strike pledge.[62] In a similarly aggressive and uncompromising fashion the strikes of 600 workers at British Aluminium in Sept-Oct 1910, 300 workers at the Port Eglinton Ironworks in March-May 1912, almost 2,000 workers at Stewart and Lloyds steelworks in September 1912 and around 500 workers at the Shawfield Chemical Works in September-October 1913 were swept aside.[63]

Labour relations policies were rarely mutually exclusive and it was perfectly possible, indeed more common than not, for employers to combine different approaches to the labour problem and exploit a range of control strategies tailored to particular circumstances. However, in response to growing competition and a decline in profitability many industrialists in the basic sectors of the Clydeside economy were increasingly concentrating upon extending their control and authority over the way work was organised and performed in an attempt to cut labour costs over c1900-1914. In the process, employers were intensifying workloads and extending the monitoring of workers at the point of production. This, again, has been examined in some detail elsewhere.[64] It took many forms: work pacing through mechanisation; increased levels of supervision; the extension of payments-by-results wage systems (such as the premium bonus scheme in metal-working); reducing the size of work teams and squads (as in the docks and at Singer); replacing skilled and higher paid workers with cheaper labour; cutting piecework rates (common in shipbuilding, engineering and coal); and crude bullying and driving by zealous foremen and sub-contractors. The tendency was for employers to look inwards, extending internal management structures and control mechanisms. This process of squeezing more out of the wage-for-effort exchange can be perceived, at various levels, in coal mining and engineering, on the Glasgow docks, in iron and steel manufacture, at Singer, Weirs, the Argyle Motor Company, United Turkey Red and across a number of disputes in the textile industry over 1910-14.

In its most advanced form pre-1914, workers were faced with intensification of their workloads and loss of control over the pace and rhythm of their work through the application of 'scientific' modes of labour management, derived from Taylorism and imported from the USA, and, to a lesser degree, from Germany.[65] Such alien work regimes were based upon systematic time study of labour processes (using a stop watch), detailed division of labour, deskilling and job fragmentation. They thus threatened to erode the pivotal power of the skilled and well-unionised craft artisans within the workplace. However, these systems were also introduced within process industries employing a large proportion of semi-skilled workers and which lacked a strong craft tradition. The Singer corporation in Clydebank, Weirs in Cathcart and Langs in Johnstone experimented systematically with such methods.[66] Other Clydeside companies embraced elements of scientific management, including premium bonus wage payment schemes (such as the Rowan system, developed on the Clyde) which incorporated an automatic price breaker. Consequently, a pincer movement – eroding paternalism and an all-pervasive intensification of work – further alienated and embittered workers. Such policies coagulated into key sources of grievance and discontent on Clydeside over 1910-14.

Conclusion

To sum up. This brief and cursory overview of the literature on Clyde employers suggests that there remains space for much more systematic research. Unfortunately, we still know very little about employer behavior, organisation and strategies across vast swathes of the Scottish economy, including clothing, transport, chemicals, food processing, personal service, administration, commerce, finance and distribution.

Relations between employers and unskilled labour, officeworkers and women remain particularly under-researched areas. Until these gaps are filled, hypotheses on regional employer behaviour – and whether Clydeside capitalists were distinctively autocratic – remain tentative and unproven.

What does appear evident is that employer organisation, behaviour and managerial strategies influenced industrial relations on the Clyde during the years 1910-14 in a number of ways. The two decades before World War One witnessed marked enhancement of the collective strength of Clydeside capitalists as companies grew larger, mergers proliferated and industry-wide employers' associations were created. Such organisational developments served to bolster employers' confidence in conflict with their workers, improving the capacity of employers' to successfully break strikes – using tactics such as labour replacement, victimisation and the lock-out – through access to increasingly sophisticated collective support networks.[67] The range of employers' organisations activities evident before 1914, across the gamut of labour market regulation, conflict management, political lobbying, the regulation of trade and product markets and the provision of mutual insurance indicates a much more vital role for such organisations than much of the literature implies. Employers' organisations on the Clyde thus performed a vital function in regulating important aspects of industrial relations prior to World War One.

Changes in company structure and ideology combined with the development of fiercer overseas competition in the years leading up to the war significantly disrupted industrial relations. Firstly, this triggered an erosion of traditional, paternalist modes of labour control, involving reciprocal rights and obligations. There emerged more impersonal (and alienating) relationships at the point of production and this fracturing of paternalism bred resentment and bitterness. Secondly, increasing competition in the market place precipitated a drive to maintain profitability by employers, achieved through cranking up productivity levels, intensifying workloads and squeezing more out of the wage-for-effort exchange. This process was multi-faceted, involving techno-logical change, wage cutting, manipulation of machine-staffing levels and increased monitoring and supervision. At one extreme within this spectrum of work intensification was old-fashioned 'driving' and 'sweating' by foremen and sub-contractors. At the other extreme, within the largest and most modern plants, was experimentation with elements of scientific management. Such 'speed up' became a major source of grievance over 1910-14, with many groups of workers utilising the opportunity of tighter labour markets to attempt to gain some material compensation for extra effort. Moreover, frequently attempts were being made to pressurise employers to grant trade union recognition and bargaining rights in an effort to exert some level of control over labour processes and work methods that were rapidly changing in the face of more hostile product markets.

These developments were occuring across the industrialised areas of Britain prior to the First World War. What, if anything, is unique to Clydeside? There is much evidence to support the prevailing notion that Clydeside employers were well organised and more domineering in their relations with their workers and their trade unions before 1914. However, some qualifications to these hypotheses are necessary. Firstly, deep divisions of interest, based on individualism, competition, company structure, industrial identity, product market experience and political orientation fractured employer solidarity. This was certainly no monolithic group. Secondly, to simply typecast Clydeside capitalists as autocratic ignores the tactical flexibility exercised by the bosses and the wide range of strategies that industrialists used to control labour – both internal and external to the firm. Thirdly, the scenario was not a static one. Employers strategies were evolving, in a state of flux. What is apparent on the Clyde – as elsewhere – is a noticeable shift towards union recognition and collective bargaining in the years leading up to the First World War.

In the final analysis, however, the evidence still points strongly towards a doggedly anti-unionist regional ethos within the capitalist fraternity on Clydeside in 1910-14. During these years Clyde employers were more likely to break strikes with force and to import replacement labour than elsewhere. Clyde industrialists remained less tolerant of trade unions – the data accumulated by the Labour Department of the Board of Trade indicates quite clearly that union recognition and collective bargaining remained weak on the Clyde compared to other regions over 1910-14. Whilst tactical concessions were made over these years, Clydeside employers proved determined, for the most part, to oppose encroachments into what they regarded as the sacrosanct right of providers of capital to manage their concerns as they thought fit. Trade union interference – what one Clyde employer termed 'inroads on the power of management in the shops'[68] – was fiercely resisted. Concessions to labour were made reluctantly and temporarily, many being dismantled when labour market and political circumstances altered in employers favour after 1920. This dogged employer intransigence incubated intense industrial conflict on the Clyde in the years leading up to the war. Accumulated grievances and bitterness with aggressive employers' attitudes and intolerant managerial behaviour thus constituted a significant element in the baggage taken over by workers and activists from the 'labour unrest' period of 1910-14 into the maelstrom of 'red Clydeside' during the war and immediate post-war years.

NOTES

1. Melling, J., 'Scottish Industrialists and the Changing Character of Class Relations in the Clyde Region, c1880–1918' in Dickson T.(ed), *Capital and Class in Scotland*, Edinburgh, (1982). For overviews of the British dimension see Garside, W.R. and Gospel, H., 'Employers and managers' in Wrigley C.J.(ed), *A History of British Industrial Relations, 1870–1914* (1982) and Gospel, H. and Littler, C.R., *Managerial Strategies and Industrial Relations* (1983).

2. The literature has focused upon relations between employers and skilled, craft labour. This somewhat distorts the overall picture, exaggerating the relative weakness of employers. Two ongoing doctoral theses will make important contributions to this debate. See Devlin R., Strike Patterns and Class Formation 1880–1914: A Comparative Analysis (forthcoming Ph.D., University of Paisley); Johnston R., Political Strategies of Scottish Industrialists, c1870–1920 (forthcoming Ph.D., University of Strathclyde).

3. Tolliday, S. and Zeitlin, J.(eds), *The Power to Manage?* (1991); Turner J. (ed), *Businessmen and Politics* (1984). Also Fitzgerald, R., *British Labour Management and Industrial Welfare, 1846–1939* (1988).

4. Phelps Brown, H., *The Origins of Trade Union Power* (1983), p. 116.

5. Zeitlin, J., 'From Labour History to the History of Industrial Relations', *Economic History Review*, XL, 2, 1987, pp. 175.

6. Reid, A., *Social Classes and Social Relations in Britain, 1850–1914* (1992).

7. Knox, W., 'The political and workplace culture of the Scottish working class, 1832–1914' in Fraser, W.H. and Morris, R.J. (eds), *People and Society in Scotland, vol II, 1830–1914* (1990), pp. 150–51; Foster, J., 'A Proletarian Nation?' in Dickson, T., and Treble, J.(eds), *People and Society in Scotland vol III* (1992), pp. 217–9; Reid, A., 'Employers' Strategies and Craft Production' in Tolliday and Zeitlin, *Power to Manage?*; Melling, 'Scottish Industrialists'.

8. Between 1870 and 1900 Scottish investment overseas ran at a rate about double that of England. See Cambell, R.H., *The Rise and Fall of Scottish Industry, 1707–1939* (1980).

9. Scott J. and Hughes M., *The Anatomy of Scots Capital, 1900–1979* (1980).

10. Melling, 'Scottish Industrialists', pp. 69–80.

11. Board of Trade Labour Department (BTLD), Directory of Industrial Associations of the U.K. for 1914 (1914: Cd7483), pp. 1–69. 'Clydeside' is here defined as Glasgow and the counties of Dumbarton, Lanark, Renfrew, Ayr, Argyll and Bute.

12. BTLD Directory, 1914.

13. The Board of Trade Directories of Industrial Associations were compiled from 1900.

14. Examples would be the Factories and Mines Acts, Workmens Compensation, the Trades Boards, the Trades Disputes Act and the National Insurance scheme, all introduced before World War One. The political activities of Clydeside employers, at a local and national level, await systematic investigation.

15. For an example of an attempt to reconstruct employers' organisation membership in one region, through cross-linkage of trade directories and membership lists see McIvor, A., *Organised Capital: Employers' Associations and Industrial Relations in Northern England, 1880–1939* (1996), pp. 59–91.

16. Reid, 'Employers' Strategies', pp. 39–40.

17. The two organisations were the Glasgow branch of the Shipping Federation and the Glasgow Shipowners' Association (whose leading members included the three big Atlantic liner companies, the Allan, Anchor and Donaldson lines). See Paterson, H., Seamen on the Clyde, 1880–1914 (unpublished MPhil, University of Strathclyde), 1992.

18. *Glasgow Herald*, 25 February 1910.

19. The weakness of employer organisation within Scottish cotton spinning and weaving is made evident by Knox, W., *Hanging by a Thread: the Scottish Cotton Industry, c1850–1914* (Preston 1995), pp. 140–3. This is in marked contrast to Lancashire.

20. Gospel, H., *Markets, Firms and the Management of Labour in Modern Britain* (1992).

21. Zeitlin, J., 'The Internal Politics of Employers' Organization: the Engineering Employers' Federation, 1896–1939', in Tolliday and Zeitlin, *Power to Manage?*

22. Joyce, P. *Work, Society and Politics* (1980); Fitzgerald, *British Labour Management*; McIvor, *Organised Capital*.

23. For a detailed, comparative and innovative investigation of employer responses to strikes, exploiting computer analysis of quantitative material, see Ricky Devlin's chapter in this book. The following section is based largely on McIvor, A. and Paterson, H., 'Combating the Left' in Duncan R., and McIvor A., *Militant Workers* (Edinburgh, 1992).

24. McShane, H. & Smith, J., *No Mean Fighter* (1978), pp. 19–20. See also pp. 8–9, 31, 44.

25. *Forward*, 13, 20 and 27 March 1909. I am grateful to Irene Maver for this reference.

26. See Kenefick, W., 'The Impact of the Past upon the Present': The Experience of the Clydeside Dock Labour Force with particular reference to the Port of Glasgow' (unpublished PhD thesis, University of Strathclyde), 1995, and *Ardrossan: The Key to the Clyde* (Cunningham, 1993).

27. See chapter 1 in this book and McIvor, A., 'Employers' Organisations and Strikebreaking in Britain, 1880–1914', *International Review of Social History, XXIX* (1984), pp 1–33.

28. *Forward*, 3 August 1912

29. *Forward*, 20 August 1910; *Glasgow Herald*, 6 September 1910

30. *Forward*, 4 February 1911
31. Discovery of this victimisation prolonged a pit strike at Uddingston. See *Glasgow Herald*, 29 July 1911; 12 August 1911; 10, 11 November 1911.
32. Selkirk B., *The Life of a Worker* (1967), pp 7–9
33. Bagwell, P., *The Railwaymen* (1963), pp. 194–5.
34. *Forward*, 25 November 1911.
35. Fraser, W.H., *Trade Unions and Society, 1850–1880* (1974).
36. See Sisson, K., *The Management of Collective Bargaining* (1987).
37. See Zeitlin, 'Engineering', in Tolliday and Zeitlin, *Power to Manage?*; Lovell, J., 'Collective Bargaining and the Emergence of National Employer Organisation in the British Shipbuilding Industry', *International Review of Social History, XXXVI* (1991), pp 59–91.
38. Melling, 'Scottish Industrialists', p 74.
39. BTLD, Directory (1914), pp. 133–62.
40. Smout, T.C., *A Century of the Scottish People, 1830–1950* (1986), p. 107.
41. Knox, 'Political and Workplace Culture', p. 151.
42. Gordon, E., *Women and the Labour Movement in Scotland, 1850–1914* (1991), p. 259–60.
43. However, the Lord Provost of the city did, on occasions, perform such a function, as during the Glasgow carters strike in January–February 1913. *Glasgow Herald*, 22, 26 February 1913.
44. London, for example, had a conciliation board for tramway employment.
45. These proportions were roughly equivalent to U.K. figures. However, this is not comparing like with like. One would reasonably expect heavily industrialised, urban areas like the Clyde to have a much higher (perhaps double the UK average) proportion of workers covered by collectively bargained agreements. These figures are derived from aggregating data on all collective agreements reported to the Board of Trade Labour Department in 1910. See Report on Collective Agreements between Employers and Workpeople in the UK, 1910, Cd. 5366, pp. 431–90.
46. Judging from the lists of conciliation boards and joint agreements kept by the Board of Trade Labour Department over 1900–1914.
47. McIvor, *Organised Capital*, pp. 118–45; See also White J., *The Limits of Trade Union Militancy* (1978).
48. See Price, R., *Masters, Unions and Men* (1980)
49. Gordon, *Women and the Labour Movement*, p. 260.
50. As Devlin's comparative inter-regional analysis of the Annual Reports on Strikes and Lock-Outs suggests. See chapter three.
51. Knox, 'Political and Workplace Culture', pp. 151, 161–2.
52. Fitzgerald, *British Labour Management*, p 9
53. There were about 22–25,000 company-owned homes in mining areas in Scotland: Melling, 'Scottish Industrialists', p. 86.
54. Melling, J., 'Employers, Industrial Welfare and the Struggle for Workplace Control in British Industry, 1880–1920', in Gospel and Littler, *Managerial Strategies*, p. 57.
55. Melling, J., British Employers and the Development of Industrial Welfare (unpublished PhD, Glasgow University), 1980; Melling, 'Scottish Industrialists', pp. 80–104; Melling, 'Employers, Industrial Housing and the Evolution of Company welfare Policies in Britain's Heavy Industries: West of Scotland, 1870–1920', *International Review of Social History, XXXVI* (1981).

56. For example, the mass evictions during the Scottish railway workers strike of 1890–91. See Duncan, R., 'Eviction, Riot and Resistance: Motherwell and the Scottish Railway Strike, 1890–1891, *Scottish Labour History Review* No1 Autumn/Winter 1989.

57. Cited in Phelps Brown, *Origins*, p. 105.

58. In the case of the apprentices strike in 1912, young workers objected to employer deductions from wage packets to pay for the provision of state welfare (under the National Insurance Act). See Knox, W., 'Down with Lloyd George: The Apprentices Strike of 1912', *Scottish Labour History Society Journal*, 19, 1984, p. 22.

59. Melling, 'Employers, Industrial Housing'; Littler, C.R., *The Development of the Labour Process in Capitalist Societies* (1982), p. 91; Askwith, G., *Industrial Problems and Disputes* (1920), pp. 353–4. The contemporary comparison would be with Japan.

60. Melling, J., ' 'Non-Commissioned Officers': British Employers and their Supervisory Workers, 1880–1920', *Social History*, V, no. 2 (1980); Burgess, K., 'Authority Relations and the Division of Labour in British Industry, with Special Reference to Clydeside, c.1860–1930', *Social History*, 11, no. 2 (1986), pp. 211–33. The 'bastards' phrase comes from McKinlay, A., *Making Ships, Making Men* (Clydebank, 1991). Foremen in Hendersons shipyard in Govan clearly had such a reputation: see *Forward*, 10, 17 December 1910.

61. For more detail see chapter 9 in this volume, and Glasgow Labour History Workshop, *The Singer Strike, Clydebank, 1911* (Glasgow, 1989)

62. *Forward*, 26 August 1911. For more detail see chapter 10 in this book.

63. *Forward*, 10 Sept–22 Oct 1910; *Forward*, 4–18 May 1912; *Forward*, 14 Sept. 1912; *Forward*, 11 Sept–2 October 1913. The Port Eglinton Ironworks supplanted the union (National Amalgamated Union of Labourers) with a Mutual Aid Society, to which the employer generously contributed £20 per annum.

64. See chapter 1 in this book, and, for a wider perspective, Price, R., *Labour in British Society* (1986) and Stearns, P., *Lives of Labour* (1978).

65. However, it should be stressed that the diffusion of Taylorite ideas was limited to no more than a handful of very large companies on Clydeside before World War One.

66. Melling, 'Scottish Industrialists', p. 77.

67. Devlin has argued elsewhere in this text that the success rate for workers in strikes over 1910–13 on Clydeside was relatively low. See chapter 3.

68. Richmond, J.R., cited in Melling, 'Non-Commissioned Officers'.

CHAPTER 3

Strike Patterns and Employers' Responses: Clydeside in Comparative Perspective

Ricky Devlin

Introduction

This chapter undertakes a comparative study of strike activity between 1901 and 1913. The study tests the continuities and differences of strike activity across a number of U.K. regions (with particular reference to Scotland). In particular focusing on the period 1910–13 as a means of providing a deeper context for the First World War labour unrest more commonly identified as Red Clydeside. One of the crucial factors to an understanding of the character of strike activity is that of employer attitudes, strategies and responses. The nature of the common employment relationship suggests that an unequal power relationship normally exists and consequently employers tend to initiate change (which often produces conflict) and workers tend to react (which often results in industrial action). It is intended to examine the causes, results and frequency of strike activity from the perspective of employer attitudes as a means of understanding the context within which such activity occurs.

Perhaps the single most influential work on strike activity in recent years has been J.E.Cronin's *Industrial Conflict in Modern Britain*. Cronin argues from analysis of U.K. strike patterns that activity for different industries runs parallel over time and that the most dramatic fluctuations in activity are those over time rather than inter-industry. Further he suggests that what is most significant in terms of strike activity analysis is not those aspects of technology and organisation which differentiate one industry from another but historical factors common to each other. I suggest that Cronin over emphasises the division between the range of influences which comprise these common historical factors and the particular technology or organisation of any industry. They are often the same thing. Changes in technology or organisation in industry spring from wider organisational and political developments – such that intensification as a process becomes a common response of British employers in the late nineteenth and early twentieth centuries. Similarly changes in work organisation spring – albeit in sporadic and piecemeal fashion – from developments such as scientific management.

More useful is Cronin's analysis that strike-waves (his metaphor for fundamental change), although probably resulting from a cumulation of short-term grievances, are the consequence of trends in economic development which operate over a number of decades which mature suddenly in response to favourable economic and political junctures. This clearly fits the long term strike patterns in Britain and Cronin identifies six such strike-waves 1889–90; 1910–13; 1919–20; 1957–62; 1968–72. One immediate problem of analysis is, as Cronin himself admits, that the fixing of start and end points of these strike waves is arbitrary and approximate. Foster makes a cogent case for great caution in the fixing of such points for analysis in his criticisms of both the McLean and Reid interpretations of events on Clydeside.[1] In this context then it is suggested that labour events in 1910–13 were linked to labour events during the First World War and immediately after, thus industrial unrest between 1910–20 might be argued to be part of one process of change.

Cronin's thesis of assessing strike trends at a U.K. aggregate level over long time periods gives the broad underlying developments of the labour movement. However such global analysis cannot give any sense of the particular meaning and nature of strike activity. Many of the variables used by Cronin for statistical analysis – union growth, un-employment, wage levels, standard of living data – cannot be applied broadly at an aggregate level since the level and range of these factors changes between locality within Britain. Whilst the general movement of direction in a U.K. strike-wave such as 1910–13 might be observable it still obscures differentiated and sometimes contradictory develop-ments within regions and across industries. Only detailed comparative analysis can describe the true complexity and diversity of labour movement development across the U.K.

Cronin's thesis suggests that working class evolution generally has followed a profoundly discontinuous path since the observably uneven character of economic growth in Britain over time has been mirrored by a comparable unevenness in industrial conflict and labour movement development. Cronin places economic growth at the core of any assessment of strike conflict suggesting that growth must be assessed in qualitative as well as quantitative terms. Thus each period of economic growth is different in character from 'what went before and what will come after'.[2] By extension then economic growth in different localities may be qualitatively different within a given period. This comparative analysis then seeks to measure localised differences in strike activity and intensity, to illustrate that an intransigent and hostile strand of management ideology was prevalent in Scotland generally, and the west of Scotland in particular. That a weaker position of Scottish workers around control issues was the result of a cruder system of industrial relations and that ultimately this situation was reflected in a less favourable context for Scottish workers than elsewhere. Finally the proposition that the dominant industry in a locality informs the general character of industrial relations in that locality will be tested.

Explaining the United Kingdom context

Price suggests that from the mid-nineteenth century U.K. capital-labour relations were characterised by a paternalistic employment relationship and considerable autonomy and independence for skilled workers.[3] Over the next fifty years that relationship was to come under tremendous strain. The U.K. context of industrial relations and consequently of management ideology was characterised – at the end of the nineteenth century – according to Burgess, by a combination of rising production costs and a less expansive overseas market during the Great Depression of 1873–1896.[4] Investment in manufacturing fell dramatically in the U.K. generally as a result of declining profit levels and the position of the staple export industries became much more difficult.[5] The quickening of global capitalist development meant that such lack of investment merely stored up pressures on British industry and society.

Burgess suggests that the actual growth of per capita incomes experienced in the U.K. in the 1880s-1890s was sustained by a 'home boom' from the end of the Great Depression. The drive by U.K. employers to maintain the rate of profit through intensification in the use of existing capital from the 1880s began to falter as the limits of efficiency were reached. The rush of imports into the U.K. more than offset any increase in overseas trade such that over 85 percent of U.K. raw materials and over 50 percent of food supplies were imported. Rising import prices (for raw materials and food) were passed on to consumers and this, according to Burgess, was the main cause of labour unrest immediately prior to the First World War.[6]

It has been suggested that Scottish labour-management relations cannot be neatly placed into such a U.K. framework. Scotland was particularly vulnerable, through a combination of factors, to this general U.K. malaise. Campbell has argued that from the Union of England and Scotland in 1707 a limited number of choices and threats were open to Scotland. The Union he argues brought an easy route to profit for Scottish capitalists by opening up the export markets of English colonies.[7] This then induced them to concentrate on exports rather than indigenous demand and as cheap food imports became available, to raise the real incomes of workers thus fuelling demand for industrial products. Campbell suggests that because of the abundance of labour from the mid-nineteenth century onwards and a lack of sufficient capital reserves Scottish industry relied on labour intensive production techniques and that this only stored up problems over labour costs which became apparent in the late 19th century. Indeed he suggests that by 1890 labour costs in industry generally accounted for 60% of total costs.[8] Additionally, the Scottish economy became increasingly concentrated in two ways:-

(a) An increasing reliance on specialist production (which meant increasing vulnerability to export markets since these goods were investment goods)in industries like engineering and ship-building.

(b) A move by generalist producers towards the coarser/low cost product markets (textiles-in particular cotton products).

Even the areas of domestic raw materials became vulnerable to international competition. However Campbell suggests that in generalist production reliance on low cost (low wage) meant only low productivity and low levels of capital investment.[9] Conversely, specialist production such as the rising steel industry, and in shipbuilding meant that profitability was tied into dependence on foreign markets for investment goods and reliance on a few large customers and suppliers. This meant Scottish industry became subject to, not different, but perhaps more intense stresses and strains.

Melling proposes an explanation of industrial development in shipbuilding from the 1860s where industrial capitalism had established a comparative economic advantage over other shipbuilding areas – from the poor organisation of existing local ironworkers. By 1914, however, a highly sectionalised, extremely well organised workforce had developed. For Melling it was this late but powerful unionisation of the area which shaped local labour relations. Employers locally remained hostile to unionisation until at least World War One preferring to bypass trade union officials, and workers relied on district officials rather than national executives as the true leaders of their organisations.[10] Foster suggests a characterisation of Scottish employers which, if true, indicates that industrial relations in the west of Scotland was significantly different from that of the industrial north of England.[11] This suggests that employers were less reliant on collective bargaining and more on the autocratic power of undermanagers, foremen and chargehands. It is to test these suggestions of a differentiated Scottish experience that the comparative analysis has been undertaken.

Methodology

Analysis of strike activity in the period 1901–13 was composed of an overall sample of 'principal industrial disputes' of which the U.K. total listing is 1672 principal disputes and my sample accounted for 55.2 percent (923) of these.[12] The sample took in *all* recorded principal industrial disputes in Scotland, Yorkshire, Lancashire and the counties Northumberland and Durham, hereafter known as N.E. England.[13] The data on which the comparative analysis for 1901–13 has been based forms part of a larger study into strike activity and comprises two distinct databases covering 1991 disputes in total (1889–90; 1896–7, 1901–13). A major change in the presentation of strike records post 1900 concerned the omission of a large proportion of the reported strikes and concentration on 'principal disputes' defined as meeting the following conditions:

(a) In mining & quarrying – more than 750 persons involved or 37,500 days aggregate duration.

(b) In building, clothing and miscellaneous trades – more than 150 persons involved or 7,500 days aggregate duration.

(c) All other trades – more than 300 persons involved or 15,000 days aggregate duration.

The effect of this change was to provide detailed information for only around a quarter of total disputes. Davidson discusses the resultant problems (not least of interpretation) with official labour statistics of the period 1886–1914 in considerable detail.[14] However, the databases devised do not simply reproduce the official records of the time but using the available information seek to develop new statistical categories and present existing categories in a particular way. Thus new classifications of employer attitudes both pre- and post strike are developed.

Strike activity 1901–13

The sample used and the total U.K. statistics are closely aligned in the broad trend of activity. Thus both sample and U.K. totals indicate declining activity in the years 1901–04, rising from the low point of 1904–05 to a peak in 1907, slumping again during 1908 before a rising trend is observed during 1909–10 and an explosion in activity from that point on, 1911–13. More interestingly it is observable from table 3.1 that the sample (comprising the 'industrial north') saw a more dramatic drop in strike activity 1901–04 (58 percent drop as opposed to 45 percent U.K. drop) but also saw more dramatic rises in activity in 1904–05 and 1910–13. The surge in activity for the sample area was of the order of a 355 percent increase(from 51 to 232 disputes annually) in comparison with a U.K. increase of 181 percent(from 531 to 1497 disputes annually).

National level analysis i.e. comparing the Scottish activity trends with that of the English sub-sample indicates greater discrepancy in activity (see Table 3.2). Of immediate significance is the observation

71

Table 3.1   1901–13 Strike Activity – Sample & U.K. Totals Compared

Year	No. of disputes (sample)	No. of disputes (Total principal disputes)	No.of U.K. disputes
1901	64	118	642
1902	58	116	442
1903	31	72	387
1904	27	60	355
1905	35	70	358
1906	42	94	486
1907	57	114	601
1908	45	94	399
1909	42	98	436
1910	51	131	531
1911	119	264	903
1912	120	225	857
1913	232	441	1497
Total	923	1672	7894

Source: Compiled from Board of Trade Annual Reports of Strikes and Lockouts 1900–13.

that the English sub-sample and the U.K. trends are very similar whereas the Scottish sub-sample differs in a number of respects. Thus between 1901–03 the English and U.K. activity indicates a significant decline in strike activity whilst Scotland remains stable, between

Table 3.2   1901–13 Strike Activity – National Comparison

Year	Scotland	England (selected counties)	British (cross national disputes)	U.K. total
1901	18	46	0	642
1902	19	39	0	442
1903	18	13	0	387
1904	6	21	0	355
1905	14	21	0	358
1906	9	33	0	486
1907	20	37	0	601
1908	14	29	2	399
1909	7	35	0	436
1910	12	37	2	531
1911	26	92	1	903
1912	43	75	2	857
1913	63	168	1	1497
total	269	646	8	7894

Source: Compiled from Board of Trade Annual Reports of Strikes and Lockouts 1901–13.

1904–10 Scottish strike activity is volatile whereas both the English and U.K. trends see continuously rising strike activity between 1904–13 (only in 1908 itself does activity fall but still remains significant). Again Scottish strike activity falls during both 1908 and 1909 whereas English and U.K. trends experience a fall in only 1908.

Clearly Scottish strike activity reflects the performance of the Scottish economy during the study period. Thus contrary to general U.K. analysis put forward by Cronin that the 1910–14 strike wave was a 'response to diverse grievances, concerning prices, working conditions and so on, built up during the previous fifteen years of boom', it is argued that the Scottish experience was very different – the confidence of English and U.K workers as evidenced by strike levels was much higher than that of Scottish workers suffering a much harsher environment.[15] Evidence for this argument can be observed in the relatively more dramatic rise in strike activity in 1905 in Scotland when as Treble indicates Glasgow experienced its only period (1905–06) between 1903–10 when cyclical depression was not inhibiting the local economy.[16] Finally it is important to note that both the English sub-sample and the U.K. totals indicate a drop in activity during the period 1910–13 (i.e. in 1912), whereas activity in Scotland remains unchecked thus producing a relatively more intense period of activity than elsewhere.

To measure the intensity of strike activity both within industries and across them I have developed an average of strike activity within my sample areas.[17] From this both an all–industry average and a sectoral average can be determined and used to show whether industries were particularly strike prone during 1901–13. Therefore in the overall sample areas for the metal, engineering and shipbuilding trades it is observable that in relation to all-industry trends in strike activity for nine of the thirteen years activity was only slightly above the all-industry average with only 1906, 1912–13 indicating appreciably higher strike activity. However within the sectoral average for 1901–13 only the years 1911–13 were well above average activity with all other years well below average. This then clearly suggests that high strike activity in this sector was concentrated into only a short continuous period (1911–13) with the norm being only average activity in line with other industries.

In mining & quarrying by contrast in eight of the thirteen years strike activity was above the all-industry average and in sectoral terms only between 1903–07 was low activity registered. An even more extreme position was noted in textiles where strike activity was above the all-industry average in ten out of the thirteen years and in six of those years was between 100–200 percent higher than the all-industry average. Sectoral analysis in textiles confirmed that the industry was extremely volatile, subject to a consistently high average, but with only three years 1907, 1911–13 showing well above average activity.

At the national level (i.e. Scotland against the English sub-sample) some interesting differences in strike activity and characteristics begin to emerge. For example in coal mining the Scottish experience is markedly different from that of the English – thus in Scotland in only three out of the thirteen years was strike activity above the all-industry average whereas in England this was the case in nine of the thirteen years. In the period 1911–13 both areas experienced a lower than all-industry average level of strike activity once the effect of the industry-wide strike is removed. For the metal trades both England and Scotland exhibit very similar relative levels of activity with 1911–13 the obvious boom period. In the case of the textiles trade the Scottish and English data remain remarkably similar with high average activity but interestingly whilst 1908 was a year of unusually low activity in the trade in Scotland 1905–08 was consistently high in the English cases. Strike activity in both the national samples was largest in the textiles trade. In overall level of strike activity the metal trades were accounting for 24.2 percent of all activity 1901–13 as opposed to 20.4 percent in the English cases.[18]

Table 3.3. illustrates that the primary concern of strike activity over the whole period was for wage increases and including all other wage matters accounted for 61.9 percent of all activity. It must be recognised that this figure accounts for only the primary reason given for strike activity and that many other reasons may be given as additional causes of conflict or brought into negotiations for the resolution of strikes.[19] The result of strike activity for the sample for the whole period shows clearly that primarily strikes ended in some form of compromise agreement (37.3 percent), with resolution totally in favour of the employer accounting for one-third of all strike activity. Clearly over the long term it would be expected that strike resolution would favour the employer given the persistent difference in power and resources between the two parties. However workers could still expect to win

Strike Patterns and Employers' Responses

Table 3.3   Overall Sample Strike Activity – Causes and Results of Disputes 1901–13.

Cause of Dispute	No.of disputes	Result of disputes	No. of disputes
for wages increase	355 (38.5%)	in workers favour	242 (26.2%)
against wages decrease	77 (8.3%	in employers favour	310 933.6%)
other wage matters	139 (15.1%)		
hours of work	31 (3.4%)		
employment of			
other workers	43 (4.7%)	compromised	344 (37.3%)
trade union			
matters	50 (5.4%)	indefinite or unsettled	27 (2.9%)
working			
arrangements			
and discipline	226 (24.5%)	other causes	2 (0.2%)
total	923 (100%)	total	923 (100%)

Source: Developed from Board of Trade Annual Reports of Strikes and Lockouts 1901–13.

outright concessions in one in four disputes and at least partial success in more than six out of ten. Conversely, employers (aside from the one-third that they won outright) could console themselves that in just under an additional four in ten disputes they need only concede part of that demanded. What this meant was that both for workers and for employers the strike process could be favourable in limiting demands and concessions from the other side – thus both worker and employer resistance became an entirely rational process.

Assessing the attitudes which strike activity exposed it is necessary to analyze the position of both sides of industry. It is initially clear that workers saw strike action as a last and somewhat risky option since only 1 in 4 disputes undertaken were completely successful. Employers were to a greater or lesser degree hostile to the existence of unions and worker rights and these attitudes informed both their initial responses to the threat and reality of strike action, and their final acceptance or rejection of those realities during the course of the dispute. The attitudes and responses of employers were clearly mediated by the experience of concerted worker opposition to managerial prerogatives, as were workers methods and attitudes to managerial determination and conviction.

Table 3.4. outlines these employer attitudes. To analyze employer attitudes to strike activity, however, two classifications were worked

Table 3.4. Overall Sample of Strike Activity – Initial Employer Responses and Final Settlement Postures 1901–13.

Initial employer response	No.of disputes	Settlement attitude	No. of disputes
authoritarian	365 (39.5%)	conciliatory	494 (53.5%)
bureaucratic	108 (11.7%)	arbitration	29 (3.1%)
conciliatory	368 (39.9%)	worker submission	267 (28.9%)
hostile:closing			
works	2 (0.2%)	hands replaced	21 (2.3%)
hostile: locking		conciliation & worker	
out	2 (0.2%)	submission	23 (2.5%)
hostile: worker		conciliation &	
replacement	35 (3.8%)	replacement	1 (0.1%)
hostile: legal		worker submission &	
redress	18 (2.0)	conciliation	63 (6.8%)
indefinite	7 (0.8%)	worker submission &	
		arbitration	3 (0.3%)
worker submission		replacement & worker	
& replacement	6 (0.7%)	submission	6 (0.7%)
		indeterminate	10 (1.1%)
total	923 (100%)	total	923 (100%)

Source: Compiled from Board of Trade Annual Reports of Strikes and Lockouts 1901–13.

up from the available data in the official strike records. The classification of settlement attitude or method was based on an earlier system used in the official statistics pre-1900, using evidence from strike reports detailing causes and outcomes of disputes. This information was not provided in later reports but after careful study of official records the basis of classification becomes apparent. I have extended the system to cover the period of study and also devised a typology of initial employer responses. The immediate reaction of employers to strike action in the overall sample is almost equally divided between a conciliatory (39.9 percent) and an authoritarian (39.5 percent) response. The classification system used for initial responses is as follows: Authoritarian – employer refusing to negotiate with workers or their representatives; Bureau-cratic – employer using formal conciliation or arbitration procedures; Conciliatory – employer showing a willingness to negotiate with workers or their representatives; Hostile – employer using positive measures to break disputes and victimise strikers(sub-classified as to most prominent method); Indefinite – disputes were information was not available. When openly hostile responses are included just under half of all employers in the sample over the period 1901–13 were hostile, to some degree, to workmen withdrawing their labour.

In contrast the final settlement attitudes or methods of employers – in the light of concerted worker opposition – show that a larger majority of strike activity was settled by conciliatory or bureaucratic means (56.6 percent). Outright employer opposition accounting for only 32.6 percent of final settlements although another 7.1 percent of disputes clearly had worker submission as the primary element of settlement even though some minor concessions were made.[20] It is clear, comparing initial with final employer responses, that changing reactions were advanced by employers generally from hostile to conciliatory, as they were exposed to the actual reality of the strike experience. Additionally, issues such as worker confidence, worker organisation and determination, and available power resources internal to the dispute were also being measured against the prevailing balance of these factors in industry as a whole.

As before, at national level a number of important divergences are observable. In Scotland the percentage of disputes primarily concerning wage matters accounts for 67 percent of total strike activity of which 47.6 percent were for wage increases. These findings are higher on both counts than either U.K. total statistics (63.1 percent and 33 percent respectively), or the English sample (59.8 percent and 34.8 percent). In terms of challenge to management authority as evidenced by the proportion of strikes attributed to working arrangements and discipline Scotland however exhibits a much lower activity level, with 17.1 percent as opposed to 27.4 percent for the English cases. This reflects yet again the much weaker position of Scottish workers around 'control' issues, a cruder system of industrial relations preoccupied with monetary resolution of grievance, and in line with the much weaker economic and unemployment context of Scotland between 1903–10. Comparison of the outcomes of disputes indicates that in Scotland workers were less likely to win outright (24.2 percent as opposed to the English sample of 27.2 percent) and that the possibility of losing completely was 5 percent higher than in the English cases. This supports the contention that Scottish employers were generally more intransigent and determined to resist strike activity than elsewhere.

1910–13 Regional Analysis

To make the case for different styles of industrial relations co-existing within different regions analysis of strike activity between and across the West of Scotland, Yorkshire, Lancashire and the North-east of England was attempted. Tables 3.5(a) and 3.5(b), 3.6(a) and 3.6(b) below develop the earlier proposed notion of a dominant industry effect characterising the industrial relations of a given locality. Thus observation of the 1910–13 data illustrates a number of facts – firstly it must be noted that of the 923 principal strikes collated in the overall sample 56.6 percent (522) occurred in this period. Secondly it must be remembered from earlier discussion that strike activity in the overall sample area (comprising the industrial north) for 1910–13 increased by 355 percent (from 51 to 232 disputes) whereas the total U.K. increase, although still dramatic, was of a lesser magnitude rising by only 181 percent (531 to 1497 disputes). The analysis indicates therefore a heightened context of conflict.

Table 3.5 (a) Initial Employer Responses by Sample Region 1910–13.

Response	West Scotland	Yorkshire	Lancashire*	North East
authoritarian	29	39	36	48
bureaucratic	15	12	17	11
conciliatory	35	75	65	39
hostile	3	6	15	3
other	0	1	0	0
total	82	133	133	101

Table 3.5(b) Final Employer Attitudes by Sample Region 1910–13.

Response	West Scotland	Yorkshire	Lancashire*	North East
intransigent	27	23	24	31
hostile	0	2	4	1
conciliatory	50	97	92	50
other	5	11	13	19
total	82	133	133	101

Source: Developed from Board of Trade Annual Reports of Strikes and Lockouts 1910–13.

Note. This table indicates only levels for the main responses to disputes. The full classification contains 8 possible responses for initial employer responses and 17 for final employer responses.

*It must also be remembered that since the raw data excluded some strikes in the immediate Manchester area caution must be exercised on sole reliance on the Lancashire figures.

Quite clearly during the period 1910–13 the West of Scotland experienced a very high proportion of employers exhibiting, at the very least, authoritarian responses both pre- and post-strike activity. Although the number of disputes finally settled by conciliatory responses rises in line with expectations – as in the other regions – a persistent trend of more conflictual industrial relations is observable. All other regions exhibit a much clearer process of employer attitude shift during the strike experience – even in the North East where the initial employer response is more predominantly authoritarian.

Research shows that these findings are confirmed year by year and not subject to any undue weighting in any particular year. Thus in 1910 the west of Scotland experienced seven authoritarian responses as opposed to one conciliatory response in initial attitudes and seven intransigent against two conciliatory in final response. This employer attitude was mirrored in the North East whereas in Yorkshire and Lancashire the process of employer attitude shift over the strike experience was much more clearly towards the conciliatory. Responses are subject to the overall industrial balance of power and this is shifting quite significantly towards labour during the period of the labour unrest 1910–14. Consequently in 1911 although it is clear that this balance of power is becoming more favourable and in West Scotland this is observed in the majority of disputes being settled by conciliatory attitudes, there nonetheless remains a persistent intransigent employer response. Similarly the North East continues to display this entrenched employer attitude in contrast to the weakening of employer attitudes in Yorkshire and Lancashire.

By 1912–13 the tide of events had swung decisively to labour and correspondingly the final settlement attitudes of employers conformed much more clearly to the expected conciliatory trend. However the proportion of disputes in both the west of Scotland and the North East that still experienced initial authoritarian responses from employers remained high. Clearly a persistent, determined employer attitude towards authoritarian industrial relations existed in these regions in contrast to that of Yorkshire and Lancashire. The explanation for such a differentiated employer response lies in the significance of the dominant industries in these localities and the character of industrial relations this implies. Tables 3.6(a) and 3.6(b) develop this argument by analysis of strike activity over the same period for different industrial sectors.

Table 3.6(a) Initial Employer Responses by Industrial Sector (overall sample)1910–13.

	authoritarian	bureaucratic	conciliatory	hostile	other	total
building trades	1	2	11	3	0	17
mines & quarries	54	12	37	4	1	108
metal, eng. &						
shipbuilding	45	16	57	7	0	125
textiles	26	13	60	9	0	108
transport	12	13	24	1	0	50
miscellaneous	33	9	64	8	0	114

Table 3.6(b) Final Employer Responses by Industrial Sector (overall sample) 1910–13.

	intransigent	hostile	conciliatory	other	total
building trade	1	0	16	0	17
mines & quarries	40	0	51	17	108
metal, eng. &					
shipbuilding	30	0	82	13	125
textiles	22	1	72	13	108
transport	10	0	35	5	50
miscellaneous	17	1	80	16	114

Source: Developed from Board of Trade Annual Reports of Strikes and Lockouts 1910–13.

N.B. Figures derived for this table indicate only levels for the *main* responses to disputes. The full classification contains 8 possible responses for initial employer responses and 17 for final employer responses.

In mining and in the metal trades a high proportion of strike activity is met initially with an authoritarian employer response – indeed in mining this forms the majority of employer responses. In final settlement attitudes this intransigent attitude is strongly confirmed in mining and to a lesser extent (although still significant) in the metal trades. Also in the metal trades a tendency among employers, when faced with determined worker resistance, for bureaucratic responses calling in third parties or setting up formalised conferences was noted. This conforms to the earlier noted tendency in the metal trades at both the regional and the national level of analysis. Outright employer hostility was most prominent in the official records proportionately in the textile trades as indeed was the most marked tendency for persistent conciliatory employer attitudes throughout the strike experience. This is suggestive of a strongly differentiated industrial relations in textiles between two extremes as indeed was the textiles industry strongly differentiated in types of textile manufacture.

Regional comparison tentatively supports the dominant industry argument, the clearly more conflictual industrial relations observable in the mining and metal trades are reflected more broadly in the North east and west of Scotland respectively. Thus for example,in the miscellaneous trades in the west of Scotland between 1910–13 out of thirteen disputes six were met initially with authoritarian responses whereas in Yorkshire only thirteen out of twenty-nine were so met. In Lancashire only eight out of thirty-seven were initially authoritarian (this rising to 14 out of thirty-seven once hostile responses are included). In the North - East this related to four (five once hostile responses included) out of twelve disputes. However, given the small number of disputes involved and the lack of any clear supportive evidence from other sectors such as transport, it must be suggested that more analysis is required to resolve this issue.

Table 3.7 indicates the causes or objects of disputes for the period 1910–13 within regions. Clearly the majority of disputes in the west of Scotland are concerned with wages increases. This is proportionately more significant than in the other regions where working arrangements are of greater importance. This confirms the findings of the earlier analysis at the national level. Closer analysis on a year by year basis suggests that conflict around these 'control' issues in the west of Scotland was of major significance only in 1910. In Yorkshire a similar effect is observed for 1910 but the issue of working arrangements remains significant in strike activity throughout the period in this region. Working arrangements in Lancashire remain significantly high throughout the period 1910–13 where additionally disputes around other wage matters and over employment of other classes of workers

Table 3.7 Strike Statistics – Causes of Disputes by Region (overall sample)1910–13.

region	wages increase	against wage decrease	other work matters	hours of work	employment other classes of worker or demarcation	trade union matters	working arrangements and discipline
W. Scotland	40	0	5	2	7	14	14
Yorkshire	65	3	18	6	2	8	32
Lancashire	55	2	23	0	12	10	31
North East	25	8	18	0	9	3	34
total	185	13	64	8	30	35	111

Source: Developed from Board of Trade Annual Reports of Strikes and Lockouts 1910–13.

are important. In the North East working arrangements are the predominant cause of disputes in three out of the four years studied and other wage matters are more significant than those of wage increase – suggestive of the issues important in the mining industry, namely, allowances for diverse working situations and manning of piecework teams.

Finally the growing importance of disputes around trade union matters and principles in West Scotland, Yorkshire and Lancashire is noted, with 1913 a key year as the strike wave reached a peak. Of twenty-four disputes eleven were in the metal trades, four in mining and three in textiles. West Scotland saw a higher proportion of these disputes with ten disputes-four were over refusal to work with non-unionists, three to obtain dismissal of workers in union subscription arrears, two over solidarity and one for union recognition. Surprisingly the North East saw little activity in this regard.[21] The results of strike activity serve to confirm the evidence of west of Scotland employers as authoritarian and intransigent in attitude and responses. Thus table 8 illustrates that throughout the period in both the west of Scotland and the North East employers determinedly resist worker demands. It is not until 1911 that workers in the west of Scotland win a majority of disputes outright and although the expected trend to increasing worker victory or partial victory is evident in Yorkshire and Lancashire, a much more persistent determination to resist workers is observed in both the west of Scotland and North East England throughout the period 1910–13.

Comparison of the result of disputes in these areas with U.K. figures shows that during the period 1910–13 in the U.K. 27.1 percent of disputes were won outright by workers, 29.6 percent by employers

Table 3.8. Strike Statistics – Results of Disputes by Region. 1910–13.

Region	in workers favour	in employers favour	compromised	indefinite
W. Scotland	25	27	29	1
Yorkshire	51	25	54	2
Lancashire	58	27	48	0
North East	21	33	45	2

Source: Developed from Board of Trade Annual Reports of Strikes and Lockouts 1910–13.

and 58.4 percent compromised. In Yorkshire and Lancashire clear majorities of disputes were won outright by workers as opposed to employers (38.6 percent to 18.9 percent and 43.6 percent to 20.3 percent respectively) whereas in the west of Scotland and the North East of England employers won a majority of disputes as opposed to workers (32.9 percent to 30.5 percent and 32.7 percent to 20.8 percent respectively). Even though Lancashire workers won far more disputes convincingly and consequently had a lower level of compromised disputes for this reason, the west of Scotland with a much lower worker success rate could not even wring a higher level of partial concessions than Lancashire.[22]

It remains only to add a cautionary note to analysis of strike activity. Research carried out by the Glasgow Labour History Workshop found that official Board of Trade statistics – because of their reliance on principal disputes – seriously under-represented the totality of strike experience in a locality. Moreover, the full range of employer policies and reactions were invariably obscured by official over-generalisations to fit crude Board of Trade classifications. The possibility remains that the full context of industrial relations in the locality is obscured by these constraints.[23] Nevertheless the official statistics remain the single most comprehensive source of strike data available at this time.

Conclusions

It is my contention then that the evidence presented here supports the view that workers in Scotland generally, and the west of Scotland in particular, were faced with a more hostile, authoritarian, intransigent employer ideology than elsewhere (mirrored in many respects in the North East). That this ideology was a characteristic of certain industries i.e. mining and the metal trades, and that the localities in which those industries were dominant consequently exhibited a more conflictual, cruder, and harsher model of industrial relations – an industrial relations focused around mainly monetary demands than 'control' issues. Whilst the struggle between capital and labour during this period intensified as a consequence of the almost unprecedented strike wave in west Scotland (as elsewhere) it failed to produce any clear winner. Employers in the west of Scotland and the North East of England were as likely to successfully resist worker demands throughout 1910–14 as workers were to win outright their demands. This was a different context from that of Yorkshire and Lancashire where the balance of power swung more decisively towards workers. Thus the cataclysmic struggle (still unresolved) between capital and labour was transported into the peculiar context of wartime where the importance of west of Scotland industrial power was critical to the war effort. Attendantly the role of west Scotland labour and its ability to disrupt war production gave it a pivotal part to play in later events of much greater fame. Indeed wartime only intensified the pressures on the labour movement and the wider community.

NOTES

1. Foster, J., 'Strike Action and Working Class Politics on Clydeside 1914–19' *International Review of Social History* XXXV – 1990. Foster utilises McLean, I., *The Legend of Red Clydeside* (Edinburgh, 1983) and Reid A., in Tolliday S. & Zeitlin J. (eds) *Shopfloor Bargaining and the State*.(1985).

2. Cronin J. E., *Industrial Conflict in Modern Britain* (1979), p.38.

3. Price, R., *Labour in British Society.* (1985), p.73.

4. Burgess, K., *The Challenge of Labour.* (1980), p. 45.

5. Burgess, *Challenge of Labour*, p.45.

6. Burgess, *Challenge of Labour*, p.79.

7. Campbell, R.H, *Scotland Since 1707; The Rise of an Industrial Society.* (1985), p.6.

8. Campbell, *Scotland Since 1707*, p. 13.

9. Campbell, *Scotland Since 1707*, p. 59.

10. Melling, J., 'Work, Culture and Politics on 'Red Clydeside': the ILP during the First World War' in A.McKinlay & R.J.Morris (Eds) *The ILP on Clydeside, 1893–1932: from foundation to disintegration* (Manchester, 1991). Also in 'Scottish Industrialists and the Changing Character of Class Relations in the Clyde Region' in T.Dickson (Ed) *Capital and Class in Scotland* (Edinburgh, 1982).

11. Foster, J., 'Strike Action and Working Class Politics on Clydeside 1914–19' *International Review of Social History* XXXV 1990 p.48.

12. The effect of this official screening was to eliminate recording of many disputes of smaller dimensions, the average percentage of principal industrial disputes equates to only 24 percent of total disputes recorded in aggregate totals (7,894).

13. The data on Lancashire excludes disputes listed as Manchester since initially it was the satellite textile towns and villages that formed the focus of analysis in this location. Geographical areas and strike locations are classified according to the 1891 Population Census of Great Britain Parliamentary Papers Session 1893–94 Vol.25.

14. Davidson, R., *Whitehall and the Labour Problem in Late-Victorian and Edwardian England* (1985).

15. Cronin, *Industrial Conflict.*
16. Treble provides extensive evidence to illustrate the persistent trade slump between 1903–10 in the capital goods industries on which the west of Scotland was so reliant. Treble, J.H. 'Unemployment in Glasgow 1903–10: Anatomy of a crisis' *Scottish Labour History Journal* No.25 (1990) pp. 8–33.
17. This average divides the sample total of principal disputes in any given year with the 6 classified sectors of occupations building trades, mining & quarrying, metal-engineering, shipbuilding, textiles, transport and miscellaneous trades. The sectoral average is calculated from the total number of disputes over the period 1901–13 in a sector divided by the number of years.
18. Strike activity in textiles 1901–13 was 27.1 percent of total activity for Scotland and 23.1 percent for the English cases.
19. The relationship between employer and worker is primarily a monetary contract thus expressions of discontent are expressed primarily as monetary demands. However it is clear from even the most cursory glance at the strikes data that either a 'shopping list' approach is used by workers or that other underlying discontents quickly surface in negotiation and resolution of disputes.
20. The classification of settlement methods indicates the primary or overwhelming settlement posture of the employer. However reality is somewhat messier than simple discrete classifications and thus where one or more attitudes were displayed by employers in the settlement of disputes I have classified these under dual headings – the first listed category however is the primary employer response.
21. Of the 14 strikes over trade union matters between 1910-13 in west of Scotland 10 occurred in 1913. In Yorkshire 6 of 8 occurred in 1913 and in Lancashire 8 of 10 occurred in 1913. The North East of England registered none of its 3 in either 1912 or 1913.
22. Both the west of Scotland and Lancashire had 35.3 percent of disputes settled by compromise in relation to 40.9 pecent for Yorkshire and 44.6 percent for the North East.
23. Glasgow Labour History Workshop, in Duncan, R. and McIvor, A. *Militant Workers* (Edinburgh, 1992).

CHAPTER 4

Philosophers in Overalls?: Craft and Class on Clydeside, c. 1900–1914

Alan McKinlay

Introduction

In April 1916 an idealistic young Marxist, R.M. Fox, offered a deeply-felt eulogy to the Clydeside craftsman, 'the Labour Thinker'. For Fox, the craftsman's daily experience made him a thoughtful materialist. Just as the craftsman used reason, experience, and skill to transform metal into useful things so he would apply the same faculties to remake the social world. Practical reasoning was at the core of craftsmanship *and* Marxism: in both, conception and execution were indissolubly linked: '"When you have a bar or iron in front of you which has to be twisted and wrought into a certain shape", he would say, "then you learn to apply ideas to things. You become practical. You cannot think the iron into the position and shape that is wanted, but you cannot do it without thought. Your thoughts, if you are to succeed in your purpose, must be limited, circumscribed, bound down to the facts of the situation. *You must not be a metaphysician'*. Craftsmanship embodied a unity of theory and practice, a productive knowledge, with a natural affinity to the praxis of Marxism. Marxism was a form of political craftsmanship whose objective was to reshape a social order no less stubborn than the iron fashioned by the artisan. The nascent Marxism of 'the Labour Thinker' was much more than abstract philosophy. The politicised artisan,

> . . . reasoned straight from the facts and the factory. He is the precursor of others who are learning analysis and precision in the workshops and will sooner or later apply these things to life. The workshop is the school of the scientists who are developing – growing – realising. The thinker in overalls; he is the hope of the world . . .[1]

James Hinton's classic account of Red Clydeside draws on a similar, if more qualified, conception of craftsmanship.[2] The 'craft tradition', argues Hinton, was a deeply ambiguous legacy. On the one hand, nineteenth century engineering craftsmen had established an occupational culture and job controls based on autonomy, limited supervision, and personal responsibility for conceptual as well as practical aspects of production. Through the late nineteenth century, however, Hinton contends that technological change and aggressive management increasingly challenged the craft tradition. And that these technological and managerial challenges opened up new spaces for Marxism and syndicalism to infuse working class political debate. On the other hand, and this is the crux of the ambiguity Hinton places at the heart of the craft tradition, skilled engineers also adopted defensive tactics which limited their ability to break with sectionalist attitudes. The defense of craft power was often directed against non-skilled workers as much as it was contrary to capital. Only exceptional, highly politicised individuals irreversibly rejected craft sectionalism in favour of class consciousness; for the majority of skilled workers, class awareness and action was born only in brief flashes. This chapter reviews developments in the labour process and worker organisation in steel, shipbuilding and engineering in the two decades before 1914. Looking beyond the experience of the skilled engineers considered by Hinton demonstrates that sectionalism not solidarity was the *leitmotif* of the Clydeside artisan.

Craft and conciliation in steel

We know relatively little about the labour process or trade unionism in Scottish steelworks. In part, this reflects the steelworkers comparative lack of militancy and the absence of any concerted managerial challenges to craft control. Steel was by no means a homogeneous commodity. Rather, there was considerable product variability as the industry responded to the booming demand from Clydeside's shipyards.[3] Equally, there was no standardisation of the iron ore, limstone, and scrap which was used to make steel. Scotland was relatively untouched by technical change before 1914: its steelworks remained markedly smaller and with much more limited mechanical handling aids than their English or German competitors. In place of mechanisation and managerial control,

Scottish steel masters relied on an elaborate system of internal sub-contracting which left the administration of production in the hands of craftworkers. In this respect, the distance between senior management and shopfloor operations was even greater than in shipbuilding or engineering. In the metalworking industries, as we shall see, the two decades before 1914 was a period of intense conflict over workplace control. In steel, however, the employers made no attempt to wrest power from the craftworkers.

The steelmaking division of labour centred on a system of dispersed control exercised through a complex hierarchy of experienced workers. The senior figure within the workgroup was the first-hand smelter, assisted by two or three 'hands'. In the dangerous, volatile environment of the steelworks, experience and split-second timing were crucial to safety and production. The first-hand smelter controlled the entire manufacturing process and was the prime sub-contractor for labour. The senior smelter was not, however, a managerial appointment but answerable to the workgroup. Both the senior craftsman's personal autonomy and his socio-economic relationship with his colleagues are captured in one steelworker's description of 'the moment of creation' at which the molten metal rushed from the furnace:

> . . . To the first-hand smelter there was great satisfaction as he watched the metal stream from his furnace into the waiting ladle. He had an awareness of creation; seven or eight hours previously this surging white-hot liquid had been one hundred tons of solid limestone, steel scrap, and hot iron. He had controlled the huge flame which played over the metal, saw that it did its work, and that it didn't damage the furnace's brick roof or linings. Hour after hour he had tended it, watched for every change in the liquid, increased the slag content with more lime, and thinned it out with iron ore. His junior smelters were every bit as interested as he was. It was their money too that was filling the ladle, and their sweat that put it there . . . [4]

No formal apprenticeship system operated in the steel industry. Rather, the steelworker entered the industry as a labourer, progressed through all the tasks around the furnace and eventually assumed responsibility for some aspect of production. The pinnacle of this extremely slow process, which typically took decades to complete, was the first-hand smelter. Throughout this long journey to full craft status, each steelworker kept his own record of every tap, noting every anomaly and corrective action. This 'hidden bible' was the cornerstone of the first-hand's expertise, buttressing his personal authority against any incursions from management technicians. Detailed technical information was monopolised by the smelters, recalled one former mill manager, and 'was passed from one roller to another – sometimes fairly openly. . . . (T)he man who was seeking the information had to acquire it over a pretty long period'. Such 'black books' distilled lifetimes of shopfloor knowledge. Craft knowledge was the core of the steel workers' ability to cope with dangerous uncertainty. Again, in the words of our mill manager, each note was a measure of a specific remedial action, 'how effective or ineffective it had been; and what measures to take this time. If they were caught out once it was an attempt not to be caught again'.[5]

Management's understanding of steelmaking, by contrast, was confined largely to a technical press which assumed the stable compostion of raw materials and ignored chance and uncertainty. The craftworkers' knowledge was rooted in years of daily observation sharpened by safety considerations and financial necessity. The experienced craftsman was capable of extremely accurate measurement of temperatures, alloy contents and the qualities of steel by a glance at the molten metal. This refined judgement eliminated the need for sophisticated instrumentation: the craftworkers were given total responsibility for making steel to exact specifications.

Skill was not restricted to the elite smelters, however. Labouring in the steelworks called for the development of high levels of tacit skills essential for the safety of the individual and his workmates. Consider the apparently simple tasks of shovelling coal, iron, and scrap, and pushing wheelbarrows. The labourer's first job of the day was to clean and grease his shovel and barrow, both of which he had personally adapted to his specific requirements. Personalised tools made it difficult to rotate these tasks within the workgroup. Even shovelling becomes an art form when tremendous weights have to shifted at high speeds. The angle of the shovel and the barrow's position were vital considerations to make this arduous task manageable. The heavy barrow, carefully loaded to spread the weight evenly, was wheeled twenty to thirty yards to the hoist ready for the blast furnace.

. . . The rain continues and I am wet to the skin and covered with sludge. The road I travel is covered with cast-iron plates unevenly laid, and as my barrow passes from plate to plate water splashes up through the joints and quickly fills my boots with water and grit. Still, on I and my mates go, heave and fill, weigh and draw, always alert that some small obstacle may throw us off our balance and cause our barrow to tip up . . .[6]

The labourers were also responsible for shovelling or throwing scrap iron or limestone into the furnace from within a few feet of the white-hot charge. Pools of molten steel were cleared up by long steel poles with huge plates attached. Within seconds these cumbersome tools would be red-hot and had to switched instantaneously. Any metal allowed to cool had to be broken with crow-bars. At this stage, labourers from adjacent furnaces could assist in clearing the melting pit, one of the few opportunities to synchronise the work of adjacent gangs.

Nor were the more senior members of the skilled gang exempt from hot, heavy and dangerous work. The gang's lieutenant – the second melter – was personally responsible for tapping the furnace and fettling. Fettling, repairing the tap hole, took between twenty and forty minutes and was perhaps the most physically demanding task in the entire steelworks. There was an equal measure of awe and disgust in one experienced comentator's description of 'the excessively exhausting work of fettling': 'The men stream with perspiration and their shirts get wet through. It is probable that an hour of continuous fettling is much more exhausting than eight hours' hand charging of blast furnaces'. Although fettling normally took around forty minutes, in exceptional circumstances it could last for up to twelve hours.[7] In sum, the division of labour in steelmaking was composed of a series of hard, dangerous tasks, controlled exclusively by craftsmen. Craft knowledge was carefully guarded by the steelworkers who controlled every aspect of production.

Employment contracts and payment systems reflected both the steel industry's long boom before 1914 and its highly stratified workforce. The skilled workers were paid a tonnage rate while their labourers were paid by the day or the hour. Tonnage rates – 'shillings for pounds' – were calculated from a sliding scale based on the selling price for the region and for the individual steelworks.[8] Labourers' wages, moreover, were paid by the skilled squad, not directly by the employer. From the late 1880's Scottish steelworks were at the forefront of unionisation of underhands. For the next thirty years the underhands' central policy was the elimination of the contracting system and its replacement by direct employment for *all* process workers by the firm.[9] While sliding scales and outside arbitration undoubtedly ate into 'managerial prerogative', there were tangible benefits for the steelmasters. For the employers, tonnage rates insulated their increasingly capital-intensive production systems against disruption by strategically placed process workers. Even during a generally prosperous period for the industry, a sliding scale made wage rates extremely plastic, but without provoking union resistance to plant-specific fluctuations which could occur every three months or regional adjustments every two or three years. For the elite smelters' union, sliding scales were acceptable on the basis of expediency as well as their perceived equity: skilled process workers benefitted financially from rising output and productivity, technical change enhanced rather than diminished their craft control.[10] Reviewing his long personal experience of wage conciliation, John Cronin, a workman's representative from Summerlee, pronounced himself 'satisfied that these great industrial conflicts which have taken place are the ruin of our country, and that every sensible man ought to do what he can to put an end to them'.[11]

The skilled men had a material incentive to increase output even if this intensified the labourers' work. Craftsman and contractor, an artisan with real supervisory authority: the skilled steelworker shared in the profits of the industry as a reward for assuming a critical managerial role in the workplace.[12] Fused with the independence which lay at the heart of the craft tradition, the contracting system underpinned a powerful unitarist ideology on the shopfloor.[13] The reciprocity between manager and senior smelters constituted a distinctive politics of production. If the craftsman sold his labour to another employer he jeopardised his skilled status while the seniority and sub-contracting systems combined to limit the employer's access to the external labour market.

> . . . I knew some good (melting shop) managers, and to respect them was a good thing for the steel one made. Then, some of one's own serenity seemed to enter the product, though I can't say that I ever heard of contented steel. But to know that a manager knew his job, and that he respected one reciprocally was a good thing all round, good for the metal, good for the smelter, and good for the manager. It created confidence, a

most important quality, for good steelmaking was as much a frame of mind as it was a job of work. . . .

The combination of a seniority system and a sliding scale squeezed out workplace bargaining and the emergence of the shop steward as a union delegate rather than as a spokesman exclusively for a specific skilled gang. For the labourers, the seniority system held out the promise of eventual promotion into the skilled gang, a promise which, when combined with their weak employment position, limited the appeal of alternative labourer's unions. The labour process, bargaining institutions, and craft exclusivism were the material bases of craft quiescence rather than militancy in steel.

Technical change and craft control in shipbuilding

In two important respects the development of shipbuilding paralleled that of steel before 1914. First, it was a craft-based production process. Second, managerial control was partly devolved onto the shoulders of artisans. But, unlike steel, craft power in the metalworking trades was consolidated by a rapid process of technical change in materials, propulsion techniques, and manufacturing technologies. The uncertainties of this process of profound technical change and the long boom in demand led to a consolidation of craft control in shipbuilding before 1914.

In contrast to the highly structured internal labour markets of the steelworks, shipbuilding was characterised by a series of overlapping local labour markets. Apart from a limited number of key artisans, skilled craftsmen were hired to perform specific tasks. Employment was limited to a defined operation rather than a given period of time. The core 'black squad' trades – all pieceworkers – consistently recorded high levels of absenteeism relative to time-workers such as shipwrights and ship's joiners. In 1899 absenteeism among time workers ranged from 4–12 percent compared to the black squad's 15–30 percent. Seasonal variations exaggerated this difference still further: annual holidays were followed by absenteeism levels of upwards of 30 percent among riveters.[14] High levels of labour mobility limited the resonance of paternalist ideologies among tradesmen accustomed to moving between yards. While the steelworker's skill was dependent upon remaining within a given internal labour market, the black squad's mobility was an essential feature of their craft culture. During boom periods skilled shipyard metalworkers 'shuttlecocked' between neighbouring firms, forcing up their earnings. This labour mobility posed particular problems for the foremen who were personally responsible for recruitment and retention. The West of Scotland Association of Foremen Engineers was founded in 1897 by two senior shipyard foremen bedevilled by footloose tradesmen.[15]

> . . . Rivalry was keen among many of the large firms, notably Elders and 'Tamsons', who were prominent in the Atlantic Trade. It was a friendly rivalry, rather like that between Rangers and Celtic, and there was a constant interchange of workmen between the two firms. Many of Tamson's best men came from Elders and similarly many of Tamson's found their way to Govan . . .

The objective of the foremen's Association, which grew quickly to a membership of several hundred, was to call 'a halt . . . to the workmen's bluff'. The employers' support of their 'non-commissioned officers' efforts to regulate local labour markets was paralleled by their own efforts to restrict nomadic labour. The cornerstone of the Clyde shipbuilders' collective presence in the labour market was the enquiry note system. Tradesmen were to be hired only if their former employer confirmed in writing that they had completed their contract. During the early years of the twentieth century the employers wrestled with how best to ensure that all firms participated fully in the enquiry note system. Stiff fines for failure to issue enquiry notes were rejected in favour of persuasion, a voluntarism which meant that comprehensive coverage was seldom achieved and never guaranteed.[16] The practical and symbolic importance of free movement to the work culture of the shipyard artisan – and employer attempts at its restriction – were to prove explosive in the context of the state regulated labour market of the Great War.[17]

The shipbuilding division of labour comprised a series of distinct but inter-dependent labour processes, each dominated by a particular trade. Here we shall concentrate on the experience of hull construction workers, specifically the boilermaking trades of plating and rivetting.[18] Plating was a composite trade of six specialist tasks. The plating squad was a durable group of six or seven tradesmen responsible for shaping and punching holes in steel plates then hanging them on the ship's frame ready for rivetting. Platers heated and shaped the steel sheets to the precise curvatures necessary for different sections of the hull. An equally precise ribbon of holes was punched in the plate before it moved from the workshop out to the berth. Although there were significant changes in plating technology, much rested on the fine judgement of experienced tradesmen working from blueprints and wooden guides. The skilled members of the plating squad, often linked by family and friendship ties, had to be able to move between their specialist tasks to maximise the squad's adaptability. The squad leader, who was chosen by and answerable only to his fellow gang members, was responsible for negotiating complex, often lengthy contracts with the foreman. Squad earnings hinged on the squad leader's astuteness in minimising any interruptions in material flows and ensuring that they were adequately compensated for any delays. The squad leader also had to decide whether to lease equipment such as trolleys and hoists from the yard or to hire additional labourers. Plating was an extremely labour intensive process characterised by the variety of manual and conceptual skills, capital equipment, and operations monopolised by the plating trades.

But the platers' skill was not exclusively defined by their mastery of tasks and tools. An important element of the platers' skill was their role as sub-contractors for temporary labourers to wield hammers to shape the steel plates and manhandle them between work stations. The skilled squad hired up to thirty helpers for contracts which could be terminated without notice. And, since plating was a trade entered after completion of a five year apprenticeship, the platers' helpers had no prospect of promotion to the ranks of the artisan. In this respect, the shipyard helper was in an even weaker position than his counterpart in the steelworks. The first significant attempt to unionise shipyard labourers was on Tyneside in 1881. The helpers struck work in protest against the boilermakers' status as sub-contractors. The Boilermakers' Society resisted this attack on their workplace power by importing some seven hundred labourers to break their helpers' protest. Although there was no similar confrontation on Clydeside, the boilermakers' hostility to helper unionisation was no less profound. Indeed, at the request of the craft union Clyde employers extended the enquiry note system to cover the helpers in an effort to prevent them leaving contracts prematurely and to deter their unionisation.[19] In order to bolster their position as labour sub-contractors, Clydeside boilermakers were prepared to forge an extraordinary alliance with the shipyard owners to disorganise the non-skilled helpers. Before 1914 Scottish unions of shipyard labourers were local, short-lived and posed no effective threat to the boilermakers' contracting power.[20] Labourer unionisation in Clydeside shipyards was achieved only during the Great War and was swept away by the inter-war depression.[21] Even so, no fundamental change to the exploitative relationship between the platers and their helpers was achieved before the Second World War. 'The method of working these team squads is entirely different in Scotland from . . . England', explained Will Sherwood of the General and Municipal Workers' union to the 1926 Balfour Committee,

> . . . in Scotland the helpers still . . . go along to the public-house and get paid out of the bag. That is where the trouble came in. These helpers were looked upon as the servants of the plater. . . . they were taken by the plater and followed from yard to yard. (The leading plater) paid his first hand . . . (and he) expected to get his whistle wetted when they were shelling out in the public-house . . .[22]

The archetypal shipyard worker of the pre-1914 era was the hand-riveter: a hard working, independent, ferocious economic militant. The manual rivetting gang comprised four people: two hammermen, a holder-on, and a boy rivet heater. The slow introduction of mechanical rivetting before 1914 did little to dislodge labour-intensive hand rivetting: rivets were heated until they were glowing white in a portable hearth, then tossed to the holder-on who pushed the incandescent rivet through the holes in overlapping steel plates, to be hammered true and flush by the two hammermen working on the outside of the vessel.[23] Riveters were time-served craftsmen but the nature of their work, their casual employment, and their uncertain habits made them unlikely labour aristocrats.

By its very nature, rivetting lent itself to counting. Each night a counter would daub the day's work with paint as the basic tally of the squad's earnings. Prices were calculated in the workplace from a complex district price list. The list specified prices for hammering down one hundred three-quarter inch rivets, plus allowances for different plate thicknesses, awkward locations, and so forth. Anomalies were normally contested in the workplace or adjudicated in a joint Riveters' Rates Committee, composed of equal numbers of employers' and workmens' representatives, plus an external arbitrator if required. The riveters sought enhanced rates to compensate for anything which disrupted their work rhythm: from poorly fitting plates to waiting time. Even when materials or techniques constituted a serious health hazard, union negotiators focussed on interruptions to customary effort. The mixture of tar, putty, paint, and yarn used to pack between plates, for instance, would drip down onto the riveters working below. The employers accepted that this volatile material 'makes a greater scab than the smallpox: it burns you and the smell is very injurious to health indeed . . . it seems to go to the lungs and chokes the men for days and days afterwards'.[24] No extra allowance was conceded in such cases. Unlike steel, which linked skilled work with the price realised in the product market, the riveters' price list was explicitly about the changing effort bargain between employer and employed. The focal point of formal negotiations – the price list – did not displace informal bargaining from the workplace but guaranteed that it was a daily reality of shipyard life. The number of referrals to the Riveters' Rates Committee rose dramatically during recessions and plummetted even more spectacularly when trade was good, an inverse relationship which confirms that the riveters perceived the workplace as the most important economic forum.

The foreman was the main pressure point in the riveters' ceaseless guerilla economic war, a role which prompted the employers to embark on a long-term strategy to increase the loyalty and dependence of their 'non-commissioned officers' to their firm through a variety of welfare provisions.[25] But the foreman's was always an ambiguous loyalty, shifting between the conflicting pulls of capital and craft. The employers' awareness of their deep dependence on the foreman as an intermediary in an essentially craft labour process, defined winning their allegiance as a central battle on the frontier of control. During an address to over three hundred foremen, Peter Denny acknowledged that for the foreman to be a useful ally of his employer he had to retain an affinity with – and the trust of – the craft community.

> . . . it would be well for the best interests of the country, if throughout the whole industrial army, from the Captains, through the Lieutenants, down to the common workman, loyalty and craft, and ambition for craft, was ever the dominant note . . .[26]

The cutting edge of riveter militancy was their power to boycott a disputed job. 'If you get a cantakerous fellow on first', explained one exasperated employer, 'then no one will go to the work. . . . There are some cases where a job lies for days'.[27] Through the first decade of the twentieth century the price list itself came under increasing pressure. This threatened not just the individual yard but shipbuilding employers as a whole. It was this generalised threat which stimulated a burst of national employer organisation.[28] It was, in other words, the vulnerability of the individual yard's cash flow to small-scale lightning stoppages by riveters which lay behind their prolonged attempts to erect a centrifugal bargaining procedure to neutralise economic militancy. But, as the Boilermakers' Society executive explained, the employers' refusal to give ground through formal bargaining contrasted with their readiness to grant ad hoc concessions to pressure from below. On Clydeside particularly, the union officials complained that the employers' formal intransigence and informal pliability 'encouraged the men to take the law into their own hands, and not leave the prosecution of their claims to their Official representatives'.[29] The immediate pre-1914 period was marked by an intensification of wage conflict in Clydeside's shipyards. Increasingly, strikes which began in individual yards lengthened and spread along the river as the employers retaliated through extensive blacklists and local lock-outs.[30] From 1910 Clyde shipyard employers were the most hawkish in Britain, ready to launch a national lock-out of the entire Boilermakers' Society to face down a seven week strike by Clyde riveters.[31] Neither the Boilermakers' Society Executive's strictures nor the employers' insistence on total adherence to formal procedure could dampen economic militancy in the yards. Spontaneous protest, scarcely restrained by official trade unionism, emerged as the dominant economic practice of riveters before 1914.

Union membership was all but universal among Clydeside boilermakers. Gaps in union organisation were restricted to individuals and small groups rather than entire departments or yards.[32] Shop stewards had a legitimate but heavily circumscribed role in collective bargaining. Formally, district delegates were tightly controlled by the union's executive. By the very nature of their work, boilermakers were accustomed to workplace militancy as their most important bargaining weapon. But the very success of the workgroup in day-to-day collective bargaining stifled the emergence of a rank-and-file movement comparable to engineering.[33] If boilermaker militancy rarely reached beyond the individual shipyard then it never escaped the bounds of a narrow economism. On the contrary, before 1914 the boilermakers' struggle for control over changing tasks and technologies was as much against their non-skilled assistants and their ephemeral unions as it was the Clyde shipyard masters.

Rebuilding craft control in engineering

Engineering workers were at the centre of industrial unrest on wartime Clydeside. And, unlike steel or shipbuilding, the wartime engineering shop stewards' movement was firmly rooted in pre-1914 developments in labour organisation and ideology. Innovations in materials and production technologies posed significant challenges to the established craft power of the skilled engineer. These technological challenges were heightened by the defeat of the Amalgamated Society of Engineers (ASE) in the national lock-out of 1897–98. Privately, leading employers saw the dispute as a way of disabling pressure from below: the ASE, in the words of one Glasgow employer, 'raise everything – save general wages questions – as so-called "Shop" questions and so render ineffectual the Employers' combination'.[34]

The 1897 lock-out was a defining moment not just for engineering but for industrial relations in British manufacturing as a whole. The 1897–98 lock-out followed a decade of rising tension.[35] Disputes over machine manning, wages, and workplace authority stimulated support for industrial unionism within the ASE and national organisation among employers. The demand for the eight hour day was the immediate cause of the 1897 confrontation but the wider issue of workshop control was clearly at stake. Confronted for the first time by a cohesive national employers' organisation, the ASE, isolated from other craft and non-skilled unions, was placed in an impossible position. Faced with a widening lock-out and diminishing reserves the ASE was forced to drop the demand for the shorter working week and accept a humiliating defeat. The 1898 Terms of Settlement enshrined 'management's right to manage' at the expense of craft protocols and established a bargaining procedure designed to remove power from the shopfloor, to draw the sting of craft militancy.

At the centre of the 1897 dispute was the 'machine question', how a series of mechanical innovations were to be introduced into the workplace. The most important of the new machines was the capstan lathe which substituted revolving tools for revolving material, which threatened many of the traditional skills of the Victorian engineer. The turner's skill lay in his ability to work from a drawing or sample component with minimal supervision or guidance.[36] Equally, the new lathes, augmented by a host of minor developments in metalfinishing technologies, could produce components of enhanced accuracy and threatened to dispense with the need for the fitter's capacity to eliminate or cope with irregularities in components. The new technologies threatened to restrict the skilled component of turning to setting the machines and the confine skilled fitting to unusually large jobs where the slightest distortion could jeopardise overall build quality.[37] Technical change, then, threatened existing craft-based patterns of work organisation and the status of the skilled engineer as a 'labour aristocrat'.

On Clydeside, the potential of the new machine technologies to redraw the engineering division of labour remained largely unrealised. The heavy and marine engineering markets which dominated Clydeside demanded products made-to-order. Fragmented demand limited the incentives for management to create integrated, machine-paced labour processes. Rather, Clydeside firms emphasised not the efficiency potential of the new machine technologies but the enhanced product quality they delivered.[38] In addition, the ASE's tradition of local autonomy and the engineers' continued power base on the shopfloor were real constraints on managerial initiatives. Before 1914 there was no sharp break with established patterns of work organisation, employer strategy or union policy but rather a complex process of small-scale conflicts to redefine the frontier of control.[39] 'Watchfulness', Clyde employers were warned, was of the first importance if the engineers were to be prevented from rebuilding their craft controls through 'insidious enccroachments' into managerial prerogative.[40]

Of the major Clyde firms, none went further than Weirs of Cathcart in rationalising work processes and factory administration. Weirs marine pumps lent themselves to partial standardisation and the firm's young managers were self-conscious advocates for the 'American system of manufacture'.[41] Between 1899–1901 Weir's factory was retooled and redesigned to introduce new automatic machinery and to tighten supervision. For the young Harry McShane, Weir's was the most modern factory in the region 'with men working in their own bays at their own machines and not moving around . . . every morning each man knew what job he was going to do during the day. The jobs were so ridiculously simple that anyone could do them'.[42]

Another engineer recalled his 'shock' at the 'regimentation' of the Cathcart factory compared to the small jobbing workshops to which he was accustomed. Contrary to local custom, in Weir's drawings and tools were provided by the firm and not left to the ingenuity of the craftsman. Weir's stress on maximising efficiency also disrupted work-time conventions which left Saturday mornings for planning and minor repairs, not for production.[43] William Weir himself remained dissatisfied that his efforts at product standardisation did not go far enough. For Weir, his customers' demands for bespoke products left him dependent upon traditional craft skills: this was the 'blind spot' of his nascent mass production strategy.[44]

A second distinguishing feature of Weirs was the development of an innovative bonus system which avoided the visible rate-cutting associated with piecework adminstered through craft foremen. Again, there were significant limits to the operation of the Weir-Halsey bonus system in practice. Before 1914 Weir's simply did not have the administrative systems necessary to introduce time and motion study. Bonus times were largely set by foremen working from historic productivity norms, rather than managerially defined best practice. But although Weir could not readily compare the efficiency of individual workmen before 1914, he could examine the relative performance of different foremen. Weir reflected in his diary: 'how *does* a foreman know he will get what he wants?'.[45]

The employers' claim that ASE foremen colluded with the men they supervised in the systematic restriction of output was an important element of the 1897 dispute.[46] Inside Weir's, management attempted to narrow the technical aspects of the foreman's role and to restrict him to enforcing discipline. Foremen bitterly resented the activities of the bonus clerks, 'the scarlet runners whose business is to find fault with all and sundry'.[47] In response, Weir established the 'Friction Club' so that foremen could air their grievances with senior managers rather than ally themselves with the craft workers.[48] No coincidence, then, that Weir's were firm supporters of the newly-formed Foremens' Mutual Benefit Society, and advocated that membership should be compulsory for all federated employers.[49] Weir's was unique on Clydeside in its pursuit of a long-term strategy to create a managerial bureaucracy based on the expropriation of productive knowledge from the shopfloor.

Just as William Weir pioneered new managerial practices, so the Cathcart factory's engineering workers were at the forefront of developments in shopfloor trade unionism before 1914. The ASE recognised shop stewards from 1892 but they remained subordinate to the union's district committees.[50] Inside Weir's, shop stewards first asserted their independence in 1899 during 'considerable' unrest over the introduction of individual bonuses: 'the chief ground for complaint was that the men were prevented from bargaining collectively'.[51] In January 1900 'the most important item on the agenda' of the 'Friction Club' was the foremens' complaints that workers in different departments were comparing earnings.[52] Factory-wide shop steward organisation emerged in response to extensive reorganisation of the factory between 1899–1901. Over the next decade, an uneasy accomodation was reached between management and the stewards: the workforce accepted that payment by results was permanent in return for management's tacit 'acceptance' of collective workplace bargaining.[53]

Clydeside was at the forefront of a general movement by engineers to establish the shop steward as the legitimate focus of workshop bargaining. But before 1914 this new form of workplace trade union-ism remained exceptional, confined to the handful of plants in which payment by results was used extensively. Even inside Weir's, steward activity was not a constant feature but fluctuated with the rhythms of industrial conflict outside the plant. After the collapse of an unofficial strike against wage cuts in 1903 in which leadership had passed temporarily to local activists, Weir's stewards redoubled their efforts to increase bonus earnings.[54] The hesitant development of new forms of workplace trade unionism paralleled widespread criticism of the ASE leadership for its attempts to increase centralised power at the expense of the local district committees.[55] The debates over the balance between local and national, between craft and industrial unionism, gathered pace from the formation of the unofficial Reform Movement in 1910. This agitation established networks of rank-and-file militants operating independently of official union structures and equipped them with a quasi-syndicalist ideology.[56] Both the ideology and independence of these organsations were essential to the development of the wartime shop stewards' movement. Despite its effectiveness as a pressure group in union politics, the unofficial movement could not dislodge the powerful grip of craft sectionalism on the engineers. Before 1914 shop stewards, while they undoubtedly gained some independence from union authority, reflected and defended the boundaries between different grades of worker.

Between 1890 and 1914 the rights of capital and labour in engineering were in constant dispute – both in the national conflict of 1897 and the guerilla war which followed inside the workshops.[57] Indeed, so pervasive was the struggle for control in the factories and so strongly disputed was the legitimacy of the industry's new bargaining structure that, for J.R. Richmond,

> . . . The position just before the outbreak of war was that, by consistent disregard of the terms of the (1898) Agreement, many of these provisions, although officially effective, had become inoperative, and these inroads on the powers of management in the shops had become so serious that, had war not intervened, the autumn of 1914 would probably have seen an industrial disturbance of the first magnitude . . .[58]

Conclusion

We began by drawing attention to the importance of the 'craft tradition' in the historiography of 'Red Clydeside'. By looking beyond the experience of the engineers it is clear that the 'craft tradition' varied significantly between industries. While all tradesmen valued their discretion in choosing working methods there was a clear spectrum ranging from the extensive expertise of the first hand smelter in the steelworks to the much more limited decisions taken by the riveter. Conversely, while labour mobility was of the utmost importance to the shipyard tradesman it was of no consequence in steel where an individual's seniority was bound to a specific workplace. Technological change raised new questions about established definitions of skill throughout the heavy industries although product market constraints muted their impact. The boundary between the artisan and the non-skilled was mediated by different labour market formations. In steel and shipbuilding, craft union policies and skilled workgroup practices hinged on the maintenance of the artisan as a labour-only sub-contractor. Only in engineering, where there was no similar contractual relationship between skilled and non-skilled labour, did the question of inclusive industrial unionism arise as a significant current in trade union debate.

That Clyde employers were under increasing competitive pressure to reduce labour costs before 1914 is beyond doubt. But employer strategies varied widely between and within the heavy industries. Only the steel masters initiated and sustained a sliding scale tying the earnings of skilled workers to product prices. In shipbuilding and engineering, by contrast, the workplace was confirmed as the forum in which the effort bargain was contested. Only in engineering, and even then only in a few exceptional cases, did this lead to the emergence of the shop steward as a representative of the workgroup as well as a lay union official. If there was no shop steward activity in steel and only the faintest traces of steward organisation in shipbuilding then we should be conscious of its limits in engineering. Shop steward organisation was most advanced in engineering but there is no evidence of permanent shop steward organisation in *any* Clyde factory before 1914 far less durable inter-factory networks. Shop steward networks were mobilised around specific campaigns for improved district wage rates and did not necessarily coincide with activist networks which established a strong unofficial presence within the ASE. The composition and interaction of the social networks of shop stewards and political activists before 1914 remains largely uncharted territory. Until research in this area is conducted it is impossible to assess the relative importance of these networks for wartime developments. What is certain, however, is that wartime Clydeside threw up significant innovations in working class organisation which far exceeded the possibilities of the pre-1914 period. One reason why the shop stewards' movement newspaper, *The Worker,* was launched in 1916, for example, was to overcome the relative isolation of factory activists,

. . . The paper was a means of communication between the different shops and yards in a manner hitherto unknown. The men in the lower reaches of the river had a chance of learning what the men in the upper reaches were thinking and doing, and vice versa. The paper itself was an organiser, and would have proved invaluable when the dilution scheme came on. I have no doubt that this was the real cause of the repression . . .[59]

There were no 'roots' to 'Red Clydeside', no organic 'natural' link between the dynamics of struggle over work organisation and wages before 1914 and those of the Great War. To search for such elusive 'roots' is to risk an appreciation of just how novel, unprecedented, and extraordinary the industrial, social and political movements of wartime Clydeside actually were. To collapse the different experiences of steel, shipbuilding, and engineering workers into a single 'craft tradition' is to lose the diversity of their experience.

NOTES

1. *The Socialist*, April 1916.
2. Hinton, J., *The First Shop Stewards' Movement* (1973).
3. Gintz H., 'Effects of Technological Change on Labour in Selected Sections of the Iron and Steel Industries of Great Britain, the United States and Germany, 1901–1939' (unpublished PhD thesis, London University, 1954), p. 48.
4. McGeown, P.,*Heat the Furnace Seven Times More* (1967), p. 10.
5. Cited in Charman D. (ed.), *Glengarnock: A Scottish Open Hearth Steelworks, The Works-The People* (Netherlands, 1981), p.78.
6. TJ, 'Barrow-Man', in Pollock M.A. (ed.), *Working Days: Being the Personal Records of Sixteen Working Men and Women Written by Themselves* (1926), p. 153.
7. Vernon, H.M., 'Fatigue and Efficiency in the Iron and Steel Industry', Report No. 5, Industrial Fatigue Research Board, 1920, p.24, 29.
8. McDonald Adams, R., 'A Comparative Study of the Occupational Wage Structures of the Iron and Steel Industries of Great Britain and the United States in the last 70 Years' (unpublished PhD thesis, London University, 1958), p. 45.
9. Wilkinson, F., 'Collective Bargaining in the Steel Industry in the 1920s', in Briggs A. and Saville J. (eds.), *Essays in Labour History 1918–1939* (1977), p.106.
10. Allen, V.L., 'The Origins of Industrial Conciliation and Arbitration', *International Review of Social History*, vol.ix, 1964, p.241; Pool A.G., *Wage Policy in Relation to Industrial Fluctuations* (1938) pp. 156, 167, 172–7; Porter J.H., 'Wage Bargaining under Conciliation Agreements, 1860–1914', *Economic History Review*, vol. xxiii, 1970, pp.467–9.
11. Proceedings at Conference, between Representatives from the Ironmasters of Scotland and their Workmen, 17,26 October 1899, p. 5 (TD171/1/6).
12. Elbaum, B., 'Industrial Relations and Uneven Development: Wage Structure and Industrial Organisation in the British and US Iron and Steel Industries 1870–1970' (unpublished PhD thesis, Harvard University, 1982), p. 129.
13. PMcG, 'Steelmen', *New Left Review*, 45, 1967, p.8.

14. Clyde Shipbuilders' Association (CSA) 'Time Lost by Workers in the Clyde Shipyards 1899–1911' (TD241/8/10). For the rituals which celebrated the boilermakers' control over working time see, McKinlay A., *Making Ships, Making Men: Working for John Brown's Between the Wars*, Clydebank, (Clydebank District Council, 1991).

15. West of Scotland Association of Foremen Engineers, Annual Report 1946–47, p. 10 (TD1115/3/3).

16. See CSA Minutes, 30 May 1900 (TD241/1/7), 20 December 1912, 20 March 1913 (TD241/1/12), for example.

17. See McLean, I.S., *The Legend of Red Clydeside* (Edinburgh, 1983), pp.38–48.

18. For a more complete analysis see, A. Reid, 'The Division of Labour in the British Shipbuilding Industry, 1880–1920, with Special Reference to Clydeside' (unpublished DPhil thesis, Cambridge University, 1980).

19. CSA, Minutes, 28 October 1901 (TD241/1/7).

20. See Amalgamated Society of Shipyard and General Labourers' of Scotland, Rules, 1882 and Financial Report, 1883–84 (SRO FS 7/13); Scottish Iron Shipbuilders and Boileramkers' Holders-Up Association, 1891–92 (SRO FS 7/13); Amalgamated Shipyard Helpers' Association, Rules, 1906–07 (SRO FS 7/50/109).

21. National Amalgamated Union of Labour, Executive Committee, Minutes, 22 March 1917. Reviewing the prospects for the post-war period, the NAUL executive was sceptical of the craft unions hostility to the labourers' unions being diluted by a wartime rise in class consciousness: 'the semi-skilled would have both the employer and the skilled trades to fight', Minutes, 16 December 1916.

22. Sherwood W. (NUGMW), *Minutes of Evidence taken Before the Committee on Industry and Trade (Balfour Committee)* vol. iv. (1926), p.1466; Schloss D.F., *Methods of Industrial Remuneration*, (1898), pp. 184–5, 201.

23. Pollock, D., *The Shipbuilding Industry* (1905), p.99.

24. Minutes of the Riveters Rates Committee, 9 March 1910, p.43 (TD241/9/21).

25. Melling, J., 'Non-Commissioned Officers: British Employers and their Supervisory Workers 1880–1920', *Social History*, vol.5, no. 2, 1980.

26. West of Scotland Association of Foremen Engineers, 14 March 1908 (TD1115/1/2).

27. Minutes of the Riveters Rates Committee, 4 April 1901, p. 33 (TD241/9/12).

28. See Lovell, J., 'Employers and Craft Unionism: A Programme of Action for British Shipbuilding, 1902–05', *Business History*, vol. 34, no. 4, pp.38–58.

29. 'Interview with Mr John Sanderson', Clyde District Delegate, Boilermakers' Society, 21 August 1906 (TD241/12/2); *Glasgow Herald*, 12 January 1911.

30. See *Forward*, 19 November, 3,10,17 December 1910 for escalating ten week strike beginning in D&W Hendersons and Fairfields.

31. National Conference, Shipbuilding Employers' Federation and Boilermakers' Society, 6 June 1910, p. 39 (TD241/2/7).

32. Minutes of the Riveters Rates Committee, 8 July 1910, p.10 (TD241/9/21).

33. See Price, R., *Masters, Unions and Men: Work Control and the Rise of Labour 1830–1914* (1980), p. 243 for an intriguing aside concerning short-lived unofficial pressure groups inside the Boilermakers' Society which sprang from platers' 'smokers' in the early 1900s.

34. Biggart to Wilson, 22 August 1896, Private Letter Book (TD1059/22/2/1).

35. Clarke, R.O., 'The Dispute in the British Engineering Industry 1897–98: An Evaluation', *Economica*, New Series 94, 1957.

36. Yates, M.L., *Wages and Labour Conditions in British Engineering* (1937), p. 12.

37. Levine, A.L.,'Industrial Change and its Effects on Labour, 1900–14' (unpublished PhD thesis, London University, 1954), pp.490–2.

38. See, for example, *Engineering*, 26 June 1901, p.795; 13 September 1901, pp.376–7.

39. McKinlay, A. and Zeitlin, J.,'The Meanings of Managerial Prerogative: Industrial Relations and the Organisation of Work in British Engineering, 1880–1939', *Business History*, vol.31, no.2, 1989, pp.32–47.

40. North West Engineering Trades Employers' Association (NWETEA), Executive Committee Minutes, 31 July 1899 (TD1059/1/1/1).

41. Reader, W.J., *The Weir Group: A Centenary History* (1971), pp.290–3.

42. McShane, H. and Smith, J., *No Mean Fighter*, (1978), pp.59–60. See Milton N., *John MacLean*, (1973), p.73 for MacLean's comments on Weir's 'Americanised' production and supervisory practices before 1914.

43. McKinlay, A., 'Employers and Skilled Workers in the Inter-War Depression: Engineering and Shipbuilding on Clydeside 1919–39' (unpublished DPhil thesis, Oxford University, 1986), pp. 46–55.

44. William Weir, 'Works Diary', June 1907.

45. William Weir, 'Works Diary', October 1901.

46. Melling, J., 'Scottish Industrialists and the Changing Character of Class Relations in the Clyde Region', in Dickson T. (ed), *Capital and Class in Scotland* (Edinburgh, 1982), pp.76–7.

47. ASE, *Monthly Report,* January 1903, p. 3.

48. Weir, W. and Richmond, J.R., 'Some Efficiency Factors in an Engineering Business', Address to the International Engineering Congress, Glasgow, 1901, p. 5.

49. NWETEA, Executive Committee, Minutes, 27 December 1904 (TD1059/1/2).

50. Hinton, J., *The First Shop Stewards' Movement*, pp.79–80; Jeffreys, J.B., *The Story of the Engineers, 1800–1945* (1945), p. 165.

51. NWETEA Executive Committee, Minutes, 13 January 1899 (TD1059/1/1/1), cited in Melling, 'Non-Commissioned Officers', p.126.

52. Weirs, 'Friction Club', Agenda and marginal notes, December 1899.

53. McShane and Smith, *No Mean Fighter*, pp. 59–60; Bell, T., *Pioneering Days* (1941), pp.107–9.

54. McKinlay, 'Employers and Skilled Workers', p.63.

55. Hinton, *The First Shop Stewards' Movement*, pp.76–93.

56. Labour Party, 'Report of the Special Committee to Enquire into the Clyde Deportations', 1917, p.12.

57. Zeitlin, J.,'The Labour Strategies of British Engineering Employers, 1890–1922', in Gospel H. and Littler C. (eds.), *Managerial Strategies and Industrial Relations* (1983), pp.26–33.

58. Richmond, J.R., 'Some Aspects of Labour and its Claims in the Engineering Industry', Presidential Address to Glasgow University Engineering Society, 1916–17, pp.5–6 (UGD 102/3/10).

59. Morton, D., 'Reminiscenses of the Clyde Struggle: Brave Stand of the Deportees', Glasgow, nd., p.4.

CHAPTER 5

'Striking Women': Cotton Workers and Industrial Unrest c.1907–1914

Bill Knox and Helen Corr

Introduction

This essay deals with industrial conflict in the Paisley and Neilston thread industry in the years running up to the First World War. At first sight, such events, taking place as they did in an intermediate sized Scottish burgh and an industrial village, may not be thought to hold much significance for historians concerned with the broader picture of national industrial relations, but such a view would be somewhat blinkered. The strikes which occurred in the west of Scotland thread industry during these years are highly important because of their representational character. Locally, they represent the breakdown of an elaborate and comprehensive system of paternalistic authority assiduously cultivated by the great thread enterprises of Paisley, such as Clarks and Coats, over the course of the nineteenth century. That system had ensured that the Paisley thread industry was almost a conflict-free zone with few recorded incidences of industrial disputes. The conflicts which erupted in the years 1907–14, therefore, are somewhat remarkable since they represented a significant leap in the class consciousness of these hitherto unorganised and seemingly passive workers. When it is realised that most of the workforce in the thread industry was made up of single, young females generally thought to have been amenable to the authority of their employers, the events of these years seem even more remarkable. However, although the rash of industrial conflict was unusual considering the history of industrial relations in the industry, questions remain as to what links the events in Paisley and nearby Neilston had with the general outbreak of industrial unrest in the country at this time, and what, if anything, do they contribute to attempts to establish a coherent theoretical framework for the period 1910–14? If linked to the other struggles taking place in Scottish industry at this times, the events in Paisley appear to point to a more general crisis in social relations in Scottish industry, and seem part of a wider movement of discontent among Scottish and British workers with liberal capitalism. But, as will see, the actions of the female thread workers had their own particular dynamic and because of this do not fit with any overarching theory regarding mass industrial unrest.

However, in order to understand why the conflicts erupted in Paisley and Neilston in this period, and how they related to the wider phenomenon of industrial unrest in Scotland and Britain, it is necessary to: firstly, delineate the process of female subordination within the technocratic regime of the thread mill; secondly, reconstruct the system of paternalism which shored-up the relations of production in the thread industry; thirdly, detail the social forces which brought the paternalist regime into crisis in the first decade of the twentieth century; fourthly, outline the nature and character of the industrial conflict which erupted during these years; and, finally, offer some conclusions as to relationship of the industrial discontent in Paisley and Neilston with the much wider pattern of industrial unrest.

The process of subordination

The process of thread-making involved a hierarchically structured sexual division of labour with each link in the chain of production requiring different skills and commanding different rewards. In addition to the subsidiary operations such as bleaching and dyeing, there were six main stages: the reelers put the bundled yarn into hanks; the winders, of which there were two kinds – cop winder and hank winder – put the yarn on to the bobbins; the yarn was then polished; after polishing the yarn was then doubled: from there it was put on to a twisting frame where it was turned into thread; the final stage saw the thread spooled on to small bobbins or spools for distribution. Unlike the more craft-based sectors of the cotton industry, such as spinning and weaving, the elaborate division of labour in thread meant that no key workers emerged to control the labour process.[1]

Most of the work in the process of thread-making was, therefore, unskilled machine minding. This was certainly the view of the employers. Replying to a letter in February 1883 from the Royal Commission on Technical Instruction regarding the benefit of technical education to their industry, Clark & Co. stated that 'as our manufacture is very much manufacture' skilled labourers were 'without much opportunity of exercising their knowledge'.[2] However, although relatively unskilled, the tasks in thread-making still involved a phased introduction to the work. At the age of thirteen young females were taken on as full-time workers in one of the various departments in the mills and there was a gradual increase in their responsibility and workload. A learner, for example, in the twisting department was only given a maximum workload when she had completed twenty-one weeks' employment. The procedure was to give the new start one or two sides of the machine to mind after two weeks on the job, then increase this to two or three after six weeks, three or four after twelve weeks, reaching a maximum of four to five after twenty-one weeks. Promotion was based on seniority and a female had to mark time until a vacancy arose in one of the mills before attaining the full load and the wages that went with it. However, most other jobs in the mills took only two or three days to learn and three months to be come fully proficient.

In spite of the unskilled nature of much of the work in the thread industry, there was a notional hierarchy of skills among the female labour force, and a clear division of labour based on gender. Surviving wage books for 1878 for the firm of Coats show that all ancillary, non-productive tasks were performed by males at substantially higher rates of pay than those earned by the females, who made the thread. Female workers earned between a third to a half lower wages than males, but there were also varied rates of pay among the female staff. Cop winders were the best paid female workers earning around 15 per cent more than spoolers. Thus, there was some degree of mobility for those females with keen eyes and quick hands.[3]

While the introduction of spinning in the 1880s added a further tier to the occupational hierarchy, it in no way altered the balance of the sexual division of labour as mule and, later, ring spinners were female. The labelling of women's work as unskilled was enormous benefit to the thread employers, for as the numbers of female employees increased the wage bill fell in proportion. Cairncross and Hunter estimate that wages as a fraction of total costs were stable at around 13 per cent until 1860, then fell under the impact of the high price of raw cotton to between 8 to 10 per cent, where they stayed, in spite of the resumption of cotton supplies from American after the end of the Civil War. The authors conclude that not only were wages a small proportion of total costs, but they were about a third lower in the early 1880s than they were in the early 1830s.[4] Thus, as the wage data confirms, the women experienced high rates of exploitation by their employers, but their ability to alter the division of the social product more in their favour was constrained by a hierarchically structured labour process which insured their subordination to men.

The subordination of female thread workers was not unique within the context of workplace relations in the Scottish textile industry. Most female textile workers occupied subordinate positions in the occupational hierarchy, but, in spite of this handicap, were able to take action to defend pay and conditions. Gordon, in her study of women workers in Scotland, is able to highlight over 300 disputes involving female textile workers in the period 1850–1914[5], but very few, if any, took place in the thread sector. This was not because female thread workers were more docile or passive than, say, their sisters in the jute industry or cotton weaving, they simply had to deal with a different set of constraints on action that other textile workers did not experienced. Much of the industrial quiescence of the female thread workers in the nineteenth century, in the face of high and sustained levels of exploitation, has to be put down to the elaborate system of paternalist authority developed by the large thread manufacturers. The system, as we will see, rewarded loyalty and service, and actively conditioned the thread workers into a strong identification with the firm's aspirations and its culture.

Paternalism and the thread industry

Paternalism underwrote the technological subordination of female workers in the Paisley thread industry. The Christian outlook and religious devotion of the main employers made it a likely strategy of manufacturing control in the workplace since, as Newby and others have pointed out, its basis was essentially moral.[6] Paternalism involved reciprocal duties and responsibilities between the superior and the subordinate. In return for the unquestionable right of the superior power to exercise economic and political control over his/her territory or domain, the subordinate were given protection from the exigencies of life. While this was generally assured in landed society, the application of paternalism in an industrial/urban context was much more problematical. In large urban centres the relationship between employer and employee was based on the cash nexus and the sheer variety of occupations and opinions to be found in such places made all attempts at social control by the employers problematic. However, in industrial villages, such as New Lanark, and small towns, such as Paisley, where one industry dominated all forms of economic and social life, paternalism was a viable strategy for controlling the workforce both within and without the workplace.

The system of paternalism adopted by the leading thread manufacturers was designed to increase the dependency of the workers on their employers beyond the wage relationship. An elaborate structure of welfare benefits and leisure facilities was erected in the course of the nineteenth century which tied the workers to their employers. Pensions were awarded to long-serving employees; facilities such as dining halls, bathing areas, hostels, and convalescent homes were provided, as was half-time and nursery education in company schools; and, lastly, leisure activities such as football and bowling were catered for. On top of this, there were the annual excursions paid for by the companies and other company sponsored events such as soirees.[7]

The provision of such a wide range of benefits and facilities was designed, in the words of Sir Peter Coats to a gathering of his workers, to demonstrate that 'Their interests and his were the same . . . namely, the prosperity and success of the Ferguslie Thread Works'.[8] Paternalism was thus used to enhance the process of internalisation within workers of company-inspired goals. It was also used to fragment worker response to developments in the labour process. Although the firms of Clarks and Coats amalgamated in 1896 to form one of the largest companies in the world, J.& P. Coats, the idea of specific company loyalty was encouraged and social intercourse with workers in other mills discouraged by the new firm. This was enshrined in employment policy as well as in recreation. Coats complained to Clarks about hiring workers from Ferguslie without their permission. In reply Clarks agreed that the practice was 'undesirable'.[9] Social separation also extended to recreation. Members of Coats' bowling club had to receive employer permission to play at Clarks' Seedhill green.[10] Such a strategy inhibited the growth of inter-workplace solidarity and maximised rivalry between groups of workers both in and between firms. Likewise, the half-time education system employed by the thread firms until the state assumed control of company schools in 1904 was used to socialise young workers into a distinct company culture. This is brought out in a song sung by half-timers in the employ of Coats at the expense of their counterparts in Clarks:

> For in Clarks they gang braw
> with their aprons an'a,
> but the Coats half-timers take
> the bray o'them a'.[11]

The paternalist initiatives seemed to have provoked a positive response on the part of the largely female workforce as for most of the nineteenth century they were successfully incorporated into the firm's notion of an organic industrial community in which inequality in the distribution of wealth and power was legitimized both in the workplace and the wider society. Company exertions to thrift, provident living and good works saw practical results in the establishment of a friendly society and a strong association with the Paisley Savings Bank. Collections for the relief of distressed workers in other occupations were common and enthusiastically contributed to. This was also true of the thread workers' support for Paisley Infirmary.[12]

Although the acceptance of thrift by the mill workers can be interpreted as functional in a pre-welfare society and, therefore, inconclusive evidence of the internalisation of what might be deemed bourgeois values on the part of the workers, when one relates this to other forms of behaviour the ambiguity seems less obvious. Primary identification with the threadocracy, particularly at important life cycle events such as marriage and death, was very strong among mill workers in Paisley. The celebration of vital family events seemed to unite employers and workers in a shared notion of an organic industrial community.[13] Opportunities to reaffirm specific attachments to firm and locality were also provided by company paid for excursions.

Naturally, locality was personified in the person of the employer. Workers would parade around the streets of Paisley on the day of their excursion with their company banners, which would be unfurled for another procession at the site of their destination.[14]

By these means the solidarities of class were transcended by the solidarities of work group culture. The strong personal identification with the culture of the thread companies and the dependency upon which this was based was also of major economic benefit to the employers. It gave them a free rein in using the most modern forms of textile technology to destroy craft-based skills, and, hence, the basis of resistance, further increasing the dependency upon them among their workers. However, after 1900 the paternalism of the thread employers began to show signs of wear and tear as new pressures began to emerge which threatened to create a new oppositional mill culture.

Paternalism under pressure

The stability of industrial relations in the Paisley thread trade was threatened in the first decade of the twentieth century by the interference of outside forces – namely the National Federation of Women Workers (NFWW) and the Independent Labour Party (ILP). Preceding, and laying the foundations for third party intervention, was the partial disintegration of the paternalist regime of the threadocracy. The amalgamation of Clarks and Coats in 1896 enlarged the scale and scope of operations and inevitably this led to greater emphasis being placed on bureaucratic methods of controlling labour. It also forced the company to tap into supplies of labour from outside Paisley. An examination of the birthplaces of thread workers covering the years 1851, 1871 and 1891 shows how the previously organic industrial community of Paisley was becoming more fragmented and less stable. In 1851 it was noted that the Irish failed to establish themselves in Paisley since they had no connection with the shawl trade, which employed half the adult male labour force of the burgh. A sample of heads of households working in the textile industry underscores the insularity of Paisley's social structure. Out of a sample of 178 heads of households in 1851, 137, or 77 per cent, were born in Paisley. However, by 1871 there were signs that

Table 5.1   Place of Birth of Thread Mill

Worker Heads of Households								
Date	Paisley		Scotland		Ireland		England	
	No	%	No	%	No	%	No	%
1871	63	51.6	50	40.9	6	5.7	3	2.5
1891	63	38.9	65	41.1	17	10.5	16	9.9

Source: Census Enumerator Books: Paisley, 1871 and 1891

the close-knit textile community was breaking up with 59.2 per cent, or 122 heads of households out of a total of 206, being born in Paisley. By 1891 the number had fallen dramatically to 44.9 per cent, or 88 heads of households out of a total of 196. If this picture is broken down to include only heads of households employed in the thread trade then the fragmentation is more acute, as Table 5.1 shows.

Mathew Blair, in *The Paisley Thread Industry*, highlighted the role of the immigrants not only in boosting the native population, but also the way in which 'The incomers brought many new ideas and practices, which have materially changed the homely style of life that previously existed'.[15] Their experience of a different process of socialisation made them amenable to alternative definitions of their social position. Moreover, the demand for labour saw an influx of daily workers from the more cosmopolitan culture of Glasgow. Coming in the main from skilled working class households, these female workers saw labour organisation as both legitimate and natural expressions of working class interests. On top of this the female workforce itself was becoming less stable and this resulted in relatively high rates of labour turnover in the key age cohorts, as Table 5.2 shows.

What is interesting is that very few of the female workers who left the employment of Coats did so because of marriage, pointing to the fact that there was a shortage of eligible marriage partners. In the age cohort of 20–25 the ratio to other causes of leaving was almost 1:4; and in the age cohort 25–30 it was just over 1:4. Greater opportunities in the labour market as a consequence of the growth of the service sector, as well as the increasing willingness of women to play by market rules, threatened to undermine the effectiveness of company aculturalisation. This process was furthered by the end of the half-time

Table 5.2   Labour Turnover in specific Age

	Cohorts at the Ferguslie Mill in 1902					
	14–20	%	20–25	%	25–30	%
Working	1060	77	586	61	370	67
Left	296	21	283	30	143	26
Married	16	1	78	8	35	6
Dead	5	1	5	1	1>	
Pensioned	0	0	0	0	1 >	1
Total	1337	100	952	100	550	100

Source: Letter Books, 1905–11 (Kinning Park) Coll., Box A2/1]

system in 1904 which denied Coats a significant role in the socialisation of its future workforce. The threadocracy's supposedly personal relationship with its workers was beginning to look more than a little threadbare. One sign of the growing disillusionment of the female workers with the paternalist initiatives was the failure of J.& P. Coats' Girls' Club. Established in 1901, the Club offered classes in dress-making, physical culture, millinery and health. The aim of the Club was to 'promote self-knowledge and self-development' among its members, but it failed to attract sufficient interest from its recognised constituency and it was deemed by the Coats' family to be a 'non-success'.[16] It was against this background that alternative, anti-employer expressions of workers' interest began to emerge and quicken the tempo of industrial conflict.

Trade unionism and industrial conflict

Although there had been a bobbin turners' strike in 1868 at Clarks' mill[17], and a strike by machine tenters at Ferguslie in 1882[18], the first major blow to the paternalism of the thread combines came in 1897 with a strike of 800 female spoolers over the introduction of a system of mechanised bobbin distribution, which created delays and led to a loss of earnings.[19] Another two strikes took place in 1900 over wages with the copwinders walking out in March and the ring spinners in November. The company on these occasions dismissed the ring leaders and posted notices warning that 'workers interfering with others who wished to continue at their occupations would be dismissed'.[20] Four years later a dispute over wages led to a walk-out of 200 hankwinders with a further 2,800 workers coming out in sympathy.[21] The employer's policy of dividing the workers by occupation was breaking down as the benefits of collective action were becoming more apparent to the former. A further strike by eighty to a hundred white hankwinders at the Anchor Mills in March 1905 for parity with winders at the Ferguslie Mill led to mass demonstrations in the streets of Paisley and the barracking and harrying of mill managers. The strikers were mainly young girls, but they were joined by what the local newspaper described as 'youths, children and others who had no connection with the strike'.[22] The organic community was in revolt against the authority and power of the threadocracy.

These developments were being advanced by the growth of Labour and trade union activity in Paisley by the ILP and the NFWW. Women's organisations had been actively campaigning among female textile workers in Scotland from 1890, particularly in the Glasgow area. The Women's Protective and Provident League (WPPL) had organised female weavers in Glasgow following a successful strike in 1890 and claimed 450 members by 1893. The WPPL, however, underwent a transformation from a trade union into a pressure group campaigning for legislative improvement in working conditions for women in general and its place was taken by the more trade union conscious NFWW led by Mary MacArthur. Although active in the Glasgow area, the NFWW was only brought into the thread mills at the request of the workers. In the aftermath of the 1905 strike the female workers of J & P Coats approached Paisley Trades Council to help them form a union and it was this which brought the thread workers to the attention of the NFWW and the ILP.[23]

A mass demonstration against the Paisley 'thread barons' was held in the Clark Town Hall by the ILP on 29 June 1906 addressed by Keir Hardie, miners' leader Robert Smillie, Mary MacArthur and local Labour leaders in response to the refusal of Coats to build a new mill at Paisley and locate it elsewhere because of the demand of the workers for trade union recognition. The chairperson, Bailie Baird, spoke of how the girls in spite of threats by the company 'had gone on quietly forming their union, which was increasing in membership at every meeting'. Hardie denounced the 'evil influences of trusts' and successfully moved a motion declaring support for an 'industrial commonwealth based on the socialisation or common ownership of land and capital'.[24] However, the minutes of the board of directors of J & P Coats noted with satisfaction that their threat 'had an excellent effect on the workers'.[25]

The policy of the thread combine was to publicly declare non-opposition to their workers 'forming themselves into a trade union for the protection and promotion of their interests', while in private resolving 'that it would be against the interests of the company to permit outside interference or recognise outsiders as representatives of the workers'.[26] However, in some ways the employers' attitude was counter-productive as their intransigence on the issue of worker representation made it impossible to resolve the growing discontent on the mill floor within an institutional framework. Sectional grievances became workplace issues and easily escalated into all out stoppages. Negotiation through strikes and other forms of industrial protest became the only means available for the workforce to express dissatisfaction with wage rates and working practices. The company had noted earlier in May 1906 that in spite of improved machinery 'production was declining' due to 'unusual sickness' and 'considerable absenteeism, especially in the mornings'.[27]

The silent protest of absenteeism gave way to all out industrial warfare in late September 1907. The strike began among the boy labourers in the turning shop of the Anchor Mills over the introduction of new machinery which threatened to bring about a reduction in piece rate payments.[28] It soon spread to the female cone-winders – a small but very important department of the mill – who also had a grievance over wages. The cone-winders complained that their wages were low in comparison to other grades in the mill and their request to either be placed on piece rate earnings, or have their time wage increased, had been ignored by management for over six months.[29] The refusal of the management to deal with their 'disaffected employees'[30] activated an unofficial agreement with the boys, the hankwinders and the block polishers and an all out strike ensued at the Anchor Mills. The hankwinders themselves had a long-standing grievance with the employers over the issuing of defective yarn which reduced piece earnings because of the number of stoppages needed made to repair the broken thread.[31]

Immediately the dispute assumed the characteristics of the

disorganised in protest. At the start of the morning shift on 2 October around 400 block polishers, shortly before joining the strike, created industrial mayhem. The *Glasgow Herald* described the scene as follows:

> . . . [The polishers] armed themselves with spoolwood sticks and smashed a large number of windows in the department . . . the management . . . deemed it necessary to summon extra police by telephone. By the time they arrived . . . the disaffected girls had been reinforced by a number of those . . . outside the gates and it was deemed prudent to send for further assistance . . . ejection was effected although notwithout considerable trouble. . . .[32]

On being driven from the mills the girls occupied the surrounding lanes and running battles took place between the 'girls' and the police. From there the strikers proceeded to the Ferguslie Mill to call out the workers there in sympathy. However, the management were able to secure the mill gate, although 'not without a great deal of effort' and with the assistance of a large police presence.[33] During the dinner hour, Ferguslie workers, who had refused to join the dispute, were 'roughly handled' by the Anchor strikers in an attempt to storm the mills. Coats responded by closing the mills. By the next day 12,000 thread workers were idle.

The success of the strike rested on the willingness of the Ferguslie workers to join forces with their Anchor workmates. However, the management's divisive tactics were to prove crucial in forestalling joint action. Paternalistic strategies had been used in the past to foster group and company identities to inhibit the growth of inter-workplace solidarity and maximise rivalry between sets of workers both within and between firms. The amalgamation of Clarks and Coats in 1896, as we have mentioned, above did not lead to an abandonment of this strategy, if anything, it intensified. Thus with the strike into its eighth day and the mills lying idle, the board of directors unanimously agreed to keep the male occupations such as, dyers, joiners, in employment and also to pay the wages of Ferguslie workers made idle because of the dispute.[34] The traditional rivalry between the workers of Clarks and Coats complicated the generation of inter-firm solidarity and the decision of the management to make good lost wages to the locked-out Ferguslie workers made it unlikely that the strike would be successful. Moreover, it was clear from the start that the strike was a spontaneous protest with 'neither organisation nor prearranged plan'.[35] Unlike the last dispute 'there was no outside interference' and the workers opted to deal 'personally with their directors', declaring their belief 'in their good intentions'.[36] On the promise of adequate police protection the Ferguslie Mills were opened on Friday 4 October and negotiations began the following day in Glasgow to discuss the grievances of the boys and the cone-winders. Around 85,000 working days were lost during the strike, which ended with a commitment by the employers to 'fully and carefully consider the grievances' of their employees. By October 9 the mills were operating as normal.

The mobilisation of protest among the mill girls and the spontaneous anarchic form it took was criticised by the press as being irresponsible and 'unspeakably ridiculous'.[37] However, it would seem that the behaviour of the Paisley mill girls was in line with their counterparts in other branches of industry which employed mainly women workers. Gordon, in her study of the Dundee jute industry, found evidence of similar actions such as parading through the streets of the town, barracking employers, assaults on workers refusing to obey the call to strike, and so on.[38] Although this behaviour was at odds with the normally sober and respectable protest of male trade unionists, Gordon sees it as simply a transportation of female leisure activities into the sphere of industrial conflict. As she argues: 'It was a flight from work, a collective expression of defiance . . . and by embuing it with a sense of fun, they underscored the fact that they were expropriating this time from the masters and repossessing it themselves'.[39] At the same time, the so-called 'disgraceful' behaviour of the striking females was a rejection of male notions of acceptable feminine behaviour and of men's ability to 'control their behaviour'.[40]

However, the contest over the possession of time between workers and management was an unequal one. The events of the autumn of 1907 in Paisley saw the Coats' management take an even tougher line on industrial protest and worker organisation. A strike of fifty-three cone-winders against a reduction in wages in May 1908 led to the dismissal of 'every woman who had shown a spark of resistance to unfair treatment', and the threat to dismiss any workers striking in sympathy to the extent of closing the mills if necessary. As the journal of the NFWW – *The Woman Worker* – remarked: 'Surely now the women workers of Paisley must realise that the only alternative to absolute serfdom is to join the ranks of organised labour'.[41] However, in spite of the efforts of the NFWW to organise Coats' workers, the major breakthrough for the union came not in Paisley, but at R.F. and J. Alexander and Co., of the English Sewing Cotton Company (ESCC) combine, works at nearby Neilston. A strike by cop winders in May 1910 over parity with wage rates paid at the Anchor Mills was taken up by the NFWW, the GTC and John Maclean of the Social Democratic Party.

There had been evidence of disquiet among the Neilston workforce two years previous when over 160 winders went on strike against a reduction in wages of 30 per cent, which led to a further 600 workers in other departments of the mill being locked out.[42] The dispute, however, was short, but there was enough indication of growing resistance among the female workers to build on. When the 1910 strike broke out on 25 May it was reported that 'The strikers are being assisted by the NFWW, who daily have representatives on the scene', and very quickly the 'majority of the workers in the mills joined the Federation'.[43] Miss Dicks of the NFWW almost immediately called on the GTC and other trades for support in the struggle. The strike also drew the attention of socialist John Maclean who wrote in the ILP paper *Forward* that ESCC had 'openly screwed down the wages of the Paisley thread workers', and called on support for the 'girls' from the rest of the labour movement.[44]

In response to the claim for parity with the winders at Clarks' mills, the management refused and further decided not to deal with the workers' representatives whom they described as 'outside people'.[45] From 6 June all the workers, numbering some 1700, were locked out by the management. Events began to turn ugly as the female workers vented their frustrations on the manager of the mills, Mr Hough. He was mobbed by the strikers and had to take refuge in the booking office of the local railway station, where some windows were broken. The windows of the mills were also smashed and the manager of the turning shop was reportedly 'roughly handled'.[46] Mass demonstrations followed and a series of meetings were addressed by leading figures in the Scottish labour movement, including James Maxton. By 8 June the foremen were forced out by the strikers so that the withdrawal of labour was total. The management offered to deal with 'representatives' of the workers but the strikers insisted on 'carrying on negotiations through trade union officials'. On 10 June a march of 5000 people from Neilston to the home of the manager of the mills at Barrhead some seven miles away took place complete with pipers, singing and banner-waving. The strikers were accompanied by a 'sprinkling' of male trade unionists from Glasgow, old 'grey-haired workers', children and young men. The language of banners carried on the march provide some insight into the level of class consciousness existing among the Neilston strikers. The largest banner carried the slogan: 'We want justice, fair conditions and a living wage'.[47] In short, it was the political language of a labourist mentality which left unquestioned the social basis of ownership, and instead concentrated on making the best bargain with capital it could in the circumstances. But in the context of the mill culture of Neilston labourism represented a leap forward in terms of class consciousness for, at the very least, it involved a break with paternalism and opened spaces for a counter-employer culture and language to emerge.

The strikers were well supported by other workers in the west of Scotland. Collections were taken regularly outside the mills of J & P Coats which yielded considerable sums. This sustained the struggle against Alexanders and the ESCC and forced the employers to accept intervention by the arbitration service of the Board of Trade. On 17 June at St Enoch's Station Hotel, Glasgow, employers and workers met in a meeting presided over by W.B. Yates of the Board of Trade. After three-and-a-half hours of talks an agreement was reached. In return for assurances that if the new working arrangements for copwinders did not improve their wages there would be a review in three months, the strike was called off.

There were no major confrontations between workers and management in the aftermath of the 1910 Neilston strike, however, at both Alexanders and J & P Coats counter-employer cultures sustained other outbursts of industrial protest. In June 1912 a strike of male black dyers over wages broke out at Coats. The company increased the wages of the coloured dyers back in January 1912, but refused to grant the black dyers a similar rise in wages on the grounds that they were less skilled than the former. Resentment festered among the black dyers and the union – the National Association of Dyers and Finishers (NADF) – prevented new men being taken on in the black dye department. Coats broke the union embargo on the hiring of new men in June when they employed a man 'at the current rate of 26s per week', and that led to an all out strike by the black dyers.[48] By employing blackleg labour Coats broke the strike after two weeks, and then used the victory to break the union. Union men were refused employment at the mills.[49] The minutes of the Board of Directors noted that the 'time was opportune to announce that only non-union men would be employed at the dye-works in future'.[50] It seemed clear that Coats had provoked the strike to finally outlaw union activity in the mills. The dyers, because of their skills and gender status, had been allowed membership of the NADF in the past, but the cost of industrial stoppages to the firm was too great to allow this to continue. As a statement of the firm revealed:

> . . . It is perfectly well-known to our workers that in the past no distinction has been made between those who belong to a union and those who do not, but when a small number strike at the instigation of a trade union secretary in Bradford, involving the risk of a general stoppage of work, we are compelled . . . to do our best to prevent a recurrence of such a strike, which may deprive many thousands of their means of livelihood. . . . It is therefore been decided to discontinue employing dyers who belong to a union. . . .[51]

The last confrontation in the thread industry of any note before the outbreak of war in August 1914 occurred at Alexanders in January 1913. Again it involved a relatively small number of strategically placed workers in the production process. Around two hundred female twisters applied for an 8 per cent rise in wages in response to new working arrangements, the first such application for five years. By the time the demand was made the Scottish National Textile Workers' Federation (SNTWF) had been established, and it was the Federation along with the NFWW that represented the strikers. The strike concluded on a partially successful note with the women agreeing to mind eight frames instead of six in return for an increase in wages. Those in the employ of the ESCC for more than ten years were granted an extra sixpence per week.[52]

The size of the huge thread mills and their integrated ownership and production methods meant that inevitably strikes in the industry would have a highly damaging effect on output. Paternalism and the social overheads that such a strategy involved were borne by the thread manufacturers because they had little choice. Although cartelisation had minimised competition with regard to price and output, market share was still fiercely contested. Disruptions of production threatened market shares and forced the thread manufacturers into compromise with their workers' demands. However, it was also true that a company such as J & P Coats with multinational status and subsidiary plants throughout the world was better able to combat worker coercion in regard to wages and conditions than the more domestically-based ESCC. Shortfalls in production in one country could easily made up in another. Thus, while the ESCC was forced to negotiate with the NFWW and the SNTWF, Coats simply refused to entertain third party interference between themselves and their workers. In doing so the company moved from a paternalism based on Christian values, to one based on authoritarianism. In future it was not simply the carrot which would be used to manufacture consent on the shopfloor, but, more as a first resort, the stick too.

The events, then, of the period 1907–12 had a contradictory impact on the balance of class forces in Paisley. On the one hand, it is undoubtedly true that the class consciousness of the workers, especially the hitherto unorganised mill girls, grew as a result of the overt clashes with capital. But the spread of class consciousness was uneven. As we have seen the workers at the Ferguslie Mill refused to join the strike and it was left to the employees at the Anchor Mill to carry on the struggle for better wages and conditions. On the other, the attempts to form a trade union for the mill girls came to nothing, with even the previously organised male dyers being forced to relinquish their craft unionism. However, in Neilston attempts at unionisation were successful and the management of Alexanders were forced to negotiate with the representatives of the workers. Thus, although class consciousness increased among the thread workers and was expressed in the rejection of management structured notions of an organic industrial community, the institutional means of directing this newly found social awareness was distinctly lacking in the case of Paisley.

Conclusion

The events in Paisley and Neilston may have resulted in a sharp increase in class consciousness among many of the female mill workers, but the question remains as to what relevance these actions had for the wider movement of discontent among Scottish and British workers with liberal capitalism. Unfortunately the pattern and timing of events in the Paisley thread industry do not conform with those occurring in other industries. The major concentration of days lost in Scottish industry seems to have been confined to the period February/April 1912, whereas the major strikes in the thread sector took place in 1907 and 1910. Moreover, due to the assiduous cultivation of specific mill cultures the disputes were confined to only half the mill workforce in Paisley. Thus Coats was able to defeat the workers without resorting to the importation of blacklegs; a policy which elsewhere in Scottish industrial disputes intensified the action and drove workers to a more militant stance vis-a-vis employers and the state.[53] Only in the case of the dyers was there any attempt by the employers to use blacklegs to break a strike. However, what did inflame the situation in Paisley was the use of the local state apparatus to protect those mill girls who refused to support the call to strike. The large police presence demonstrated the degree to which employers were increasingly relying on the state to assist them in subordinating their workforces. It was a development which was leading to the increasing politicising of industrial relations in Paisley and elsewhere. A trend which reached its culmination during the First World War in those industries brought into temporary state ownership.

As to the causes of the outbreak of industrial protest during the years 1910–14 the experience of the thread industry of the west of Scotland seems contradictory. Economistic explanations of industrial unrest stress the knee-jerk response of workers to years of falling standards of living due to rising prices and falling real wages. The labour unrest which characterised the period 1910–1914 was the result of workers making good the losses they had incurred in the first decade of the twentieth century in a period of full order books and a high demand for labour. In Cronin's elegant phrase, it allowed workers to translate 'oppression into protest'.[54] However, as we have noted the multinational status of Coats by-passed these problems. The workers never enjoyed a position of strength as paternalist strategies divided them, and the ability of the company to switch production to different sites throughout the world undermined the effectiveness of any action taken in defence of wages and conditions. There is also little evidence to suggest that the thread industry was experiencing serious deficiencies in supplies of labour. The labour market was anything but tight.

More convincing as an explanation of industrial unrest is that linked to the attempts by management to assert greater control of the labour process through intensifying the working rhythms of the labour force. Novel methods of work intensification such as Taylorism, payments by results, and so on, were implemented throughout British industry in this period. Indeed, in the thread sector it was attempts to speed up production and/or increase the workload of the workers which led to the strikes. The rewards for accepting new working arrangements were either too scant, or involved a loss of earnings, and this led to strike action by a supposedly passive workforce. But unlike other workers in dispute in these years, thread employees, with the exception of those in Neilston, were largely unsuccessful in redressing their grievances. This cannot simply be put down to the use of the employers of the coercive arm of the state, since the female workers in Neilston did achieve positive gains in this period. The main reason for the success of the Neilston thread workers lies in their ability to initiate with the assistance of the labour movement a community-wide challenge to the authority of capital. Mobilisation of similar community interests in Paisley was forestalled by the traditional policy of divide-and-rule practiced by the thread employers. Indeed, Coats was able to use the incidence of industrial unrest among the dyers to establish a completely non-union establishment. Therefore, while changes in the labour process initiated the unrest, industrial militancy had a contradictory impact; success in one site of production was more than offset by defeat at another.

The experience of Paisley and Neilston demonstrates, generally, the importance of local studies, and, more specifically, the particularness of industrial sectors. No set of causal factors were reproduced in each location and sector beset by industrial conflict in the years running up to the First World War. The thread industry shared some of the wider causal features which promoted industrial unrest in Britain in this period, but also proved exceptional in many respects. As in most cases, the largely female labour force of the thread industry experienced a rise in class consciousness, but it was contradictory and far from universal. Inherited patterns of social relations shaped by paternalist managerial strategies inhibited labour protest in at least half the female workforce in Paisley, as well as creating a major barrier against the construction of institutions of worker self-defence. During the war years themselves the high demand for thread provided employment for the women and a steadily improving standard of living. Out of their profits the thread manufacturers paid war bonuses which defused any potential for industrial unrest and largely pacified the thread workers. In 1915 alone thread workers enjoyed three separate increases in wages. In March a bonus of 1s per week was paid; in July a further 2s per week was paid; and in November a 10 per cent increase in wage rates was introduced, with married men and women with children of school age receiving significantly more.[55] These actions brought industrial peace to the thread industry for the duration of the war and made the likelihood of establishing a trade union an unrealistic proposition. However, the realisation among the workers that their interests were not the same as their employers was shown in the political field. The normally safe Liberal seat was threatened in 1918 when the candidate of the Co-operative Party, J.M. Biggar, came within half a percentage point of winning Paisley. Of course, Labour finally won the seat in 1923 when Glasgow lawyer, Rosslyn Mitchell, defeated the Liberal leader, Asquith, in a straight fight. Therefore, while Paisley mill girls did not provide the challenge to capital and the state which characterised the shipyards and engineering shops of Clydeside during the war, the experience of industrial conflict in the run up to 1914 indelibly shaped their consciousness. Weaknesses experienced in the sphere of productive relations, however, were from 1918 compensated by the pursuit of a class agenda in the political arena. The granting of the franchise to women was the poisoned chalice for the Coats' political ambitions and provided their female workers with the means to exact revenge for previous industrial defeats and humiliations.

NOTES

1. Watson, J., *The Art of Spinning and Thread Making* (Glasgow, 1878), p.112; I.W., 'Cotton', in *Encyclopedia Britannica*, VI, (Edinburgh, 1877), p.502.
2. Royal Commission on Technical Instruction, *British Parliamentary Papers (BPP)* *xxxi*, (1884), p.660.
3. Coats Letter Books, 28 June 1878, (Kinning Park Collection, Box A1/2)
4. CairnCross, A.K. and Hunter, J.B.K., 'The Early Growth of Messrs J. & P. Coats, 1830–1883', *Business History*, Vol 29, (1987), pp.157–77.

5. Gordon, E., 'Separate Spheres', in *People and Society in Scotland, Vol.11, 1830–1914*, ed. Fraser W.H. and Morris R. J. , (Edinburgh, 1992), p.222.
6. Newby, H., (*et. al.*), *Property, Paternalism and Power: class and control in rural England* (Wisconsin, 1978), pp.27–8.
7. Coats' Works Committee, Minute Books (1897–1903), (Paisley Museum and Art Gallery [PMAG], files 1/10/1, 4/1/1)
8. *Paisley Daily Express*, 7 February 1880
9. Coats' Letter Books (1905–1911), (Kinning Park Collection, Box A1/2).
10. Board of Directors, Minute Books, 24 May 1898, (Kinning Park Collection, Box A1/2).
11. *Ferguslie News*, April, 1954.
12. *Paisley Daily Express*, 1 March 1879; *Ferguslie News*, Feb/March 1954.
13. See for example the reports in the *Paisley Daily Express* of employee participation in Coats' family weddings (22 April 1876, 18 September 1879)
14. Descriptions of these events can found in the *Paisley Herald* and *Renfrewshire Gazette*, 1 July 1878, and in Keir D., *The Coats' Story*, Vol. 1 (unpublished company history, Glasgow, 1964), pp.183–4.
15. Blair, M. *The Paisley Thread Industry* (1907), p.183–4. See also Gordon, E., *Women and the Labour Movement in Scotland, 1850–1914* (Oxford, 1991) p.211, for a discussion of the impact of migration on Dundee's social structure and the disruption of family relationships.
16. Coats Letter Books, 1905–11, (Kinning Park Collection, Box A1/2).
17. *Paisley* and *Renfrewshire Gazette*, 19 May 1868.
18. *Paisley* and *Renfrewshire Gazette*, 18 March 1882.
19. *Glasgow Evening Times*, 1 November 1897.
20. Board of Directors, Minute Books, 29 March 1900, (Kinning Park Collection, Box A1/2).
21. Board of Trade, Reports on Strikes and Lockouts, (1904), (Public Record Office [PRO], LAB 34/22).
22. *Paisley and Renfrewshire Gazette*, 18 March 1905.
23. *Glasgow Herald*, 9 May 1906.
24. *Glasgow Herald*, 30 June 1906.
25. Board of Directors, Minute Books, 14 June 1906, (Kinning Park Collection, Box A1/3).
26. Board of Directors, Minute Books, 14 June 1906.
27. Board of Directors, Minute Books, 3 May 1906, (Box A1/2).
28. *Glasgow Herald*, 24 September 1907.
29. Wage Complaints Book, No.1, 2 October 1907, (PMAG, f.1/5/45)
30. *Glasgow Herald*, 25 September 1907.
31. Board of Directors, Minute Books, 16 May 1907, (Kinning Park Collection, Box A1/3).
32. *Glasgow Herald*, 3 October 1907.
33. *Glasgow Herald*, 3 October 1907.
34. Board of Directors, Minute Books, 3 October 1907, (Kinning Park Collection, Box A1/3)
35. *Daily Record and Mail*, 3 October 1907.
36. *Daily Record and Mail*, 5 October 1907.
37. *Glasgow Herald*, 4 October 1907.
38. Gordon, *Women and Labour*, pp. 177, 179, 192.

39. Gordon, *Women and Labour*, pp.209–10.

40. Gordon, *Women and Labour*, p.210.

41. *The Woman Worker*, 5 June 1908.

42. *The Woman Worker*, 28 August 1908.

43. *Glasgow Herald*, 26 May 1910.

44. *Forward*, 4 June 1910.

45. *Glasgow Herald*, 7 June 1910.

46. *Glasgow Herald*, 7 June 1910.

47. *Glasgow Herald*, 11 June 1910.

48. *Glasgow Herald*, 23 July 1912.

49. *Glasgow Herald*, 23 July 1912.

50. Board of Directors, Minute Books, 18 July 1912, (Kinning Park Collection, Box A1/3).

51. *Glasgow Herald*, 23 July 1912.

52. *Glasgow Herald*, 30 January 1913.

53. Glasgow Labour History Workshop, 'Roots of Red Clydeside: labour unrest in the west of Scotland, 1910–1914', in *Militant Workers*, ed. Duncan R. and McIvor A., (Edinburgh, 1994), pp.93–4.

54. Glasgow Labour History Workshop 'Roots of Red Clydeside', p.97.

55. *Glasgow Herald*, 12 July and 9 November 1915.

CHAPTER 6

A Struggle for Control: The Importance of the Great Unrest at Glasgow Harbour, 1911 to 1912

William Kenefick

Introduction

The events that were to unfold along the Glasgow waterfront during 1911 and 1912 were orchestrated and managed by the Scottish Union of Dock Labourers (SUDL). Over this relatively short period Glasgow's dockers gained formal trade union recognition by all employers at Glasgow harbour and established the Glasgow Harbour Joint Negotiating Committee. There is little doubt that this period was to prove a major watershed in the history of dock-labour relations at Glasgow, as it did for the rest of Scotland and the United Kingdom generally. It is perhaps ironic, therefore, that some six months earlier, around December 1910, dock trade unionism at Glasgow appeared to be about to collapse. James O'Connor Kessack, the Scottish Organiser of the National Union of Dock Labourers – which at that point represented the dock labour force at Glasgow – made an appeal to the Glasgow Trades Council to assist in "getting the men back" into the union.[1] By January 25, 1911, however, the Glasgow branch of the NUDL was officially closed down by James Sexton and the links with organised dock unionism had been broken at Glasgow for the first time in over twenty years.[2] After 1910 the task of reorganising Glasgow's dockers lay with a 10-man committee of the Glasgow Trades Council. Within six months the SUDL was formed at Glasgow and the dockers proved they were sufficiently reorganised to take part in a national strike of seamen, dockers and other transport workers between June and August 1911.[3]

The main aim of this chapter is to provide a case study which will attempt to highlight the importance, and assess the impact, of the period of labour unrest along the Glasgow waterfront between 1911 and 1912, and place it in some historical perspective, before returning to the analysis of the events of that period themselves. It is important, therefore, to consider the reasons for the decline of the NUDL as well as the resurgence of dock unionism under the SUDL. This requires a brief analysis of the economic conditions from the turn of the century onward, which help explain why the NUDL fell into terminal decline at Glasgow. The economistic argument is also one used to explain the causes of the 'Labour Unrest' between 1910 and 1914, therefore this theory can be tested by considering the experience of the Glasgow dockers during this period. It will also be shown too, however, that there were significant differences in opinion between the rank and file at Glasgow and the executive of the NUDL in Liverpool as to the correct industrial strategy to adopt in wage bargaining. Rank and file discontent played an important part in the NUDL's decline at Glasgow and this factor needs to be considered closely.

Secondly, I will look closely at the methods used to reorganise the Glasgow dock labour force after they had left the NUDL in 1910. The first phase in this process was founded on the basis of a 'rolling' strike wave, which took place from early May through until August of 1911, and it was this strategy that laid the firm foundations upon which to rebuild dock unionism at Glasgow. The third part of this chapter will consider the events of 1911 as preparation for the extensive general strike and lockout which was to take place over January and February of 1912. This analysis will be less concerned with the actual technical details of the strike, than the political concerns that this strike raised. The experience of unrest, and the dockers' open challenge to the employers' managerial prerogatives, forced the employers to re-appraise the traditional, and somewhat draconian, industrial strategies adopted to deal with organised labour, and it was the fear of politically-driven discontent that influenced this shift in attitude. The employers' concerns about socialism and syndicalism as a cause of unrest are therefore an important part of this chapter. The chapter will conclude by considering the aftermath of this period of industrial conflict; whether the fears of mass insurrection and revolt were in fact warranted; and finally, how politically significant this episode was in the long term, both in relation to dock unionism at Glasgow and the dockers political evolution.

A Struggle for Control

The roots and the decline of dock unionism at the port of Glasgow

The roots of dock trade unionism along the Glasgow waterfront stretch back to the mid nineteenth century. One of the first dock workers' unions to emerge in Britain was formed at Glasgow in 1853 as the Glasgow Harbour Labourers' Union (GHLU), composed mainly of shipworkers.[4] The GHLU union began to open-up its ranks to all regular dockers at the port by the early 1870s and thereafter embarked on a three-week strike for higher wages. The strike proved unsuccessful and was broken by introducing imported labour into the docks.[5] The GHLUs membership thereafter fell by over two-thirds, declining to 230, around the time of the formation of the National Union of Dock Labourers (NUDL) at Glasgow in February 1889.[6] The NUDL were composed mainly of quayside workers – the most distinct difference between the two organisations. Over the following three to four years these two bodies entered into a bitter dispute for the right to organise dock workers at Glasgow.[7] The details of this battle are not relevant to the present study, but the dispute seriously threatened dock unionism at Glasgow between 1889 and 1893 and coincided with a vigorous employers' counterattack along the British waterfront, which saw many dock unions and dock branches around Britain fail completely. The GHLU and the NUDL both survived this counterattack. Indeed, by 1899 the GHLU had joined the ranks of the NUDL, which resulted in the dock labour force being brought together within one trade union organisation.

The NUDL was one of the first general organisations of dock workers to be formed in Britain during the period of 'New Unionism' and was in existence some six months before the start of the Great London Dock Strike. Sydney and Beatrice Webb described the NUDL as 'an antagonistic society organised on the idea of including every kind of dock and wharf labourer in a national amalgamation'.[8] By 1891 the NUDL had established 34 branches throughout the United Kingdom since the foundation of its first branch at Glasgow in February 1889.[9] At the Fifth Annual Congress of the NUDL, held at Liverpool in 1893, the NUDL's President, John McHugh, described the union as a 'pioneering organisation for what came to be called New Unionism', and even in the aftermath of the employers' counter-attack was still "solvent, independent and full of vital energy".[10] Even at this stage, however, the NUDL was having problems and by the mid-1890s the number of branches nationally had dropped from 34 to 14, and at Glasgow (which now had two branches) the membership dropped considerably from 4,000 to 1,400 over the period 1889 and 1895.[11] Nationally the NUDL was to make a resurgence and at Glasgow the NUDL was further strengthened by the amalgamation with the Glasgow Harbour Labourers' Union into the union in 1899- bringing the combined membership at the port to around 3,500.[12] They had not quite realised the high membership levels they had reached at Glasgow around 1889/90. The union had come through a difficult period, which combined a sustained employers counter-attack between 1890 and 1893 and a trade depression which followed in 1894/5. By the end of the nineteenth century, therefore, the NUDL at Glasgow seemed to be in a particularly strong position. However, the new century would ensure that the future of the NUDL at Glasgow would be a troubled one.

The first decade of the twentieth century saw the fortunes of the NUDL change dramatically for the worse, a fact which is partly explainable in economistic terms and the effects of two particularly severe depressions between 1903–5 and 1907–10. Jim Treble has described these crises as having 'devastating economic and social effects' on the communities around Glasgow.[13] Dock work was seriously affected by the depressions of the period, and the problems were exacerbated by unemployed men from other occupations descended on the docks to seek work.[14] A report in the *Glasgow Herald* in March 1908 noted that 'dullness in trade deprived the *bona fide* docker of what he considered his regular work, because of the influx of men from other walks of life'. By September the *Glasgow Herald* was reporting that 'dock labour were experiencing worse conditions than at any time over the previous thirty years'. The report concluded that some 2,000 dockers at the port were idle and that their wages were at half their former levels. It was during this particularly difficult period that the NUDL was attempting to maintain its foothold at the port of Glasgow, and despite the best work of organisers such as Jim Larkin, and later James O'Connor Kessack, the situation only worsened.

Economic arguments for the NUDL's decline at Glasgow are, then, particularly powerful ones. But they do not fully explain the union's collaps by the later months of 1910. There is strong evidence to suggest that there was deep division between the Glasgow rank and file and the Liverpool executive of the NUDL during this period. The NUDL executive were conciliatory by nature, none more so than James Sexton, the NUDL's leader. Indeed, Sexton's conciliatory approach was legendary and this brought him into direct and often bitter confrontation with the membership in general and Jim Larkin in particular. Sexton recognised that the ordinary docker 'seemed to thrive on strikes and lock-outs', and that this strategy also proved a profitable recruitment device; he nevertheless disapproved of the arbitrary use of direct action and the violence that often followed in the wake of such an industrial strategy.[15] Larkin on the other hand accused Sexton of hampering his work because he would not back up talks with strike action.[16] The feud between Larkin and Sexton ended with Larkin being tried and jailed for conspiracy to defraud the NUDL, Sexton himself being called as the main prosecution witness.[17]

Larkin was later to be released from prison after serving only three months of a twelve-month sentence. But the affair created some divisions within the ranks of the NUDL nationally, and left a bitter legacy at Glasgow. Glasgow Trades Council, for example, stated that they denounced the attempt 'to crush Mr Jim Larkin', and 'declared their belief in his honesty and integrity.'[18] It may be suggested that the dock labour force at Glasgow felt similarly. As previously noted, Larkin accused Sexton of not backing up talks with industrial action, and in the final analysis it was this very point that moved the Glasgow membership to leave the NUDL by late December 1910. During December the Glasgow dockers went on strike in order to push through their demands for new working conditions at the port – the first strike of any significance since the late 1890s – but Sexton refused to approve any further strike action on the part of the men. O'Connor Kessack was to report later to Glasgow Trades Council that because of the Liverpool executive's position, the membership considered 'there was no use of being in the union', and they therefore left the union in great numbers.[19]

Within six months of the NUDL's collapse at Glasgow, however, the SUDL was formed, and by September 1911 the new union could boast a total membership of 6,400, of which around 5,000 were Glasgow dockers.[20] These levels had never been previously reached in the history of dock union organisation at Glasgow and surpassed those recorded at the height of the period of New Unionism. The dockers of Glasgow were now better organised than ever before and the SUDL's position had been considerably strengthened by overseeing a series of successful disputes over the remaining months of 1911.

The SUDL and the great strike wave of 1911 – 1912

> ... The historian, with his ampler opportunities of taking long views, may be able to state the value and the significance of the labour movement of our time. In the meantime with our more limited horizon, we may be forgiven for tracing some of our troubles to the disintegrating effect of the Trades Dispute Act and . . . the fermentation of a socialist leaven in untutored minds. . . . Practically every outstanding upheaval of recent days has been an insurrection . . . [21]

The strike wave of 1911 was very sporadic with different dockers striking in different parts of the port at different times, and while it is unclear if this was a clearly thought-out strategy, it certainly proved effective. For example, dock labourers who worked for the Allan and Donaldson Line were on strike for only 24 hours – between 27 and 28 June – before wage increases were conceded. Like other strikes at this time, the dispute resulted in the SUDL becoming firmly established among the dockers employed by that line. [22] A one-day strike among dockers of the Clan Line which ended on June 28, not only secured wages rises but the SUDL and the dockers forced the employers to concede increasing squad sizes from 12 to 16. [23] Indeed, the general Clydeside strike of January and February 1912 was specifically fought over the issue of gang sizes. The employers by then were determined to reduce gang sizes. The dockers, on the other hand, not only wished to defend this position, but also demanded the absolute right of control over gang sizes. This issue was to become a critical and central demand of the 1912 strike.

During July 1911, as the rolling strike wave continued, the SUDL's influence began to spread within a growing group of dockworkers. The employers operating the ultra- modern purpose built mineral port at Rothesay dock conceded to the demands of 400 workers on July 3, including official recognition of the SUDL. [24] By July 12 the *Glasgow Herald* was reporting on the mixed successes of the dockers, but the general impression is that many gains were now being made across Clydeside as a whole. Dockers at both Queen's and Princes' docks had won wage increases of between 20–25 percent. Dockers were also continually reported to be refusing to work with non-union labour and this became a central element to the dockers' demands thereafter: particularly during the general strike of transport workers over July and August of 1911. The *Glasgow Herald* had no doubt who was to blame for this turn of events:

> . . . Dockers have no direct cause for complaint against the shipowners, who have already satisfied their demands, but out of sympathy with the Seamen's union the dockers refuse to load or discharge certain steamers because they allege that their owners employ non-union seamen and firemen . . .[25]

Despite the condemnation by the press of the dockers' sympathy action, there seems little doubt that it was proving effective. By July 31 it was reported that the seamen's strike was over, and that every shipping line and shipping firm had granted recognition to the Seamen's union: firstly, and significantly, the North Atlantic Trade Line owners, then the overseas cargo steamship owners and latterly almost every other firm at the port of Glasgow.[26] This event was to have significant ramifications for the dock labour force of Glasgow also. Basil Mogridge argues that the main achievement of the transport workers by August of 1911, particularly the seamen and dockers, was 'the measure of recognition' they gained, and that in the long term this was the most significant effect of the strike.[27] In the short term, however, the strike, which came to involve over 13,000 workers on Clydeside, engendered a high degree of solidarity among the dockers and the seamen there, and this would prove important to future developments in dock unionism.[28]

The general strike of transport workers also had a significant effect on trade union membership. Emanuel Shinwell informed Glasgow Trades Council on August 16 that the SUDL at Glasgow had a membership of 5,000.[29] As noted previously, dock trade union membership in Glasgow had never been this high before, but the trend was to continue upwards. By the end of September the SUDL were fully affiliated to the Glasgow Trades Council, and Joseph Houghton informed that body that they now numbered 6,400 in Glasgow, and that the SUDL had organised both Dundee and Ayr.[30] At the beginning of November, Houghton reported to the Glasgow Council that a transport workers' committee had been set up for Clydeside, comprising the SUDL, the Seamen's union, the cranemen, ships riggers and cooks and stewards, and that it had met with the coasting shipowners 'for the first time in their history'.[31] The ground was now being prepared for the extensive general strike that was to take place during the early months of 1912.

Glasgow port employers' attitudes to the unrest

Many employers at Glasgow, like the writers of press reports of the period, felt that the industrial problems they encountered after 1910 were directly related to the Trades Disputes Act (1906), specifically those provisions of the Act which prevented a trade union from being sued for damages, and which legalised 'peaceful picketing'. As a result, it was argued, there was not only a significant increase in picketing, but that this was now accompanied by a considerable increase in levels of coercion, intimidation and violence, on the part of strikers. The trade unions were now perceived to be in a much more powerful position, and many employers felt that this created the impetus for the strike wave they were experiencing. William Raeburn – a leading and active supporter of the Shipping Federation – in the aftermath of the transport workers strike of July and August, 1911, called on the Clyde Navigation Trust to demand that the government repeal the Trades Disputes Act. It is clear, however, that the employers did not unanimously agree on the reason for these disputes, or the best methods to combat them. The *Glasgow Herald* noted that the treasurer of the Clyde Trust, Mr Graham, voiced his disapproval of Raeburn's general attitude to the labour force; the resolution Raeburn moved to petition the government to repeal the Trades Dispute Act, and his explanation as to why the transport workers strike had begun in the first instance:

. . . If any individual was responsible for what occurred at Glasgow Harbour, then that man was Mr Raeburn. . . . Had not he and his Federation declined talks . . . the outrages that had been complained about would not have happened. The shipping trade was in a very good position, and when the workmen who had miserable starvation wages asked for some increase, the Shipping Federation, of which Mr Raeburn was a burning and shining light, would not meet with them . . .

Another Trustee, Mr W.F. Anderson, stressed the Shipping Federation's 'miserable handling of trades disputes'. He argued that Raeburn and his Federation never granted the men an opportunity to air their grievances and treated their employees with 'all sorts of contempt'. One port employer and Trustee agreed, and added,

> . . . It was his opinion that shipowners had made the biggest mistake of their lives when they failed to recognise trade unionism. From his own standpoint he would rather deal collectively than individually with his men . . .

Another employer added that if the Trust were to approach the government and demand changes to the law, then they would only 'further ferment political feeling'. But Mr Raeburn could not accept that the blame lay with him, the shipowners, or their Federation:

> . . . There was no doubt that syndicalism, accompanied with rioting and anarchy, had swept over the land, and if they could not do anything as peaceful citizens to get some repeal of the Act . . . that was surely a straight forward piece of business which no man need be ashamed of . . .[32]

The central importance of this debate is that at this point there was no single discernible employers' attitude at this time. On the one hand there are those who obviously felt that the time for joint negotiation had come, while the Raeburn camp remained stubbornly anti-union and draconian in their attitudes. However, despite what seemed to amount to a rather confused industrial policy on the part of the employers at this juncture, such debates did signal a decisive movement away from the repudiation of trade unionism and towards formal recognition, while at the same time moving ever closer towards the establishment of a joint procedural agreement. It had taken the Glasgow port employers almost twenty-five years to get to that stage and it was to prove a significant development in future industrial relations along the Glasgow waterfront.

The strike of 1912 and the 'Struggle for Control'

The strike wave which swept over Clydeside in 1911 acted to weld together again the vast majority of dockers within one trade union body. Thereafter the SUDL strengthened its position on Clydeside generally and Glasgow in particular. The upturn in trade was no doubt of great importance, as was the long tradition of combination on Clydeside. But, it would seem that the political agitations of the period also had some impact on events at Glasgow. On Clydeside the role of the Glasgow Trades Council – in conjunction with many other political and trade union organisations – was central to the campaign. The Seamen and Firemen's union, close allies of the dockers and the leadership of the SUDL, for example, arranged, through the Glasgow Council for Madame Sorgue – a leading spokesperson for the French Syndicalist union, the Confederation General du Travail (CGT) – to address the Council on the need to organise an 'International Federation of Trades Unions'.[33] Captain Edward Tupper of the Seamen's union, too, addressed Glasgow Trades Council at the time of the 1912 strike.[34] Indeed, Tupper was to make a special mention of the dockers strike in his own autobiography. He stated that the seamen 'had come out in support of the dockers there', and that the strike was to become 'a very bitter battle where there was serious rioting and grave disorders'[35] – what Shinwell later described as the 'great unrest at Glasgow Harbour'.[36] Tom Mann, too, was active in Glasgow at this time, speaking enthusiastically 'on the solidarity that was growing in the labour movement generally'.[37]

The fact that there was a considerable degree of political activity at this time is not in doubt, and it did act to draw the SUDL and its leadership into a close and sympathetic alliance with the seamen in particular, and the broader Clydeside labour movement generally. But it is not clear to what extent the ordinary docker was influenced by such political campaigning, or whether politics came to influence the dockers' industrial strategies during this period, particularly during the dispute of January and February of 1912. Although there were many inter-related issues involved in the dispute, the pivotal factor concerned the dockers' demands to control gang sizes, and to force the foremen into membership of the SUDL. These demands served to create a high degree of solidarity within the Clydeside dock labour force. It may well prove to be the case that these central issues were politicised in the first instance in order to achieve that end – although this is far from clear. What is clear, is that the strike had a significant impact in respect of labour relations along the

Glasgow and Clydeside waterfronts, and had a significant effect on the general community within Clydeside in so far as the strike raised many concerns about public safety and law and order. The Board of Trade noted that some 7,000 port transport workers became involved in the strike, of which around 600 were seamen striking in sympathy with the dockers. In order of magnitude this meant that only the strike at Singers at Clydebank, during March and April of 1911, and the general strike of Clydeside transport workers over July and August of 1911(which included the Glasgow dockers), had involved more workers up to that point.[38]

The strike of 1912 began on 29th January after the employers initiated a lock-out around Glasgow harbour. The first phase of the dispute was brought officially to an end on 10th February, following an agreement between the employers and the trade union officials.[39] However, the dockers rejected this agreement, and 6,400 dockers came out on strike against their leaders' advice on 12th February.[40] The second, and unofficial, phase of the strike was short lived, and within two days, after the intervention of George Askwith at a meeting at the Central Hotel in Glasgow, the matter was referred to arbitration. Captain Tupper, in his autobiography, wrote of this particular meeting with Askwith, at which he, Shinwell, and Joseph Houghton were present, along with Glasgow shipowners. He also notes that Winston Churchill became involved in the talks on his arrival from Belfast. Tupper argued that Churchill's involvement showed the concern of the government with this particular dispute. 'It was strange to relate', wrote Tupper, 'but that night, the owners gave way to some of the demands of the union negotiators'. He could only conclude that 'the Glasgow owners were up against something new – and it was too much for them'.[41]

The *Glasgow Herald*, at the outset of the dispute, reported that the dockers' actions' were 'a slightly varied form of the old question of shop management'. The dispute had taken on the same character as the engineers' lock-out in 1897–98, noted the report, and, as then, the employers refused to recognise the bargaining rights of trade unions. Even if recognition were to be achieved, however, it was not expected that the employers would budge on the right to manage:

> . . . so long as they [the employers] are responsible for financing and conducting their works . . . they must retain in their own hands the management of their establishments. . . . The right of combination may

be freely granted to all workmen, but the right of dominion must be refused. The Glasgow dockers, in their newly found enthusiasm for trade unionism, have adopted one and usurped the other . . . The Dockers had an organisation stronger and better managed than anything of the kind which has ever existed a the port. If it had not got out of hand it may have been a power for good. But it has got out of hand. Its great weakness has been proved to lie in its strength. . . .[42]

It was argued that the 'shipowners could hardly call their boats their own' and the SUDL was now suffering from an 'exaggerated idea of its own importance'. The dockers also insisted that foremen be forced to join the SUDL. *Forward* was to report that certain employers had already conceded to these demands and offered the example of the Anchor Line having to pay £1 per head to the SUDL for each of its 18 foremen. The report concluded, however, that the employers at Glasgow were naturally inclined to 'rebel against such impositions'.[43] The reason for forcing the foremen into the union seemed to be to place some curb on their power and aid the dockers in their fight against any reductions in gang sizes – principally an attempt to control the level of work intensification. As noted in *Forward*, 'the dockers had been brutally overworked, badly paid and sworn at sometimes in a most disgusting manner'. A common phrase was 'you lazy Irish bastard!'[44] The root of such 'brutality' was inevitably, and in most cases correctly, laid at the doorstep at the foremen, and one reason that the dockers would have sought to exert some control over them. In the final, analysis, it was the foreman who held sway over the system of employment and recruitment. It was the foreman who decided who worked and who did not. As executor of the employers' business, the foreman thus personified the worst excesses of the system. If the dockers could control the foremen, then they had direct control over the hiring system, a critical element of the system of casualism.

There was also a considerable level of propaganda circulated by the employers about the dockers and their habits at this time – not least their hard drinking reputation. One employer, reported by *Forward*, made his views on the matter very clear. The report noted 'that the employers thought that the dockers were more fond of liquor than they were of work, and if the men drank less whisky, things would go more smoothly'.[45] This attitude was well illustrated in an open letter published in *Forward* on the 3rd of February 1912. It was titled 'The

Dock Strike: Questions By an Employer'. The writer claimed to be 'in sympathy with the ideals of *Forward*', but felt it necessary to raise certain questions regarding the dockers' general attitude to work. Among other things he accused the dockers of not only being well paid, but lazy, and this was clearly seen in the 20 percent increase in the cost of unloading a ship. Some men also got "helplessly drunk" and were protected by their gang mates, who threatened to strike should the offending docker not be paid for being there. He also stated that a union official 'on seeing a man sweating' insisted that the dockers were being overworked and demanded that gang sizes be increased. He concluded by stating that the employers had the right to manage their own business and signed himself 'Fair Do'. The whole question of who had control over gang sizes was now the central and the most important issue of the dockers' demands, and the employers were not prepared to concede this point.

The *Daily Record* also reported extensively on the dispute. It noted Joseph Houghton's analysis of the dockers' determined stance, that all the men understood what they were doing, and knew full well the serious consequences that might ensue.[46] The battle lines in what the *Glasgow Herald* was to describe as 'the labour war at Glasgow' were thus firmly drawn, and the 'struggle for the control' of the industry was now well underway. The employers refused to budge on the matter or their right to reduce gang sizes and were determined to resist pressure on this point. On Saturday January 27 they stepped up their campaign and initiated a lockout. Notices to that effect were posted around the port and under-signed by 132 shipowners with business interests at Glasgow harbour. It was generally believed, noted *Forward*, that the dockers had been spoiling for a strike for some time, but the report also stressed that the employers seemed equally 'anxious for a lockout.' It was the lockout notice which signalled the beginnings of the dispute.[47]

It is at this point the employers, like the press, were noting that agreements relating to working conditions had been accepted at ports such as Dundee and Liverpool, but that at Glasgow the dockers refused to accept the agreement thrashed out by the leadership of the SUDL. 'Glasgow had now come into line with other employers', noted the *Glasgow Herald*, 'the employers had now learned their lesson', they stressed. All the shipowners wanted now was for the dockers to accept the conditions of the joint agreement. What was occurring within the ranks of the SUDL, therefore, was 'the tyranny of the majority'. 'Mob rule was now in effect', they posited, 'and when the dockers rejected the recommendations of the leaders they merely became an uncontrollable mass'. The report promoted the view that the dockers' actions were evidence of syndicalism, a point that was reiterated in almost every report between January 29 and February 15 1912.[48] By the time the strike was coming to an end the *Glasgow Herald* was to advise the dockers 'that they had gained the machinery of conciliation and that it was up to them to see that it was a success'.[49] The *Daily Record* underlined this when it reported on a speech by William Raeburn, given at a function sponsored by the Glasgow Shipowners and Shipbrokers' Benevolent Association Dinner on the evening of February 2 1912. 'The great cry had been recognition of the union, and the great demand, collective bargaining. The Shipowners had conceded both', argued Raeburn. They would not, however, give over to the docker 'the management and control of their businesses'.

The conflict finally came to an end when the case about who had the right to control gang sizes went before a court of arbitration. The arbiter was Lord Mersey and he found in favour of the employers. He stated clearly that the employers had the absolute right to decide on gang sizes. With this decision the shipowners brought the lockout to an end and while there remained, for a time, some pockets of resistance around the port, the dispute was effectively over. The decision of Lord Mersey seemed to suggest that the employers had effectively won 'the labour war at Glasgow', but perhaps the outcome could be better described as a draw. The leadership of the SUDL were not entirely displeased with the outcome and in the immediate aftermath of the strike the leadership of the SUDL professed themselves to be generally quite happy with the result of the dispute.[50] Joe Houghton reported to the Glasgow Trades Council that, while they had some difficulty in getting the men back to work, the negotiations with the shipowners were positive and that the men had achieved an advance in wages. He also argued that the reduction in gang sizes had little effect on the men.[51]

In the long term, however, the most significant achievement for the SUDL was the creation of joint-negotiation machinery within the Glasgow port transport industry, and this thereafter spread to other ports on Clydeside. This had a critical impact on the future of industrial relations along the Glasgow and Clydeside waterfront. The formulation of Lord Mersey's decision also illustrates that the dockers themselves had won considerable concessions at Glasgow, despite losing the point regarding gang sizes. He argued that, 'if any hardship resulted from the practice of the shipowners in relation to gang size, then the dockers had the right to appeal to the joint committee, by virtue of paragraph four of the conditions of employment'. Similar to the arrangements between employers and dockers at Liverpool, as noted by R. Bean, the recognition by employers at Glasgow was to prove 'the start of a continuing relationship with the union', and as with other ports, helped bring about 'a new era of collective bargaining and joint negotiation'.[52] The new bargaining structure was implemented throughout the British port transport industry, but the employers at Glasgow had proved to be among the last major group of port employers to concede to this, and only did so reluctantly.

The role of syndicalism, socialism, and industrial unionism

In order to assess fully the nature, or the extent, of syndicalism, socialism, or industrial unionism, and the impact of these in relation to this dispute, it will be necessary to discuss in greater detail particular elements of the dispute. The unofficial nature of the second part of the 1912 strike, and the rank and file rebellion against the recommendations of the leadership at that juncture, could suggest a strong syndicalist impulse. This would conform well with John Lovell's definition of syndicalism, which, in the trade union sense, can be taken to mean the use of 'direct industrial action intended to wrest control of industry through workers' own organisations'.[53] It may have been the fear of this perceived syndicalist factor in the dispute which brought the Glasgow shipowners to the conference table in the first instance, and this may have been 'the something new' – as noted by Tupper – that the employers were up against.

There are other elements of the dockers dispute in which displayed syndicalist traits. The strike was first and foremost a general strike of dockers in the Clydeside region, and this was accompanied by a significant degree of sympathy action on behalf of the dockers. The seamen's union refused to work alongside any non-union docker or any blackleg, where blacklegs had managed to gain entry, and for a time some 600 workers struck in sympathy on behalf of the dockers. The carters stated that they would help the dockers 'gain a glorious victory', and that in the name of 'brotherhood, trade unionism and solidarity, they would stand by the dockers', while Jim Larkin sent similar messages of support from Dublin. Indeed, it was reported early in the dispute that arrangements were in place to 'hold up ships of the Anchor Line at New York'.[54] Apart from the seamen, however, it is unclear whether other offers of support were ever backed up by action, but such propositions no doubt had an impact on events. Emanuel Shinwell stressed in 1911 that 'sympathy action was an effective weapon, which helped sow the seeds of revolution on Clydeside.' Shiwell argued that socialism may have been rarely mentioned at this time, but he had little doubt that its influences was widely felt.[55]

It was clear, however, that it was the dockers' intention to have a greater say over who controlled the process of work and recruitment, and, more fundamentally, who had the right to decide on gang sizes and determine local working conditions. The dockers did, in the words of Joseph Houghton, leader of the SUDL, throw down the guantlet to the employers.[56] Moreover, if the press reports of the period are to be believed, the role of syndicalism, socialism and industrial unionism all seem to have played some part in bringing the dockers to that position. Certainly the employers on Clydeside, as noted previously, were fearful that such political influences were acting on the minds of their workers. This is perhaps best illustrated in the employers' concerns about the dockers' rejection of their trade union leadership's recommendations, and after having reluctantly conceded to joint negotiation with the SUDL the employers were angry at the dockers' refusal to accept the agreement that had emerged from those discussions.

From the standpoint of the foregoing analysis, can it be argued that the actions of the Glasgow dockers, or the attitude of the SUDL leadership, be described as characteristic of a syndicalist position? It is clear that the dockers did attempt to exert greater control over their industry than at any other time in their history. There is little tangible evidence to suggest, however, that their actions were intended and determined to undermine the capitalist system. The dockers did not actively vocalise their rejection of parliamentary politics or exhibit a strict adherence to any other radical political philosophy. As for the leadership of the SUDL, they were happy to accept joint-regulation of the port transport industry on Clydeside, and this fact in itself would seem to undermine any proposition intended to promote their actions, over the period of dispute as a whole, as anything other than orthodox political, or industrial activity. There is little doubt that Joseph Houghton, like his close associate Emanuel Shinwell, was a convinced socialist, and although he and Shinwell consorted with well known syndicalists such as Tom Mann and Madame Sorgue, it was never claimed that they were syndicalists themselves. In the final analysis, it is a fact that the leadership enthusiastically endorsed joint negotiating, and were willing to enforce the agreements thereafter reached, and this position is clearly not indicative of syndicalism.

The actions of the dockers themselves during this period could perhaps be best described as a type of 'proto-syndicalist behaviour.' As defined by Bob Holton, proto-syndicalism can be taken to mean an industrial attitude falling somewhere between 'vague revolt and clear cut revolutionary action'.[57] The unofficial nature of some of the disputes at Glasgow could, for example, be construed as direct militant action, in so far as the rank and file did defy the recommendations of the SUDL leadership. As reported by *Forward* in January 1912, the strength of the dockers lay in their ability to down tools at any moment without notice. The dockers knew this, and so did the employers,[58] as did the SUDL leadership. But apart from a short-lived period of rank and file rejection of the leadership of the SUDL's recommendations, and the dockers' use of direct action – a traditional characteristic of their industrial strategy in any case, as intimated by the report in *Forward* – their actions do not seem to conform with specifically syndicalist principles.

In the final analysis, neither the dockers nor the leadership of the SUDL exhibited any rigid set of political goals, and despite evidence of a very resolute industrial stance there is little to suggest a determined syndicalist impulse. As for socialism, to paraphrase Shinwell, the principles of socialism, as he saw it, may have been apparent at the time of the unrest, but it was never to become an intergral part of the dockers industrial strategy in 1912. Shinwell himself argued that socialism was rarely mentioned and this proved to be very much the case with the dockers dispute in 1912. It was only in press reports that the influence of socialism was considered to be of significance in relation to the dispute at Glasgow harbour at this time.

The industrial strategies of the dockers can, perhaps, be more clearly defined as industrial unionist, in so far as they would back the use of the general strike as an industrial weapon, manifested in their involvement in the general strikes of both 1911 and 1912. There are further manifestations of this type of industrial philosophy evident in the support of the dockers, and the SUDL leadership, not least Joseph Houghton, for their affiliation to the National Transport Worker' Federation, and to agree to NTWF's later amalgamation with the Miners' Federation and the National Union of Railwaymen in setting-up the Triple Industrial Alliance. However, as John Lovell argues, even with the launching of the Triple Alliance in 1914, 'this did not in any way anticipate or entail an imminent general strike, or that concerted action between the three industries was a possibility'. The only time the Glasgow dockers, or the SUDL leadership, called for such concerted action on the part of the NTWF, or the Triple Alliance, was in 1921, when they actively argued for a general strike in order to come to the aid of the miners.

After the strikes of early 1912 there are only sporadic reports of labour disputes on the docks at Glasgow, and on Clydeside generally, normally over wages and usually very quickly settled. The only exception to the industrial peace thereafter was the ten week strike which took place at the Ayrshire port of Ardrossan between October 1912 and January 1913. This dispute was in many ways a re-run of the early strikes experienced at Glasgow and the same political content was to be identified. Ardrossan was perhaps somewhat different, however, in so far as the Ardrossan Harbour Company, who owned and controlled the port, attempted one of the few concerted employer counter-attacks to be seen along the British waterfront during the period of the labour unrest. Despite a considerable degree of violence and the importation of labour into Ardrossan, the strike ended with the employers and the SUDL reverting back to joint negotiation.[59] On Clydeside generally industrial relations along the waterfront settled down and more or less remained that way through to the First World War and beyond. Thus the employers, and the SUDL leadership, had achieved stability along the waterfront in the long term, something that the employers clearly thought impossible before and during the disputes of 1911 and 1912, and before the employers formally recognised the SUDL and accepted the principle of joint procedural agreements.

Conclusions

Despite the relative industrial peace that was to descend upon the Clydeside waterfront after 1912 it should not be forgotten that, for a time at least, there was a considerable degree of discontent, and that some of this was considered to be politically directed. When the dockers and the seamen of Glasgow openly challenged the might of the Clyde employers, and, more importantly, the then monolithic ranks of the shipowners, it forced a major rethink on how best to regulate industrial relations. This was perhaps even more necessary when the employers could see that almost every meeting of dockers and seamen around the Glasgow's docks and wharves was accompanied by speeches from well-known leaders of the labour movement such as Tom Mann, Ben Tillett, Madame Sorgue, Father Hopkins and John MacLean.[60]

In the final analysis, given the political activity that was apparent at this time, the conciliatory nature of the employers may have been a simple strategy which was intended to 'placate the labour force and prevent them from being taken *en masse* by growing socialist and syndicalist ideologies'.[61] It may be strongly argued that this is what occurred along Clydeside – a politically-motivated movement towards collective bargaining by traditionally authoritarian employers. As noted above, many employers patently felt that syndicalism and socialism were a major cause of the unrest. They also felt that if recognition was not granted to the trade unions further political feeling would be fomented. Perhaps because of fears about political influences, recognition was granted to the SUDL, and with this recognition came the formalisation of joint procedural agreements. In the long term, and in the industrial arena, this was the most significant outcome of the disputes of 1912.

In the short term, however, the strikes of 1911 and 1912 did cause great alarm and while the historian can argue strongly that it did not lead to further discontent, there was, for a time at least, a genuine feeling that the 'labour war' at Glasgow could have acted as a prelude to widespread political unrest, revolt, and insurrection on Clydeside. This was clearly articulated by the press and in the widely reported remarks of various employers at the port of Glasgow at this time, and it was evident too in the wider social context. For G.D.H. Cole the labour unrest was real, possessing both direction and determinism, and without doubt was syndicalist in form.[62] H.G. Wells was to write of the times,

> . . . The discontent of the labouring mass of the community is deep and increasing. It may be that we are in the opening phase of a real and irreparable class war. . . . New and strange urgencies are at work in our midst, forces for which the word 'revolutionary' is only too faithfully appropriate. . . .[63]

Even if there was little chance of the Glasgow dockers going over to syndicalism *en masse*, or that the possibility of this happening was, in fact, more apparent than real – at least in the eyes of the historian today – the fear was nevertheless genuine enough between 1911 and 1912 in the eyes of the employers, the press, and society in general. After these disputes, however, relations along the Clydeside waterfront were placed on 'a more orderly and stable basis' – a pattern which was projected along the British waterfront.'[64]

By the time war broke out in 1914 the SUDL were firmly established along the entire west coast of Scotland, had organised several east coast ports, including Dundee and Bo'ness, and various north west English ports. For the first time, in a history of dock trade unionism which stretched back to the period of new unionism, and beyond, formal recognition had been granted by all the employers at these ports, and joint negotiating machinery was now firmly in place. This last factor alone suggests a watershed in the development of dock unionism in Scotland and the Clydeside area. At Glasgow it was perhaps even more significant given the stern resistance of Glasgow port employers' to any type of collective bargaining before the unrest. They were also one of the last major groups of port employers to accept that such concessions were necessary. But once in place this joint procedural structure was to remain more or less unchanged.

The war years only served to broaden and enhance the profile of the SUDL and the dock labour force generally. However, despite the dockers' considerable achievements and their active participation within the Glasgow Trades Council, the STUC, the NTWF and the Triple Alliance, they still principally concerned themselves in matters relating to port work and dock life in general. SUDL Executive Minutes do testify to wider considerations in the political arena: concerns over housing, education, and food prices, particularly during the war years. These minutes, however, do not give any real sense that such factors came to form the basis of a radical political philosophy. This suggests that the dockers were concerned with defining and defending their own territory, and protecting first and foremost those who belonged to their own very distinctive occupational community. Perhaps this is why the dockers, and the SUDL, did not come to figure in any prominent way in the events which came to characterise 'Red Clydeside', and the main political and industrial developments of that period. It was not until the dockers lone sympathetic action during the miners' dispute from April 1921 onward – in the wake of the collapse the Triple Industrial Alliance, and the failure of the leadership of the NTWF to call a general strike of transport workers – that their industrial strategy discernibly changed. This dispute was financially to ruin the SUDL and would lead to its eventual collapse by December 1922. The events of 1911–12 can hardly be considered a prelude to the heightening class-consciousness characteristic of the Clyde region during and immediately after World War One. If the dockers of Glasgow had come to know and experience 'Red Clydeside' it was more likely that this was achieved by their industrial actions, and the political stance they adopted, during the strike of April to June 1921, than at any other time in their history.[65]

NOTES

1. Glasgow Trades Council Minutes, 21 December, 1910.

2. Glasgow Trades Council Minutes, 21 December, 25 January, 1911. James Sexton's notification of the official close of Glasgow Branch read out as correspondence February 15 meeting 1911.

3. By its conclusion the National Strike of transport workers came to involve some 120,000. Mogridge, B., 'Militancy and Inter-Union Rivalries in British Shipping, 1911–1929, *International Review of Social History* (*IRSH*), Vol. XI – 1961. p 382.

4. It would seem that the GLHUs correct title was the Glasgow Harbour Labourers' Friendly and Protective Society, which was dissolved under that title in September 1886. The union is actually only referred to as the GHLU under the terms drawn up in a new constitution in May 1890. Registrar of Friendly Societies in Scotland, Scottish Records Office, FS. 7–10.

5. Royal Commission on Labour, Minutes of Evidence – Group B – Dock. Wharves, Shipping and Canals, Second Report June 1892, *British Parliamentary Papers* (*B.P.P.*), C-6795 – Vol. II xxxvi pt III, Q. 12,789 and Q. 13,417. The outcome of the strike of 1872 was noted in the testimony of Mr J. Smith Park, representing the Glasgow Shipowners' Association, and Mr William Hannay Raeburn; evidence given before the Royal Commission on Labour.

6. For membership levels of GHLU see Lovell, J., 'Sail, Steam and Emergent Dockers' Unionism in Britian, 1850–1914', *IRSH*, Vol. XXII – 1987 – 3, p. 237; see also Webb, Sydney and Beatrice, *Industrial Democracy* 1913, pp. 120–121. Reference to the formation of the National Union of Dock Labourers, *Glasgow Herald* 6 February, 1889, report entitled 'A New Union for Glasgow'.

7. Indeed, there is undisputable evidence to show that the GHLU at this time began to act as strike breakers in their efforts to save themselves from being absorbed by the larger NUDL. The NUDL by 1889 was reported to have a membership of over 4,000; Glasgow Trades Council *Annual Report* 1888–1889, p 8.

8. Webb, Sydney and Beatrice, *Industrial Democracy*, pp. 120–121.

9. Taplin, Eric., *The Dockers' Union: A Study of the National Union of Dock Labourers, 1889–1922* (Leicester University Press 1985), chapter two and appendix page 168 for numbers of NUDL branches.

10. Executive Report by John McHugh, the General Sectretary, and Richard McGhee, the President, of the NUDL to the Fifth Annual Congress, Liverpool 1893.

11. Calculated from TUC affiliated trade union membership list for individual branches in 1895. Glasgow No1 branch had a membership off 1,000, while Glasgow No2 branch had 400. It is also the case that it was only total paid up members who were included in these calculations and as dockers had a habit of paying their union subs retrospectively, because of the casual nature of their employment, this arguably gives a more dismal account of the state of the membership than perhaps was the case.

12. Amalgamation of GHLU and NUDL noted in Board of Trade Report on Trade Unions, 1899, *B.P.P.*, 1889: 1900, Cd 422 lxxxii, pp. 74–77. GHLU membership for 1899 was 670 according to the STUC affiliated membership list for that year. The NUDL sent no delegates to that years congress, but based on the 1897 membership numbers of 2,850 the total membership for Glasgow when joined with those of the GHLU was over 3,500.

13. Treble, J., 'Unemployment in Glasgow 1903 – 1910: Anatomy of a Crisis', *Scottish Labour History Society Journal* No 25 1990, p. 21.

14. Treble, 'Unemployment in Glasgow', p. 21.

15. Taplin, *Dockers Union*, pp. 71 to 74. Larkin's successes were significant. He increased the NUDLs membership by 6,000 between 1906 and 1908, reorganised Aberdeen, formed a new NUDL branch at Govan, and at Belfast set up two branches of 3,000 with a combined Cathoics and Protestant membership.

16. Larkin, Emmit., *James Larkin: Irish Labour Leader 1876–1947* (1965), pp. 18–19.

17. An event that W.P. Ryan argued was 'scarcely credible', see Ryan, W.P., 'The Rise of Larkinism', in *The Irish Labour Movement* (New York 1920), pp. 209–215.

18. Glasgow Trades Council Minutes, 29 June, 1910.

19. Glasgow Trades Council Minutes, 21 December, 1910.

20. Glasgow Trades Council Minutes; for Glasgow membership see Minutes 16 August, 1911, statement made by Emanuel Shinwell: for total membership, see 27 September, 1911, as stated by Joseph Houghton.

21. *Glasgow Herald*, 31 January, 1912.

22. *Glasgow Herald*, 27 and 28 June, 1911.

23. *Glasgow Herald*, 29 June, 1911.

24. *Glasgow Herald*, 3 July, 1911.

25. *Glasgow Herald*, 19 July, 1911.

26. *Glasgow Herald*, 29 July and 31 July, 1911.

27. Mogridge, 'Militancy and Inter-Union Rivalries', pp 382–3.

28. Duncan, R. and McIvor, A. (eds) *Militant Workers: Labour and Class Conflict on the Clyde, 1900–1950* (Edinburgh 1992), p. 83 (see Table 1 for list of principal disputes).

29. Glasgow Trades Council Minutes, 16 August, 1911.

30. Glasgow Trades Council Minutes, 27 September, 1911.

31. Glasgow Trades Council Minutes, 21 December, 1 November, 1911.

32. *Glasgow Herald*, 8 November, 1911; report of Clyde Navigation Trust Meeting. Mr Reaburn's concluding remarks on his resolution to Call on the Government to repeal the Trades Disputes Act.

33. Madame Sorgue's address was reported in the 31 May, 1911, minutes of Glasgow Trades Council. Joseph Houghton, prior to his election as General Secretary of the SUDL, moved that the Council would "render all assistance possible" to help her and the International Federation to secure that end.

34. Glasgow Trades Council Minutes, 14 January, 1912. It was noted that Captain Tupper was addressing a large meeting of seamen and dockers and their rejection of the shipowners new conditions concerning manning levels on ships and on the loading and discharging of vessels. Emanuel Shinwell and Joe Houghton also addressed the meeting, stating that a strike was imminent; due to the desire of the men to refuse to work alongside any non-union labour.

35. Tupper, Captain E. *Seamen's Torch: The Life Story of Captain Edward Tupper, National Union of Seamen* (1938), p 74.

36. Glasgow Trades Council Minutes, 15 May, 1912.

37. Glasgow Trades Council Minutes, 17 January. 1912.

38. Duncan and McIvor, *Militant Workers*, p. 83 (see Table 1 for list of principal disputes).

39. The agreement referred to was noted in full in the February edition of the Board of Trade *Gazette*, p 43. The agreement covered the loading and discharging of all types of vessels and cargo at the port such as Liners and ocean steamers and coasting vessels. The agreement also decided on gang sizes on all vessels dependent on tonnage and type of cargo handled, such as mineral ores and coal, etc.

40. Board of Trade *Gazette*, March 1912, p 86.

41. Tupper, *Seamen's Torch*, pp 75–6.

42. *Glasgow Herald*, 29 January. 1912.

43. *Forward*, 27 January 1912.

44. *Forward*, 3 February 1912.

45. *Forward*, 27 January 1912.

46. *Daily Record and Mail*, 29 January, 1912.

47. *Daily Record and Mail*, 29 January, 1912.

48. *Daily Record and Mail,* 29 January, 1912, 3 February and 8 February, 1912.

49. *Daily Record and Mail,* 12 February, 1912.

50. *Glasgow Herald,* 21 January, 1912.

51. Glasgow Trades Council Minutes, 21 and 28 February, 1912.

52. Bean, R., 'Employers' Associations in the Port of Liverpool, 1890–1914', *IRSH,* Vol. XXI – 1976 – 3, p. 382.

53. Lovell, J. *British Trade Unions 1875–1933* (1977), pp. 46–7.

54. *Daily Record and Mail,* 1 February and 3 February, 1912.

55. Duncan and McIvor, *Militant Workers,* p. 98.

56. *Daily Record and Mail,* 29 January, 1912. Part of a statement made by Joseph Houghton, General Secretary of the SUDL, in reponse to the employers' lock-out notices around Glasgow Harbour January 1912.

57. Duncan and McIvor, *Militant Workers,* p. 98; see also Holton, B., *British Syndicalism 1900–1914* (1976), p. 76.

58. *Forward,* 27 January, 1912.

59. Kenefick, William, *Ardrossan, The Key to the Clyde: A Case Study of the Ardrossan Dock Strike 1912–1913* (Irvine 1993) *passim.*

60. See *Glasgow Herald* and *Forward,* January to February 1912 for illustrations of the extent of political activity at this time; and *Ardrossan and Saltcoats Herald* for later examples of political speeches and appearances of both Tillett and Mann during dispute at Ardrossan between October 1912 and January 1913. Refer also to Kenefick, W., 'The Dock Strike: The Labour Unrest of 1910–1914; With particular reference to the Ardrossan Dock Strike, 1912 to 1913', section three of chapter one (unpublished part of Honours Year Dissertation, University of Strathclyde), and Kenefick, *Ardrossan,* pp.13–14.

61. McIvor, Arthur., 'Employers Organisations and Strikebreaking in Britain, 1880–1914', *IRSH,* Vol. XXIX, 1984, 1, p. 12.

62. Cole, G.G.H., *The World of Labour* (1913), p. 33.

63. Wells, H.G., 'The Labour Unrest', in Wager, W.W., (ed), *Journalism and Prophecy 1893–1946* (1965), p. 43.

64. Bean, 'Employers Associations', p. 382.

65. Kenefick, W., The Impact of the Past Upon the Present: The Experience of the Clydeside Dock Labour Force c.1850 to 1914 with particular reference to the Port of Glasgow' (unpublished Ph.D Thesis, University of Strathclyde), 1995, pp. 306–323.

CHAPTER 7

Militant Miners?: Strike Activity and Industrial Relations in the Lanarkshire Coalfield, 1910–1914

Sandy Renfrew

Introduction

Britain, in the years before the Great War, witnessed an unprecedented level of industrial unrest. Workers, whether through their trade union or on their own initiative, rose to challenge capital in many sectors of the economy. A distinctive characteristic of strikes in 1910–14 was that many were spontaneous, unofficial and the result of rank and file action. Industrial relations were no less turbulent in mining. Indeed, the first ever national strike of coal miners took place in 1912. Furthermore, much of the unrest in mining mirrored what was happening elsewhere in the country. Mineworkers challenged coal owners on wage issues, non-unionism, working conditions, intensification of work, and over control at the point of production. Much of the attack was orchestrated by local and national unions but a significant proportion of labour unrest in the pits also originated from rank and file workers. Labour unrest in Lanarkshire was at least as tempestuous as elsewhere in Britain.

This case study of labour relations in Lanarkshire pits will seek to ascertain the reasons behind the unrest. Firstly, a brief overview of labour relations in Lanarkshire mining during 1890 to 1910 will help place in context the stormy years immediately prior to the outbreak of war. Next, the issues and outcome of the 1912 National strike and the effect this stoppage had on labour relations in Scottish mining is investigated. Thirdly, the paper will consider how far the changed economic position of miners influenced labour relations. In a similar vein the role played by alternative ideology is analysed. Following that an in-depth study of strike activity during 1910–1914 will seek to determine what factors lay behind these years of virulent industrial unrest. For example, how big a factor was work intensification and speed-up in pitwork in explaining the increase in strikes? Did the continuing switch to mechanised methods of coal extraction have an impact on industrial relations? This chapter will conclude by considering the impact of the unrest before 1914 and whether a link existed between this era and the years that followed the Great War.

The historical context

From the mid 1870s to the early 1890s labour organisation in Lanarkshire mines was characterised by numerous, small, short-lived trade unions organised on a local basis. In 1886 an attempt was made to organise a national union – the Scottish Miners National Federation. One of the main forces behind this movement was Keir Hardie. This also proved to be as ephemeral as earlier attempts. On the plus side, however, this short lived national body did help stimulate a movement toward county unions and this, along with the exceptional organisational work of William Small, led to the formation of the Lanarkshire Mining Federation in 1893. This union subsequently became the Lanarkshire Miners' County Union in 1896.

A primary aim of this body was to gain recognition from employers. This was achieved in 1899–1900 when a Conciliation Board was established. Another objective was to get a minimum wage for miners. This goal was also achieved and a minimum of 5/3d per day, with a 7/- maximum to last for six months, commenced in January 1900. Further negotiations saw this increased to 5/6d and 8/- respectively. This new settlement to last until July 1901.[1] These advances had been secured during the economic boom of 1889–1900 which saw Scottish pithead prices reach 14/- per ton, their highest pre-war level.[2] By 1902, however, owing to a downturn in trade, coalmasters were successful in linking the minimum wage to a sliding-scale. Between 1902 and 1909 various wage agreements were concluded, generally on advantageous terms to the owners. In 1909 the minimum wage was 6/- per day. This was the absolute minimum recognised by the British national union, the Miners' Federation of Great Britain (MFGB). Indeed, according to the rules of the MFGB if Scottish owners tried to reduce wage rates below this datum English and Welsh miners were duty bound to come out on strike in support of the Scots. This was the position in August 1909. Thus, the first ever national strike of British mineworkers was on the cards.

The threat of an all-out general strike led to government intervention. Winston Churchill and George Askwith succeeded in getting miners and owners to put the dispute before an independent chairman, Lord Balfour of Burleigh. The final outcome was that the six shilling a day minimum was recognised but it was tied to a much harsher sliding-scale. If, for instance, economic conditions warranted that the minimum should be less than six shillings for a period of (say) six months then following an economic upturn which merited a wage rise the increase would not be paid for six months. Thus coal owners would have been compensated for their earlier 'loss'. The inequitable terms of this wage settlement and the feelings of hostility to owners and the Government was a major ingredient in the level of unrest.

The national strike, 1912

The first national strike of mineworkers in Britain occurred in 1912. The main bone of contention was the issue of abnormal places, or, as this was known in Scottish pits, deficient places. Miners working these places were unable to make a living wage through no fault of their own. For example, geological conditions may have been such that hewers were unable to cut their required *'darg'*, or daily quota. Other factors included excessively wet conditions or production hold-ups outwith the control of the men for instance, machinery breakdowns. Disputes over such conditions were usually settled through individual negotiation between the miner(s) concerned and management. Scottish coalowners acknowledged that pitmen in these situations were entitled to a fair wage but there was no agreement as to what constituted a deficient place or, indeed, a fair wage. As this issue was outwith the remit of the various conciliation boards it was decided at national level to campaign for an individual minimum wage. The minimum wage achieved by miners in 1900, it should be noted, was a guaranteed wage when working under normal conditions. It took no account of men working in abnormal places unable to earn the standard wage. Negotiations with employers continued throughout 1911 and into 1912 when a ballot on whether to strike over the issue was taken. At national level the majority in favour of strike action was 4:1. In Scotland it was 5:1.[3] The first ever national strike of mineworkers in Britain began on 1st March 1912 and ended six weeks later with the loss of 30 million work-days. Again the seriousness of the situation prompted government intervention. A week before the strike Prime Minister Asquith stated in a letter to the M.F.G.B.:

> The Government recognises that it is not right, it is not just, that it is not in the interests of the community that this great interest of yours should be carried on without adequate securities and safeguards for the attainment by underground workers of a reasonable minimum wage.[4]

The Government, who were also consulting with the employers proposed that a Bill be enacted which encompassed four main points. The principle of an individual minimum wage would be established. The wage would be set taking district circumstances into consideration. They would be set by district boards. If a failure to agree was reached Government representatives would arbitrate. Mining unions were completely against compulsory arbitration. They also wanted a schedule of district minima incorporated within the legislation to guarantee minimum wage levels. Lloyd George, during negotiations with Robert Smillie, president of the M.F.G.B., advocated they should take a more moderate line emphasising that this would be the first time in history a minimum wage would be legislatively established. Smillie answering stated that a minimum wage had been established by Lloyd George in 1911 when he passed a minimum wage act for Members of Parliament:

> £400 per annum irrespective of their efficiency, lunacy or malingering propensities . . . and if you can put figures in a Minimum Wage Act for M.P.s without objectionable clauses, surely you can do the same thing for miners.[5]

The wily Welshman, it was noted, replied in silence.

The Bill, in its original format, became law on the 29th of March which prompted a second national ballot. A narrow majority of members were in favour of continuing industrial action, Scottish mineworkers voting 244,000 to 201,000 for continuation of the strike.[6] Union leaders advocated a return to work to await the outcome of the

District Boards. Smillie argued that the men returning *'en bloc'* would be taken as a show of strength by the independent arbitrator. A sectional return may be viewed as a weakness and could reduce the amount of settlement. Smillie was also concerned that further action by Scottish and Welsh miners would deplete union funds and thus, the union would be unable to strike again if the arbiter's award was insufficient.

Scottish coalmasters who, along with their counterparts in South Wales, had steadfastly refused to concede the principle of the individual minimum wage, did take part in the District Boards but still refused to give ground on the issue. David Gilmour of the Lanarkshire Miners' Union stated at a conference on the minimum wage question that in Scotland:

> just as before the strike our owners would concede nothing and they have continued in the same spirit from the beginning to the end. We were not able to agree upon anything. If we looked through the window and said the sun was shining or a statement of that kind we could not agree . . . our owners have never given the slightest intimation of trying to carry out the Act. Hardly a single colliery has recognised the Joint Committees . . . We have got rather less than nothing. We are in this difficulty that some of the strongest companies in our county have absolutely violated the spirit of the law, they have dismissed men of thirty years of age unless they would sign an agreement to be outside the Minimum Wage Act. We have almost 20 percent of the men employed at one big company in which the men have been dismissed or forced to sign outside the Minimum Wage Act or through threats of dismissal.[7]

Once again the draconian attitudes of coalmasters and government intervention had left mineworkers feeling cheated and betrayed. Page-Arnot posits the view that, 'this feeling of betrayal had the effect of welding them [miners] more closely together both within Scotland and throughout the British coalfields'.[8]

However, coal owners and Government ministers and officials were not the only targets for resentment from mineworkers. Trade union leadership both at county level in Lanarkshire and at national level was increasingly under attack from some sections of the workforce. Indeed, this point was underlined at a M.F.G.B. conference in April 1912 by a Scottish delegate who commented 'the rank and file in Scotland felt sold down the river by leaders.'[9] This split between trade union leadership and some sections of the rank and file will be considered in more depth below when the patterns, nature and causes of industrial unrest during 1910–1914 are investigated. Before that some consideration should be given to the changing economic conditions during these years and the presence of alternative, more radical ideologies and the impact these may have had on levels of unrest.

Causation: the impact of economic change and ideology

Improving economic conditions undoubtedly played a part. Wage levels in Lanarkshire mines had remained fairly static between 1902 and 1912, daily rates averaging from 5/6d to 6/- per shift. This period of stagnant wages was also one of rising real prices. Indeed, the cost of living was reckoned to have risen by at least 10 percent.[10] It should come as no surprise then that disputes over wage issues were the most common cause of strike action in these years. From mid 1912 market conditions changed. Rising demand for coal in domestic and foreign markets saw wages and coal prices escalate. Daily wage rates stabilised at 7/3d in 1913 and pit-head prices averaged 9/6d per ton. Tight labour markets led to an increase in trade union membership. The Scottish Miners' Federation, for example, witnessed a growth in members from 78,000 in 1912 to 90,000 in 1914.[11] This expansion in membership increased the bargaining position of mineworkers. The increase in industrial unrest in Lanarkshire pits undoubtedly reflected the efforts of miners to claw back ground lost in the preceding decade.

From an economic standpoint miners and coalowners were in a better position at the beginning of the century. Daily wages were 8/- and pithead prices stood at 14/- per ton.[12] At this time, however, mining unions were completely unsuccessful in their attempts to abolish contracting or to gain closed shop agreements, two areas where they achieved notable success in 1910–1914. Profit mark-up per ton in 1900 was more than double that at the later date. Thus employers had much more to lose at that time. Why then did they concede so much ground to labour in 1910–1914? Furthermore, the Lanarshire Coal Masters' Association (LCMA) had fewer members at the earlier date. Several large mining companies, Archibald Russell Ltd; for example, remained outside the association thus weakening its control! During the interim period membership grew. Following the national strike in 1912 membership increased from 36 to 61 companies and the association then claimed to control 90 percent of output in the district.[13] The strength and extent of organisation of mineworkers and their solidarity during the strike was an obvious factor influencing combination amongst employers. The presence of such a well organised, numerically and financially strong union was a major factor behind the victories won by mine labour before the war.

Debate on the influence of ideology on labour unrest in this era continues. At one end of the spectrum authors such as Hunt, in his study of British labour, attribute little significance to the role of ideology in the growing industrial unrest in pre-war Britain. Others, Price and Cronin, for instance, take the opposite view. They argue the presence of alternative ideologies was a major ingredient of militancy. Syndicalism, Price contends, had permeated practically every major trade union by the outbreak of war.[14] The extent of syndicalist influence on unrest in Lanarkshire is difficult to quantify. No direct mention of syndicalism or syndicalists appears in the county union records for this period. At national level Robert Smillie contended that syndicalists had no influence on the national strike 'the connection only existed in the imagination of Capitalist Pressmen'.[15] However, connections did exist. Campbell noted that in 1912 the Welsh syndicalist, W.F. Hay spoke in favour of reconstruction of the LMCU, at a meeting in Hamilton organised by the 'Miners' Indignation and Reform Committee'.[16] Thus connections did exist between Lanarkshire and the strong hold of syndicalism, South Wales.

It appears, however, 'revolutionary socialism', as propounded by John MacLean and James MacDougall, had a greater impact on Lanarkshire pitmen. These two ran Marxist economic classes throughout the county. These classes had become so popular, as Harry McShane stated in his autobiography, that by 1911–12 all other socialist organisations were trying to run similar classes. MacLean regarded miners as the political wing of the movement.[17] The close relationship between MacLean and the miners continued up to his death in 1923. It is not without coincidence that seven of the first eight full-time students to graduate from the Scottish Labour College in 1921, were miners. Several of them, John Bird and John McArthur in Fifeshire and William Allan in Lanarkshire played prominent roles in the

Reform Movement in the early twenties. These activists all began work in the years before the war.

The idea that labour unrest was escalating at an unprecedented rate was commented upon by various contemporary observers. George Askwith, the Government's industrial relations 'trouble shooter' who had been closely involved in the threatened strike in 1909 and the national strike, was concerned with the growing militancy of labour.[18] Coal owners too were apprehensive about the increasing organisation and strength of mineworkers. F.L.McLeod, Glasgow Coal Company, acknowledged this fact in 1909 when he cautioned fellow LCMA members that not only did they face the local union but also the organisational and financial power of the M.F.G.B.[19] Robert Small, a Lanarkshire miners' agent, commenting on the aftermath of the 1909 wage settlement noted that 'a spirit of revolt was abroad'.[20] The spectre of revolt seemed even more likely in the months before the outbreak of war when meetings of miners, railwaymen and transport workers were called to discuss forming a 'Triple Alliance'. This potential coalition of three large, well organised unions which posed a considerable threat to the whole country was, as Hinton has argued, 'widely seen as a portent of a revolutionary general strike'.[21] The following advertisement, undoubtedly a light-hearted attempt to drum up custom, nevertheless shows just how far the feeling of growing militancy and escalating strike action had permeated society as a whole.

ALARMING NEWS
of industrial war having broken out in all trades and prices for groceries and provisions are abnormally high

RUSSELL AND SMITH
have looked well ahead for their Christmas Club customers and secured for them a supply of goods which will again give unbounded satisfaction. you are invited to

STRIKE
a bargain now. Join our Christmas Club at once. All you have to do is ask for a club card free and be enrolled as a member. Only a limited number of cards will be given out. Secure one today and prevent being **LOCKED OUT.**[22]

Levels of unrest in Lanarkshire pits, 1910–1914

Let us now consider in detail strike levels and patterns in Lanarkshire mines during the 1910–1914 era. When analysing the extent of strikes during this period it should be noted that official figures shown in Board of Trade data generally understate the level of unrest. Board of Trade statistics take no account of strikes involving less than ten workers or which lasted less than one day. For example, government statistics for Scotland during this quinquennium, for all areas and all occupations, record the total number of strikes as 131. Earlier work by the Glasgow Labour History Workshop (GLHW) has shown this to be a gross understatement. Indeed, this group found that 243 strikes had occurred in West Central Scotland alone.[23]

The number of strikes in mining shown in the GLHW column in Table 1 is for West Central Scotland, that is, Renfrew, Dumbarton, Ayrshire and Lanarkshire whereas the rest of the table concentrates on Lanarkshire alone. Provision of data on industrial unrest by companies to the Board of Trade was on a voluntary basis. Some firms chose to ignore requests for such information.[24] Others, like some members of the Lanarkshire Coal Masters' Association opted to be selective with their data.[25] Consequently, the level of strike activity in the Lanarkshire coalfield unearthed from the LCMA minute books, while greater than official or GLHW figures, most probably also understates the actual level of unrest.

Table 7.1 Strikes in Lanarkshire Coalfield, 1910–1914.

	GLHW	LCMA	Compensation
1910	3	10	£1,082
1911	16	7	£7,128*
1912	8	4	*
1913	15	17	£6,857
1914	11#	47	£11,611
TOTAL	53	85	£26,678

*Compensation of £7,128 is for years 1911 and 1912. # Figure is for the first seven months only. National strike of 1912 not included.
Source: Number of strikes shown under GLHW from a trawl of the Glasgow Herald and Forward newspapers by members of the Glasgow Labour History Workshop, and subsequently published in Duncan R. and McIvor A., *Militant Workers*, (1992) p 89, Strikes and compensation payments shown in second and third columns from the Annual Reports of the Lanarkshire Coal Masters' Association, 1910–1914.

When the incidence of strikes in Lanarkshire is considered it can be seen that 1913 and 1914 were years of increased industrial conflict. This fact is borne out by both the frequency of strikes and the amount of compensation paid to members of the employers' association. However, figures in columns two and three cannot be directly correlated because the LCMA only compensated members under certain conditions. The following criteria had to be met before they could be recompensed. Strikes had to last three or more days. Disputes had to involve the entire mine, partial stoppages did not qualify. Furthermore, the issue had to be deemed of general interest to the coal trade. In other words, matters judged as local management issues did not qualify for compensation. If coal producers could meet these conditions then they would be compensated for profits lost during a stoppage. The actual number of stoppages that qualified for compensation payments has only been recorded for 1914. That year 27 coal companies received £11,611 for profits lost during 34 disputes.[26] Furthermore, industrial unrest, in this sector of Scottish industry at any rate, was not stemmed by the outbreak of war. Just over 25 percent of stoppages in 1914 took place after the outbreak of hostilities.

Closer inspection of strikes indicates the type of dispute was also changing in the latter years. In the months following the national strike there is increasing reference in the LCMA's minute books to miners holding morning meetings and then taking the rest of the shift off. In 1912 these meetings were invariably about the presence of non-union labour. In order to combat this practice employers decided to impose a lock-out for a further two days.[27] This entitled member firms to receive compensation. It is difficult to calculate the total number of days lost from stoppages because the starting or finishing date of disputes is invariably missing from the LCMA's records. However, these dates are known for the 31 morning meetings which occurred during 1913 and 1914. Of this total 21 lasted for four or more days, and a few for as long as two weeks. These token strikes, Smillie argued at a meeting of the Conciliation Board in 1912, were in response to management reducing rates or making changes in methods of production without joint consultation with mineworkers, which was the traditional custom.[28] In essence the conflict can be seen as the right to manage versus traditional custom and practice. These stoppages were unofficial in nature, taken by the miners at the pithead – where notice of management changes were posted the night before. When employers changed their tactics and began to lock miners out the union became involved and in the majority of cases financially supported their members throughout, and beyond the lock-out, usually for a week. Therefore, the majority of morning meetings began as unofficial wild-cat action, became an employers' lockout and ended as official strikes.

Unofficial action: the fight against non-unionism, supervision and contracting

Before looking at the issues which lay behind this industrial unrest some explanation of the limitation of the sample from the LCMA's records is necessary. Although the data is quite explicit on the duration of stoppages classed as morning meetings it is much less reliable on the reasons behind them albeit, as is mentioned above, the main problem seemed to be one of control. Of the remaining 54 cases, where the cause of the strike is known for 51 stoppages, the main points of conflict were as follows; wage issues, generally opposition to wage reductions, accounted for 44 percent of stoppages. The next biggest area of discontent, responsible for 19 percent of strikes, arose over proposed changes to working conditions or work methods, that is, over control in the workplace. Victimisation of mineworkers and the presence of non-union members in the pits caused 13 percent and 11 percent of downtime respectively, with sympathetic strike action and opposition to the system of contracting in mining accounting for the remainder. It is clear then that wage and control issues were the focal point for much of the unrest.

A more in depth investigation of some areas of discontent should prove instructive at this stage. The fight against non-unionism is one area where organised labour achieved significant success. One of several examples of this type of struggle was the dispute at the Summerlee Coal and Iron Company's Bellshill mine in 1913. This strike, which had been an ongoing source of conflict since early 1912,[29] finally erupted in early January when 1,000 workers struck work over the company's continued refusal to deal with the problem. Mr D Mowat, general manager of the Summerlee Co; stated 'that he would never compel men to join the union'.[30] This attitude ties in with the long anti-union tradition at Summerlee. Summerlee was also one of the large concerns mentioned earlier which were forcing their workers to contract out of the Minimum Wage Act agreement. John Robertson, vice president of the Scottish Miners' Federation (SMF), was at Bellshill to negotiate but, true to form, Mowat refused to see him. Robertson then threatened to extend the dispute to other mines in the Summerlee group which could have resulted in 5,000 workers downing tools. The strike ended within a few days. Management conceded defeat and agreed that all non-union workers would be given four weeks to join the union. If they refused then the company would *deal* with them. Also any new workers would be made to join the Lanarkshire Miners' County Union as soon as possible. In effect the miners had won a closed-shop agreement, an amazing victory over such an anti-union employer!

Why had such a staunch, anti-union company capitulated over this issue in a matter of days? Rising demand for coal products was one factor which favoured labour in this period. Coal prices had been increasing since the summer of 1912 and rose even more sharply with the onset of winter. The Summerlee Company would have faced a large cut in profits if 5,000 miners had gone on strike. Also they could not rely on compensation payments from the employers' association to offset this loss as the LCMA had decided against recompensing members because some other companies within the association, and nationwide, had already conceded closed-shop agreements. Indeed, at national level 65percent of disputes in mining and quarrying were settled in favour of workers and as the following statement from the Report on Strikes and Lock-outs, 1913, shows this was due in large part to the success of trade unions against non-union workers:

> The high proportion of disputes settled in favour of the workpeople in the mining and quarrying trades was mainly due to the success which attained strikes against the employment of non-unionists in the coal mining industry.[31]

Other examples of successful action against non-union labour in Lanarkshire pits in 1912–1913 include Summerlee mines at Braidhurst and Hattonrigg, Dixon's Carfin pit, Baird's Bedlay mine, the Kenmuirhill pit owned by the Glasgow Coal Company and Russell's Ferniegair mine.[32] These victories over one of the most draconian of all employers' organisations stem in part from the growing strength and organisation of coal miners and the increased militancy of many groups of workers in the period.

Organised labour made further inroads in the fight for control in the work place by forcing supervisors to join their union. The first tier in management in the mines was the fireman. As well as being responsible for safety in the pit firemen also allocated work to the men. These supervisors were the people mineworkers negotiated with over any problems concerning work in the pit. For example, in cases of deficient places workers would first negotiate with firemen over rates. Thus, to get this group of key workers to join the union was a significant achievement for organised labour. The majority of disputes over this issue happened in 1913 and 1914. For instance, strikes in early 1914 at Priory, Parkhead, Shotts and Baton collieries all resulted in firemen joining the LMCU. Perhaps the most telling case was at Russell's Ferniegair pit. Here a fireman refused to join the union. The ensuing strike was only settled when management sacked the supervisor![33] The fact that some coal owners were forced to accept their supervisors joining the miners' union and in the case of Ferniegair management played an active role in this process again highlights the successful assault on managerial prerogatives by mining labour in this era.

Contracting in the mines was another bone of contention with colliers. This system of working saw owners subcontracting various sections of a mine or an entire pit to contractors. These middle-men in turn hired miners to carry out the work. Mineworkers were against this system for several reasons. Coal companies paid the contractor and, thus had no responsibility to ensure that colliers received the correct remuneration, or, indeed were paid at all. Robert Smillie stated at a meeting of the Conciliation Board in 1911, that during the last two decades he knew of 40 or 50 cases of contractors absconding with miners' wages.[34] Also when work was sub-divided between several contractors it proved difficult for union organisation. In effect union officials had to deal with several different employers of relatively small squads of workers which made union recruitment difficult. It was also relatively easy for contractors to get rid of union members and activists. Contracting appeared to be declining in the decade before the war. Indeed, in 1908, the LCMA declared that they had abandoned contracting for ordinary coal getting, that is hand-hewing of coal.[35] Despite this statement contracting caused numerous disputes during the period in question, on example was the Blairmuckhill Colliery in early 1913, where management tried to re-introduce the practice. They tried again a year later. Other strikes occurred at Loganlea and Howmuir mines and at Kenmuirhill where management eventually agreed to abolish contracting, conceded a five day week and forced non-unionists to join the LMCU. The fight to end contracting was another area where miners' union gained considerable success.

Work intensification and mechanisation

A particular feature of industrial unrest in this period was the level of unofficial action instigated by rank and file workers. The strike at Earnock Colliery in July 1912, was started by men at the coalface when management refused an extra payment for working double shifts. The union later authorised this action and granted official support.[36] In July 1911, three pits at United Collieries, Nackerty mine in Uddingston, came out on strike over several grievances, including contracting, the introduction of outside labour, victimisation and improved wages and conditions. Although not initiated by the rank and file, the stoppage was prolonged by activists who campaigned against the union's call to return to work pending negotiations.[37] The strike, involving approximately 600 workers, began on the 29th of July. The union executive called on the men to return a week later. A report in a local newspaper stated of the men:

> They have practically thrown down the glove to the local agent (Mr Murdoch) and the executive, demanding their dealing with the grievances on which they were brought out, and have sent the agent back to the executive with that message.[38]

This strike continued until November. Only a few of the LMCU executive minutes for 1911 have survived, therefore it is not known whether the union continued to pay strike money to the men. Whether this was the case or not for mineworkers to remain out for this length of time shows the depth of feeling on the issues in question and, perhaps more importantly, it highlights the growing opposition of rank and file members to the policies being pursued by the union hierarchy.

Indeed, in several instances pre-emptive action by the rank and file led to stoppages getting official union support. This again being more likely to happen in 1913 and 1914. For example, in December 1913, mineworkers at Muiracre mine struck over a proposed wage reduction. This unofficial action later received union backing. Another case occurred in May 1914, at Cadzow Colliery when a wildcat strike by machinemen resulted in other workers at the pit being locked out. The union made the strike official and, thus miners received strike pay whilst fighting the case. Similarly, at Newton Colliery rank and file action over a fireman resigning from the county union also received official support. However, not all unauthorised disputes gained official blessing. The case at Monklands pit in the summer of 1914 is a typical example. Twenty colliers had 'lifted their graith' and walked off the job due to low wages. The LMCU in this instance refused to investigate the dispute until the miners returned to work.[39]

The case at Monklands is just one of many examples where trade union leadership clamped down on wildcat action. Indeed, many potential stoppages were prevented by the union hierarchy opting to settle disputes through negotiations with employers. Often reaching agreements which ignored the wishes of their membership.[40] Indeed, this approach to industrial relations adopted by the LMCU supports Zeitlin's hypothesis that union leaders, due to the nature of their agreements with management 'adopted an active role in sustaining managerial discipline in the factory', or in this instance, the mine.[41] The increasingly institutionalised structure of collective bargaining which was being pursued by union executives was a constant source of friction within the industry and led to increased independent action by rank and file members over 1910–14. The case of Lanarkshire miners, at any rate, supports Hinton's argument that the emergent system of collective bargaining in this period 'strained the relationship between trade union officials and their more militant workers'.[42]

However, other elements were also present which affected the high level of unrest. Intensification of work was another important contributory factor. Coal mining, like many other sectors of British industry, was facing stiff competition from overseas producers. Colliery managements throughout the industry attempted to increase output through wage cuts, increased supervision, a greater move to mechanisation and a general speed-up in the pits. All of these cost reducing methods created friction in the workplace and soured relations between management and mineworkers.

The two main sources of discontent in Lanarkshire were, without doubt, the implementation of the Eight Hours Act of 1908, and greater use of machine coal-cutters and mechanical conveyors underground. The Eight Hours Act resulted in mine managers increasing the tempo of work in an attempt to achieve the same production in an eight hours shift that had been gained previously in nine hours. Introduction of mechanical aids to boost production quotas generally resulted in changes to traditional work systems. Shift patterns had to be altered. For example, when coal-cutting machinery was introduced a move to a two shift or three shift system was seen as the most productive method of working. Under these new systems any delay to one part of the mechanised cycle would delay succeeding shifts. Mechanical breakdown of cutting or conveying equipment, which was a fairly regular event, meant disruption to the work system and loss of output. When breakdowns occurred machinemen would be coerced to work longer than eight hours.[43] This created friction in the workplace. In 1910, at the Broomfield mine seven miners were dismissed when they refused to work over the eight hours. Similarly, at Russell's Greenfield mine in 1913, machinemen were working 12 to 16 hours continuously.[44] These are just a few examples of this constant source of discontent in mining. Adding to this discontent was the fact that new shift systems also impinged on the mineworker's social life.

The LMCU were constantly at odds with mine management over the issue of long hours. These disputes frequently ended in strike action being taken. Union leaders also tried to solve this problem through official channels but with little success. Following a breach of the Act at Woodhall Colliery in December 1910, the union took the matter up with the Chief Inspector of Mines but to no avail.[45] (Indeed, it was 1935 before a special enquiry was held to investigate this problem.) Also, following another infringement of the law at Auchengray pit, Longriggend, the LMCU brought the matter to the attention of the Police and Procurator Fiscal. However, the authorities, as noted in the LMCU's minute book, 'were diffident about raising a prosecution'.[46] The continual flouting of the act was one factor ensuring relations between management and workers were forever strained. This tension between the two sides frequently erupted and resulted in strike action.

Greater diffusion of mechanisation in Scottish pits meant traditional customs and practices of colliers were persistently threatened. New technology also led to deskilling in pitwork. John McArthur, a leading figure in the United Mineworkers of Scotland during the inter-war period, recalled that in his father's time colliers used a diverse range of specialist tools. Indeed, the miner had so many tools that he needed a hutch, that is, the tub used for transporting coal underground, to move his gear from place to place. With the move to machine cutting, strippers, the term used for miners who brought down the coal after it had been undercut by machine, now used just two or three different picks.[47] This is an indication of how new technology led to the division of labour and deskilling in mining.

Many men who worked coal-cutters were new to pit work and unskilled in the eyes of the traditional collier. Employment of unskilled men was a cause of concern at both local and national level. Enoch Edwards, in his presidential address at the M.F.G.B.'s annual conference at Edinburgh in 1910, poured scorn on the idea that any type of untrained labour could be used to work coal cutters. Furthermore, a resolution was passed calling for a clause to be introduced in the forthcoming Coal Mines Regulation Act that employment of unskilled labour in mines be made illegal.[48] It is significant that the proposition was made by Yorkshire and was seconded by Scotland – the two most highly mechanised areas in the British coalfields at that time, and those, in the miners' view, where skills and traditional methods were under threat from new technology. The above resolution, therefore, can be viewed as an attempt to defend skill and traditional practices in mining.

These changes to traditional work practices often resulted in disputes over control at the point of production – the right to manage versus traditional custom and practice. A dispute at Nimmo's Auchengray mine near Airdrie being a typical example. Miners working a section of the pit by traditional hand-hewing methods struck work over disputed tonnage rates. Management extended a nearby machine run into the disputed section. Colliers subsequently 'blocked' the whole section claiming that 'management had no right to take by machine any coal which had previously been wrought by pick'. Coalowners contested 'the right of the workmen to interfere with their right to say by what method the coal should be worked' and in retaliation imposed a lockout. This dispute was viewed by the employers' association as a

Table 7.2. *Frequency of Strikes in Mechanisaed Mines, 1910–14*

	Strikes	Mechanised Mines
1910	10	6
1911	7	6
1912	4	1
1913	17	13
1914	47	32
TOTAL	85	58

Source: Strikes column from Table 6.1. Number of strikes occurring at mines which were mechanised calculated by cross referencing data in Lanarkshire Coal Masters' Association minute books, which named pits on strike with pits designated as using coal cutters in the List of Mines, an annual Board of Trade publication.

serious point of principle and, thus Nimmo & Co; qualified for compensation.[49]

Table 7.2 provides some statistical evidence which shows that a correlation exists between high strike rates and pits which employed machine mining techniques. The table compares the number of strikes which occurred at pits using machine cutters to the total number of strikes in Lanarkshire mines during 1910 to 1914. Out of a total of 85 stoppages 58, or 68 percent of strikes happened in mines engaged in machine mining. Not all of the 58 strikes that took place in mechanised mines were directly linked to the use of machinery. Some for example, as shown above, stemmed from problems of contracting, non-unionism or indeed from disputes over wage rates. However, these issues were also present in mines which still relied on traditional hand methods to extract coal. Yet, in 1914, only 42 percent of mines in Lanarkshire used coal cutters. It is evident, therefore, that the level of industrial unrest was significantly higher in mechanised pits. It seems reasonable to argue that changes and pressures which went hand in hand with new working methods resulted in a more militant labour force. Thus, technological change and the concomitant intensification of pitwork were significant causal factors of strikes in this period.

Conclusions

This case-study of industrial unrest in the Lanarkshire coalfields in 1910–1914 has shown that the level of strikes was much higher than official statistics suggest. Labour challenged managerial prerogatives on a variety of issues and achieved considerable success. No single reason can account for the extent of unrest, indeed, a wide variety of causal factors have been identified. The battle for control at the point of production was very significant, especially in relation to mechanisation. Statistical evidence has shown that pits which adopted machine techniques were much more prone to labour unrest. The tendency toward unofficial, independent action by rank and file miners was a prominent feature of industrial activity as the period wore on. A growing section of colliers seemed to have become increasingly dissatisfied and disenchanted with their union leadership and the policies pursued by these bodies. The emergent system of collective bargaining being a notable source of friction and discontent. The presence of alternative ideologies seems to have been another component of unrest. Alan Campbell has shown that more than one third of Lanarkshire mineworkers were under the age of twenty five in 1911.[50] Arguably, this group would have been more receptive to new ideas and more inclined to oppose the cautious approach advocated by the older union leadership. The ability of miners to gain concessions over such a wide front from one of the most draconian of employers' associations reflected the growing strength and organisation among mineworkers. Solidarity of labour, for example on the issue of non-union labour in the pits, surpassed that of the Lanarkshire Coal Masters' Association. The formidable onslaught of mineworkers and of labour in general forced this autocratic combination of employers to cede ground hitherto unthinkable.

To say the 'Roots of Red Clydeside' can be found in the 1910–1914 period would be extremely difficult to prove. High levels of labour unrest were present in other sectors of the mining industry. The coalfields of South Wales being the obvious example. Strike levels also increased in other Scottish coal producing areas – Fife and Ayrshire in particular. To argue that mining unrest was a phenomenon unique to the Clydeside basin would be innacurate. From a Scottish standpoint, however, although the unrest in the pits was increasing and widespread a significant difference existed in the magnitude of strike activity. The level and intensity of conflict was considerably greater in Lanarkshire than in any other Scottish district. In this sense Lanarkshire was unique. Similarities and linkages can be found between the pre and post war periods of conflict. Strikes were fought over similar issues. Nonunionism, contracting and the practice of morning meetings caused stoppages in both periods. Disputes arising from work intensification and mechanisation were, if anything, greater in the years following the war. Hostility to the government continued, especially over decontrol of the industry in 1919.

A link also exists between some main players in the industry. Activists prominent in the war-time struggles, William Allan and Andrew Fagan, first joined the industry in the years prior to the war and these would have been crucially formative years for these men, and would have had some influence on the attitudes and stance they, and others like them, adopted in the later period. The experience of the war was without question a major factor which shaped the attitudes and actions of workers post-1914 and was perhaps the main cause of unrest in post-war Clydeside. The linkages above suggest that a connection does exist between both periods of labour unrest in Lanarkshire mining. The roots of Red Clydeside may indeed be traced back to the unrest experienced in the 1910–14 period.

NOTES

1. Page-Arnot, R., *History of the Scottish Miners from the Earliest Times*, (1955), p 99–100.

2. Page-Arnot, *History of the Scottish Miners;* see table facing page 110.

3. Page-Arnot, *History of the Scottish Miners*, p 121.

4. Miners' Federation of Great Britain, *Annual Proceedings*, 1912, Executive Committee meeting, 25/2/1912.

5. *Forward*, 6/4/1912; Interview of R.Smillie by Patrick Dollan.

6. M.F.G.B. *Annual Proceedings*, 1912, Special Conference, 6/4/1912.

7. M.F.G.B. *Annual Proceedings*, 1912, Ibid, Special Conference on the Minimum Wage, Blackpool, 15/16th August, 1912.

8. Page-Arnot, *History of the Scottish Miners*, p 131 & 132.

9. M.F.G.B. *Annual Proceedings*, 1912, Special Conference, 6/4/1912.

10. Board of Trade, *Investigation into the Changing value of the Sovereign*, p 235.

11. Page-Arnot, *History of the Scottish Miners*, p 133.

12. Page-Arnot, *History of the Scottish Miners*, All wage rates and pithead prices taken from figure facing page 110.

13. Lanarkshire Coal Masters' Association,(LCMA), *Annual Report*, 1912, UGD/159/2/1.

14. Hunt, E.H., *British Labour History, 1815–1914*, (1981). Price, R.,*Labour in British Society*, (1986). Cronin, J.E., *Industrial Conflict in Modern Britain*, (1979).

15. M.F.G.B. *Annual Proceedings*, International Miners' Federation conference in Brussels in May 1912, Smillie notes only a few syndicalists in South Wales and just 10 of the 150 M.F.G.B. delegates were syndicalists.

16. Campbell, A., 'From Independent Collier to Militant Miner: Tradition and Change in the Trade Union Consciousness of the Scottish Miners, 1874–1929', *Scottish Labour History Society Journal*, No. 24, 1989, pp 12.

17. McShane, H., *No Mean Fighter*, (1978), p 54.

18. Askwith, G., *Industrial Problems and Disputes*, (1920).

19. LCMA, Minute Books, Executive Committee meeting 24/2/1909.

20. Small, R., *The Cry From The Mine*, (1911), p 2.

21. Hinton, J., *Labour and Socialism: A History of the British Labour Movement, 1767–1974*, (1983), p 92.

22. *Motherwell Times*, 29/9/1911, p 1.

23. Duncan, R. & McIvor, A.(Eds), *Militant Workers* (1992) see Table 3, p 85.

24. Kenefick, W., 'The Labour Unrest of 1910 To 1914, with particular reference to the Ardrossan Dock Strike, 1912–1913' (unpublished Honours Dissertation, University of Strathclyde,1990), p 74 & 81.

25. LCMA, Board Minutes, 1909 to 1910, UGD/159/1/7, Executive meeting of November, 1910, J.M.Strain of John Watson Ltd; chairman of the LCMA, stated that members should supply the Board of Trade with the information in case the government made it compulsory. He added that his company only gives information on the important strikes.

26. LCMA, *Annual Report*, 1914, UGD/159/2/1.

27. LCMA, Minute Book, 1911 – 1912, UGD/159/1/8. Strategy proposed by J.M.Strain, John Watson Ltd; at an executive meeting, 11/12/1912, as a way of eradicating the "idle–day" practice.

28. Board of Conciliation Minutes, UGD/160//1/1, 2/8/1912

29. *Daily Record*, 7/1/1913, p 3.

30. *Glasgow Herald*, 8/1/1913, p 9. Mowat also claimed at a strike committee meeting of the LCMA that if the men were not forced to join the union then 30 percent of them would be outside the union.

31. Report on Strikes and Lock-outs and on Conciliation and Arbitration Boards, 1913, *B.P.P.*, Cd 7658, pp xx & xxi

32. *Glasgow Herald*, July, September and October 1912, October 1913, and the Lanarkshire Miners' County Union (LMCU), Minute Book, 13/1/1913 – 22/12/1913, DEP 227.52.

33. LMCU, Minute Book, DEP 227.56, Executive committee meeting, 21/3/1914.

34. Board of Conciliation Minutes, UGD/160//1/1, 13/3/1911.

35. LCMA, Minute Book, 1908, UGD/159/1/6, Executive Committee meeting 4/3/1908. Association declare they have stopped contracting for ordinary working but not for machine cutting.

36. *Airdrie and Coatbridge Advertiser*, 6/7/1912, p 6.

37. *Glasgow Herald*, 29/7/1911 to 10/11/1911.

38. *Motherwell Times*, 11/8/1911, p 3.

39. LMCU, Minute Book, All examples from Dep 227.56, 1913/14.

40. LCMA, Annual Report, 1914, UGD/159/2/1. Records note that a number of disputes had been settled by joint conferences with the miners' representatives, thus saving on compensation payments.

41. Zeitlin, J., 'Rank and filism in British Labour History: a critique', *International Review of Social History*, Vol 34, (1), 1989, p 46.

42. Hinton, *Labour and Socialism*, p 93.

43. LMCU, Minute Book, Executive Meeting, 2/8/1910. Dep 227.53.

44. LMCU, Minute Book, Executive Meeting, 16/8/1913. Dep 227.55.

45. LMCU, Minute Book, Executive Meeting, 7/12/1910. Dep 227.53.

46. LMCU, Minute Book, Executive Meeting, 13/12/1913. Dep 227.56.

47. McDougall I.,(Ed) *Militant Miners*, (1981), p 6.

48. M.F.G.B. Annual Proceedings, Annual Conference in Edinburgh, October, 1910.

49. LCMA, Minute Book, District Committee meeting, 5/8/1914.

50. Campbell, *Independent Collier*, p 17.

CHAPTER 8

The United Turkey Red Strike – December 1911

George Rawlinson and Anna Robinson

Introduction

In this chapter we will look at the strike which took place in the United Turkey Red (UTR) combine in the Vale of Leven in December 1911. We will discuss briefly the period in which it occurred, the womens' organisation which was involved in the strike, before considering the strike and its outcome. Finally, we analyse the roles of the principal players in the dispute. It will be shown that the strike was not an isolated incident but rather just a more public and heightened form of the struggle than was evident in the Vale, and that while the strike did improve the conditions of the workforce it did not satisfy the demands of the women workers. Also, while the unions did achieve the recognition which they sought they were unable to maintain the degree of discipline over the workforce that they would have wished.

The strike was not spectacular. It did not have any features that made it outstanding in any way, but the fact that it was well reported has led to it being cited in many works which have tended to see it as an isolated example of militancy in what was normally a quiet, almost passive, area.[1] Macintyre notes that in the immediate pre-war years the apparent tranquility of the Vale had been seriously disturbed, but he makes the point that the Vale seemed to provide a very good example of the patronage and social control that were practised widely in the nineteenth-century. He supports this by quoting a Scottish socialist writing about the workers of the Vale in 1912:

> . . . They are an example of frugality and respectability and docility to the entire world. On 18/- a week for men and less than half of that for women, they manage to keep themselves alive and work ten hours a day. They went to the kirk on Sundays, and won football matches on Saturdays. Scottish thrift found its apotheosis in the Vale of Leven . . .[2]

Far from being an example of docility the evidence suggests that the Vale was, prior to the First World War, exhibiting aspects of dissent which were to became far stronger in the post-war years, so much so that it constituted one of Macintyre's 'Little Moscows'.

The 1911 dispute can in fact be seen as a microcosm of the political and industrial situation that existed in the West of Scotland – the struggle of the unions to be recognised as legitimate partners in the industrial arena, the attempts by the employers to resist this and to try to ensure that any gains obtained by the workers were matched by productivity increases, and the struggle of the workers to better their conditions. It is in this period that the final fracture with paternalism was seen in the Vale, albeit a paternalism which had only really extended to the skilled male workers and which had been eroded by the series of take-overs and mergers which had resulted in the creation of the UTR combine in the late 1890s. It was a strike started by the workforce, run by the unions and settled more in the interest of the unions than of the workforce – the result was a partially unionised but undisciplined workforce which continued guerrilla-like tactics against the employers.

It should be borne in mind that these were formative years for the developing labour movement, particularly in relation to general unions and organisations of unskilled women, and that the debate between different styles of unionism and labour politics was ongoing, as is seen in the UTR dispute. There were many rival factions and groups active within the labour movement at that time, and while socialist papers would report on labour issues, we cannot assume that they were impartial, any more than we can assume the impartiality of the mass circulation papers. The 1911 strike needs to be seen as taking place at a time when the labour movement was still in its infancy (less than 1 in 5 workers were in trade unions at this time) and against a back-drop of working class forces that were pulling in the same general direction, but were also peeling off at different tangents.

The National Federation of Women Workers

A central player in the strike was the National Federation of Women Workers (NFWW). In order to understand the role of this organisation we will give a brief outline of its origins and development and, most importantly, of the way that it tended to operate. While the Federation was a women's' organisation it would be wrong to view it in terms of a feminist organisation. The Federation was just one of a number of organisations which concerned themselves with the position of women within society. Many of these organisations were interlinked and while they may have had separate fields of activity the personnel were often the same. It could also be said that the dominant political philosophy within these organisations was often the same. Mary MacArthur, for example, who as General Secretary of the NFWW came to the Vale during the dispute, retained secretaryship of the Women's Trade Union League (WTUL) when she took up the position of President of the Federation following its formation in 1906.

As early as 1892 a Women's Trades Council was established in Glasgow and many other organisations were formed around the same time. For example there was the Women's Protective and Provident League,[3] founded by Emma Paterson, this had a Scottish Branch and shared premises with the Glasgow Council for Women's Trades and the National Federal Council of Scotland for Women's Trades. These organisations were linked to the Glasgow Union of Women Workers which was itself linked to the National Union of Women Workers. Many of these organisations were not what we would now term women's organisations and frequently had men in leading positions. Most were dominated by middle class attitudes and often had little connection with the realities of working class life. As Sheila Lewenhak says:

> . . . Emma Patterson did not make the mistake of appealing directly to working women. She first sought middle class support, which she knew existed, for the setting up of a National Union of Working Women . . .[4]

This view is emphasised by a comment made at the National Council of Women Workers conference in 1911 by a branch worker who said, 'it seems to me that we should not always be weaving schemes for working people without coming into touch with them'.[5]

Perhaps the attitude of many of these organisations is best expressed by an observation by Serena Kelly:

> . . . The National Union of Women Workers interpreted this [the idea of work] not as paid employment as wage earners, nor work in a household

as wife or mother. For the NUWW work meant putting into practice the duties and responsibilities middle class women felt towards society. Not only was this work respectable, it was obligatory. . . .[6]

It could also be said that many, if not all, of these organisations often protected the position of men within the labour market. There has been much written on these societies/organisations and we do not intend to dwell on this area, suffice to say that it was from this mixture of organisations that the Federation sprang.[7]

The tactics of the National Federation of Women Workers were to go into an area identified as suitable for recruitment and to hold local meetings, recruit members and then move on to another area. This style of work led to rapid growth in membership but it was a membership which could not be sustained. After a relatively short time many branches ceased to operate or, as in the case in the Vale, members were transferred wholesale to the male trade union in the respective industry. The strike in the Vale of Leven came at a time when the NFWW was very active in Scotland. Since 1909 the NFWW had been represented on Glasgow Trades Council initially with three delegates; five from 1910, and reports were regularly given to the Council by Kate McLean, the Scottish organiser of the Federation. By 1911 the Federation claimed 48 branches in England, Scotland and Wales, with a membership of over 10,000.

The minutes of Glasgow Trades Council show that there were a number of strikes throughout 1910 and 1911 involving the Federation. In June 1910 Mary MacArthur, the Secretary of the NFWW, addressed the Trades Council on a dispute in Neilston. As was common at the time it was a strike over unionisation. MacArthur hoped that the Board of Trade would be able to arrange a meeting and hoped for an early settlement, a view which she expressed again during the UTR dispute. Further disputes were reported by Kate McLean throughout 1910 in Neilston, Airdrie, Kilummey and Larkhall.[8] In January 1911 McLean reported on a dispute at the UTR works in Alexandria and told the council that a branch of 600 had been formed as a result. Again in March 1911, McLean reported on a strike at Alexandria which had been resolved following her intervention. The strike at UTR in late 1911 was not, therefore, an isolated incident, rather it is an example of the type of struggle that had been going on for over a year and which would continue up to, and even beyond, the outbreak of the Great War.

Background to the dispute

The United Turkey Red works were situated in the Vale of Leven along the course or the river Leven. UTR was created in 1897 with the amalgamation of the three principal firms in the Vale. The other two works in the Vale (Dalmonach and Ferryfield) were absorbed by the Calico Printers' Association. The resultant programme of rationalisation which followed the 1897 amalgamation caused job losses, periods of short time and unemployment in the Vale.[9] The rationalisation, in fact, reduced the workforce from 6,000 in 1898 to 3,000 in 1911. Conditions were worsened at the turn of the century by a decline in the Indian markets and increased competition from the rest of Europe. The net result was a reduction in income brought about by short time working compounded by the 1908–10 recession.[10]

UTR was basically a family owned company, the main share holders being members of the Orr Ewing, Gilmour, Christie and Wylie families, Families which had a history of paternalism, at least up to the amalgamation. In Jamestown, for example, Archibold Orr Ewing had built houses for his workers, a school and public hall, and provided half the cost of a new kirk building.[11] The provision of houses did, however, reflect the division of labour at the works, skilled workers being provided with company houses, while the poorer dye hands were forced to live in slum areas like the Burn in Bonhill.[12] As well as housing, the employers were closely involved within community organisations, for example being elders of the church. The main families also provided the Members of Parliament for the area: Alexander Orr Ewing in the period 1862–1892 and Alex Wylie from 1895 to 1906. In 1868 John Orr Ewing donated 100 tonnes of coal to the 'deserving poor' and in 1878 the workers in the Vale were given a holiday when Archibald Orr Ewing's daughter got married. In 1882, William Ewing Gilmour presented the community with the Ewing Gilmour Institute for men, followed by one for women in 1891.[13]

The owners of the works lived in the Vale in the 19th century and Alex Wylie became very involved with the welfare of his skilled workers to the point of writing papers on good management. He believed a more educated skilled workforce was to be gained by bringing his workmen 'into personal contact with superior, and more highly trained minds' and that this would help eradicate 'erroneous and subversive' doctrines.[14] While there is obvious evidence of paternalistic attitudes on the part of the employers it is important to stress that this was almost exclusively directed towards the male skilled workers who formed a minority of the workforce. Indeed Wylie ignored the less skilled workers, except to regard the Irish immigrant population as drunkards and unworthy of attention.[15] By 1911 what paternalism had existed within the component companies of the UTR had disappeared. What did continue, however, was the differentiation between the skilled workers and the semi or unskilled workers. The skilled calico printers were organised in their association and were recognised for collective bargaining purposes by the company. The rest of the workforce prior to the 1911 dispute were not organised and any negotiations were conducted directly with the workers.

The roots of discontent and the 1911 strike

As has been noted earlier there had been a history of small disputes in the UTR works in the year or so preceding the December 1911 strike. Even the *Glasgow Herald* reported that 'the district was simply seething with discontent.'[16] Sworn statements taken at the time of the dispute give a clear picture of what life was like in the UTR factories. One worker described how she worked in the yarn department where they stripped off polls, lifted 25 hanks weighing a pound each, tied them together and carried them, against her side, to the ware room. Sometimes she carried them down five flights of stairs and sometimes up two. Her pay was 10 shillings and 6 pence a week, she started work at 6am and finished at 5-30 or sometimes 6pm. She had previously worked in the tamping department four years earlier and her hands had still not recovered from the damage caused by the chemicals used. A past foreman in the black ageing department of the Levenbank works told how he had been ordered to screw down windows (which were opened by the workers for ventilation) which he was instructed to open again when the manager knew that the factory inspector was coming. Yet another worker recorded that her feet were constantly wet and that she had a hole in each big toe caused by liquid (chrome). It was not as if the managers did not know how bad conditions were as another worker reported that the foreman moved the girls when the

Factory Inspector called so that those with bad hands were behind the machines.[17]

Not only was the position of the company in relation to health and safety very poor, but also any attempt by the workforce to improve their wage rates was met with a demand for work intensification. For example when the stove women demanded a rise in wages of two shillings and one penny per week the company responded:

> . . . This demand was considered today and I am advised to inform you that the advance has been conceded. The advance, however, is granted on the understanding that each girl carry from the dye house, spread, carry into the stove, hang, take out of stove and convey to the conditioning shed at least 1,000lbs a day . . . I am instructed to ask that you will see that the above quantity is obtained from each girl and that when production is reduced the number of stove women will be reduced also. . . .[18]

The strike of December 1911 can be traced back to at least the January of 1911, when the NFWW became involved in a major way in the area. The NFWW called a meeting on 24th January 1911 in the Co-Op hall in Alexandria. The meeting concerned the unfair dismissal of two girls at the UTR which had led to a strike by 200 of the workers. The meeting attracted over 800 women and men and was addressed by Kate McLean and Miss Brown of the NFWW and by Mr J O Connor Kessack of the National Union of Dock Labourers. After the meeting a committee was formed, comprising one member of each department, in order to make arrangements to bring the Turkey Red workers of Alexandria into the union. The committee must have been very active, and the workers at UTR keen to join the union for by February 11th *Forward* could report four branches of the Federation and by February 18th a further three were formed giving a membership of an estimated 2,000. Membership was further increased in February with the formation of a branch at the Calico printing works in Bonhill.[19]

A mass meeting in early February was addressed by Kate McLean and George Dallas (ILP secretary). At this meeting, attended by about 300 men and women, Dallas gave an address on the rules of several unions and a discussion took place on the respective merits of industrial unions and trade unions. The meeting took a vote in favour of the principle of trade unions and a motion was passed to form a branch of the Amalgamated Society of Dyers, Bleachers, Finishers and Kindred Trades (ASD). It is interesting that while the male workers assisted the women to organise it was only through pressure exerted by the women workers and the NFWW that the ASD agreed to take in the unskilled workers at UTR, and this was not until late March of 1911.[20]

The next identified dispute occurred in March 1911 again over the dismissal of a female worker and again reinstatement was achieved through the negotiation of Kate McLean. This was after 50 workmates had come out on strike. Similar disputes occurred through the year, *Forward* reported a dispute in April again involving wrongful dismissal and again it was resolved through the intervention of Kate McLean of the Federation. In July it was reported that a strike in Alexandria had been settled to the advantage of the union members.[21]

The series of skirmishes linked with the growth in trade union organisation came to a head in the winter of 1911. On November 4th 1911 the NFWW and the ASD made a formal request to the employers, the UTR Co (it should be noted that neither union was officially recognised by the management of UTR). The request was for a 10 percent increase in wage rates, to be paid weekly and not fortnightly, a 55 hours week, and for time and a half rate for overtime. The company did not reply or even acknowledge the request and the unions told them on 27th November that a ballot of the workers had resulted in 91 percent in favour of sending notices to cease work. On the strength of the ballot the unions no doubt felt that they were in a strong position and they asked for an interview with the directors to discuss the situation before any further steps were taken. The company continued to ignored the request.[22] Hayhurst (Dyers union official) stated that he had written to the Company three times and got no reply, even when he telephoned the Company Secretary he was likewise refused.[23] The notices were posted, they ran out on 9th December and the strike started. It was to last about two weeks.

On 30th November a meeting was held in the Alexandria Co-Op hall attended by about 1000 and addressed by George Dallas and Kate McLean for the Federation and Hayhurst and Webster for the ASD (Dyers union officials who came up from Yorkshire). The platform also included representatives, male and female, from the various works. One of the important points about this dispute, and a point which is common in this area of labour history is the anonymity of the organisations within the workplace. There was obviously organisation in the works, mention is made to it, in passing, in various reports, but it has proved impossible to get anything other than vague impressions.[24] The result of this is that perhaps more emphasis than should be is given to those who appear to be the main actors, in this case, Kate McLean and George Dallas from the NFWW. Given the history of victimisation and sackings it is understandable that those employed in the work place would not wish to attract attention or publicity. This leads to an over emphasis being put on the role of the full time union officials.

The response of the company to the demands was to express surprise that any dissatisfaction existed, to post their own notices on the Wednesday refuting the wage rates as stated by the unions (and widely reported in the press), and added that the directors were always ready to meet with the employees and that they had met and resolved matters in the past.[25] It seems that at this early stage in the dispute the company believed that they could ride out the storm and that if they kept a firm line then the dispute would dissapate. This attitude was reflected in the way that they put out notices saying that the works would be open as usual on the Monday for those willing to work. In this the company made two serious mistakes. Firstly, they underestimated the strength of feeling amongst their workforce, and secondly, they underestimated the public support which the workers had, and which was reflected in the attitude taken to the strike by the *Lennox Herald* and the *Glasgow Herald*.

On 6th December the directors met in Glasgow. The outcome was not made public but the local paper, the *Lennox Herald*, reported that it was understood that the company would negotiate with the workpeople but not with the union.[26] When such an idea was put to a meeting of workers the next night it was rejected by the strike committee even though the union officials present were prepared to accept it.[27] On Monday 9th December the strike began and was solid. The *Glasgow Herald* reported that by 5am on the Monday crowds numbering 7,000 were at the gates, bringing the works to a 'virtual standstill'. The workers formed an impromptu band, behind which men and women marched to the largest of the works at Croftengea. At each of the six works pickets lined the streets to jeer strike breakers. Women burned effigies of company directors and carried banners claiming 'white slaves, Vale of Leven, no surrender', and the slogan 'We dye to live' were in evidence.[28] In the evening there was a meeting of 2000, mostly women, in the Co-Op hall at which Kate McLean, in what was described by the *Lennox Herald* as a fighting speech, urged picketing, and reference was made to the rail strike which was seen as an omen 'which might be followed in the Vale of Leven'. A resolution was passed which empowered one delegate from the Dyers and one from the NFWW to attempt to get an interview with the directors.[29]

It is perhaps worth noting that the strike committee had previously rejected such a move. What had happened to change this position is not clear. The fact that the matter was put to a mass meeting where the union officials may have had more sway than they had over a strike committee is perhaps worth bearing in mind.[30] The strike held firm and on the Tuesday there was a large demonstration in Renton at which all the strike leaders were present and it was disclosed that the directors would consider the request to meet with the delegation. The strike continued for the next week with mass meetings being held regularly and picketing being organised at a very high level. Mary MacArthur, arrived in the district on the Wednesday and while she participated in the final agreement which was reached there is no report of her addressing the strikers. But it was not just the unions who were organising meetings. The well known anarcho-syndicalist Madame Sorgue addressed a meeting in Alexandria, a fact which was not looked upon with any enthusiasm by Mr Webster of the Dyers union who told a meeting that they wished to conduct the strike on their own and dissociated the strikers from the meeting being addressed by 'a foreign lady named Madame Sorgue.'[31]

As would seem common at the time – particularly in disputes involving women – the strike created an almost carnival atmosphere within the Vale It was evident in the Singer dispute earlier in the year, and has been observed in disputes within the cotton industry as late as the 1930's, and is perhaps linked to the liberating feeling that comes from collective action. It was almost as if the tradition of celebrating St Monday had not died out. This carnival atmosphere was seen when 5,000 marched from Alexandria to Renton, escorted by 4 bands and displaying two dummies, one representing the director of the company the other the firemen-clerks.[32]

While there were no reports of any extensive violence during the strike there were hints of incidents and the police were deployed in more than usual numbers within the district. Of the 100 constables in the district 60 had been drafted in from various parts of Dumbartonshire. Indeed it would seem that the unions, be it the NFWW or the Dyers, did not have total control of the way that the strike was run as pickets had to escort an undermanager into the Cordale works past a crowd of women.[33] The *Glasgow Herald* reported how:

> . . . the Clerks from head office in Glasgow were subjected to a lively time by female strikers, who threw flour and peasemeal at them, and a number were carried to the river and thrown in . . .[34]

From such evidence it would appear that the women workers were prepared to carry our militant action, despite contemporary reports stressing the docility and respectability of the workers.[35]

Resolution and aftermath

While the dispute developed in the Vale, in London the matter was raised in Parliament on behalf of the local MP Acland Allan with the President of the Board of Trade. The reply given was that the Chief Industrial Commissioner, (George Askwith) was 'at present in communication with the parties in the dispute'.[36] The strike was brought to an end through the intervention of the Board of Trade and the organisation of a conference in early 1912 on the matter. From the company records it would seem that it was the unions who broke the deadlock between the two sides by offering to the UTR managers to end the strike if negotiations were set up.[37] A conference being agreed the unions then persuaded the workers to go back to work which they did on December 25th.

To the casual observer the dispute was over but newspaper reports from the 6th January note a split between the terms of settlement negotiated by the two unions. At the beginning of the dispute the men and women demanded the same increases. The NFWW, however, put forward the demand for a minimum wage for females working at UTR of 14 shillings a week. The ASD did not seem to support the women's case and they accepted the companies terms of settlement. The women's case was put at a further conference which took place on 6th February 1912. The result was that the women not only failed to obtain a minimum wage but they were given less than the men. The men over 18 and earning less than 25 shillings a week, got a one shilling advance, the women got sixpence a week if they were over 18, with some minor increases at plant level.[38] Not long after the dispute was settled the NFWW turned their branches over to the ASD as they began to admit women in 1912 (whether this was a consequence of the 1911 strike is not known). Reports from union officials show that the female ASD membership began to decline considerably after 1912[39] whilst nationally the NFWW continued to grow, with a membership of 11,000 in 1914 rising to 60,000 in 1919.[40]

Perhaps more interesting than the fact of the strike occurring are the comments and attitudes of those involved, reflecting, as they do, the many strands of thought at the time. Take for example the main players in the dispute on the Federation side, Kate McLean and George Dallas. Kate McLean was one of the Scottish organisers of the NFWW, she was active in Glasgow Trades Council, was on the General Council of the STUC 1911–1913, and on its Parliamentary Committee. She had been very active in organising the NFWW throughout Scotland. She represented the STUC on the Women's National Suffrage League and was a workers' representative on the shirt-making Trade Board. Yet while she was so obviously concerned about the organisation of women she would seem to have not been opposed to the transfer of the Vale of Leven women to the male union shortly after the strike. Neither are there signs of any continued involvement with the women of the Vale after the return to work. Kate McLean continued to work for the Federation and was active in a number of strikes, most notably the 1913 strike of networkers in Kilbirnie which lasted from early April through to September. She went on to become a Labour Councillor in Glasgow in the inter-war years.

The role of the ILP, and in particular of George Dallas, is also interesting. A key figure in the dispute and credited in press reports as working for the NFWW, Dallas was secretary to the Scottish divisional council of the ILP. According to research notes on the National Union of Dyers, Bleachers and Textile Workers he is credited with the organisation of the ASD in Scotland – according to these notes Dallas contacted the union regarding unorganised dye-house workers in 1911. The notes saying:

. . . This first contact was made by Mr George Dallas who was organising for political Labour societies in Glasgow and the surrounding areas. He appealed to the union for advice as to organising workers in the dying trade in the Vale of Leven. The workers in that area had decided to form a union of their own but Mr Dallas asked them not to do so until he had sought advice from ADS. This resulted in Joe Hayhurst and an executive council member travelling to Scotland to hold meetings of dyehouse workers in the Glasgow area . . . The union also enlisted the services of George Dallas to assist in organising the dyeing trade in Scotland . . . the union had formed seven branches with a total membership of 1,947 . . . The branches were at Alexandria, Renton, Jamestown, Glasgow, Thornliebank, Barrhead and Lennoxtown. . . .[41]

In early 1912 Dallas was appointed as chief organiser of the NFWW and took up a post in London.[42] His career in the labour movement continued when in 1913 he took up a full time post with the Workers' Union.[43] He went on to became a Labour MP.

Of particular interest is the way that both the ILP and the unions played down issues in order to achieve arbitration and union recognition. By the start of the strike the UTR company had started legal action against George Dallas, Tom Johnson and Forward over reports that had appeared in *Forward* regarding conditions and pay in the UTR works. The company summons claimed the Defenders had slandered the Pursuers and that, 'The Defenders having by their said unfounded statements held the Pursuers up to public hatred and contempt . . .' and sought compensation of £2000 with interest at 5 percecnt per annum and £100 expenses. Dallas and the ILP responded to the summons, defending the statements which had appeared in Forward and produced sworn statements from workers as to wages and conditions at UTR. Given the wide publicity that the dispute had it would seem that UTR did not relish the thought of exposing their workers' wages and conditions to full public scrutiny and the case was quietly dropped by the company. Yet the action may have had some effect on the ILP or at least on Dallas and Johnson as they seemed to impose self-censorship on the reporting of the strike. In *Forward* there was the following statement:

. . . We have been asked by the union officials to withhold reports dealing with the Vale of Leven strike as there is some prospect of a successful settlement. The ordinary press has dealt fairly with the Strikers, and has reported their side of the case. It is felt that no good purpose will be served this week by carrying the war into the enemy's camp. . . .[44]

Conclusion

This study of the UTR strike has been informative, but frustrating. It is informative in that it gives an insight into the way that the trade unions were organising prior to the First World War. It is frustrating because of the information that is not available, particularly the fact that the records of the NFWW were not able to be tracked down, and that no trace could be found of strike committee records or of the records of Dumbarton Trades Council. We are left to wonder what the organisation at factory level was like, who were the members of the shop and strike committees and what were their political affiliations or persuasions? Our main sources are mostly linked to local press and the ILP, and while the ILP, the NFWW and the Dyers union could be said to represent the workers side, we are left with a feeling that a fuller picture would have been given if other records were available.

From the evidence available it can be argued strongly that the strike was not an isolated incident but rather a slightly more dramatic example of what had been happening previously and was to occur in the years to follow. The unions may have won a victory in achieving recognition but they had certainly failed the female workers. They had also failed to bring the workers into line as can be seen from the UTR dispute book for March 1914 which states:

> . . . On Tuesday 10th strikers with the help of women and children from Renton succeeded in stopping two of the new male workers and on Wednesday 11th only one male worker appeared and on that day the girls also were absent. The Department was therefore shut down on Thursday 12 th March. . . .

This is supported by an extract from McIntyre's book when he is talking about relations at UTR a year after the strike:

> . . . The boys and the female hands were particularly troublesome, and the manager of Cordale works printing department complained that his workers were abusive to the point that they 'believe they have only to demand to get what they want', when the union organiser reproached

them for their indiscipline, they replied 'they were not members of the bloody union' and walked out. 'When we are going to educate these people God alone knows', lamented the official. . . .[45]

Yet the strike must be situated within the developments of the time and it must be remembered that at the time of the strike there was a feeling that society was not at ease with itself.

Many newspapers were warning of the dangers of industrial anarchy and unrest. In December 1911 the *Lennox Herald* had a review of strikes in Britain likening them to French syndicalism. At a national level there was concern at the industrial situation, how much of this was feigned and how much was real is debatable. It is true, however that between the summer of 1909 and the autumn of 1911 British society underwent some major developments. Bernard Porter notes in his book on political espionage that it was in this period that:

> . . . MI5 and MI6 were both born, the modern Official Secrets Act was passed: the 'D-Notice' system for vetting newspaper stories bearing on 'national security' was devised: a register of aliens living in Britain was set up: blanket interceptions of certain categories of mail at the Post Office began: and the Special Branch was brought close to being a proper domestic counter-subversive agency on modern lines. These develop-ments marked a crucial stage in the transformation of Britain from a relatively open liberal democracy into the far more restrictive one we have today. . . .[46]

In the mainstream press there were stories of general unease and industrial unrest. The *Glasgow Herald,* in August 1911, carried an article on the nature of syndicalism:

> . . . It is beyond dispute that a sea change has come over labour politics within a very recent time. The supreme question is whether the public, now that it is cognisant of the direction in which labour is tending, intends to cultivate a criminal apathy or to awake, before it is too late, to the fundamental immorality and lawlessness of the forces by which the State is menaced? . . .[47]

The period can be seen as the formative years for those who went on to figure so prominently in the 'Red Clydeside' era. The political climate was in a state of flux, particularly as far as the labour movement was concerned. Trade unions were seeking to establish their legitimacy, some labour politicians were seeking acceptance within the system, others were seeking the legitimisation of their cause within the established order while others sought the overthrow of the entire system. Yet non of the trends which existed had coalesced and while today we can relatively easily (thought sometimes erroneously) categorise labour figures as of one hue or another, it was not possible to do that in 1911. An individual could be involved with a mix of organisations, movements and groups which today we may well think of as contradictory. Not only was the labour movement in a state of flux, so was the women's movement. As has been noted earlier many of the women involved in both the suffrage movement and in the area of working women were members of, and active in, a cross section of organisations. Women such as Mary MacArthur who, as Gordon notes. became 'more influenced by notions of inter-class co-operation' than by class action.[48]

On the political front there were vying forces and this period could be seen as the point where the battle between industrial unionism and trades unionism was at it highest. Yet there is little evidence to suggest that syndicalism, or industrial unionism, played anything other than a minor role, if that, in the dispute. That is not to say, however, that the ideas of syndicalism were not present, but rather that they did not take organisational form. The fact that Dallas debated industrial unionism with the workers, the presence of Madame Sorgue, and the proximity of the Singer works (where industrial unionism sank deep), would indicate that there would have been some knowledge of syndicalist organisation and beliefs in the area.

When looking at the 1911 dispute we have, as is always the case, been restricted by the material evidence that we could gather and while there is considerable evidence both from the company and the unions side, there is little or no evidence directly from the workers side. It is important to stress this as we believe that the actions and motives of the unions involved were not synonymous with those of the workers. Indeed the impression given is that the workers were used by the unions in an attempt to establish their own credentials. While we would argue that the workers used the unions as a way of addressing their grievances, we do not believe that one can read into the actions of the workers or the unions a full commitment of the one to the other. As we have said the strike itself was not spectacular, it had no particularly outstanding features, there were some rowdy scenes, and effigies were made, but such things were not new to the area. It was not an isolated example of workers' struggle but rather an example of the continuing struggle. The fact that the dispute was widely reported allows us some insight into the way that disputes were conducted at that time and of particular interest is the insight that it gives us into the way that the fledgling labour movement operated at a time when the 'Red Clydesiders' were themselves in their formative years.

NOTES

1. McIntyre, S., *Little Moscows (1980)*
2. McIntyre, *Little Moscows*, p 84 quoting William Stewart in *Clarion*, 5 January 1912.
3. The Women's Protection and Provident League had its first meeting in 1888 which was sponsored by Glasgow Trades Council. See Gordon, E., *Women and the Labour Movement in Scotland 1850–1914* (1991).
4. Lewenhak, S., *Women in the Trade Unions* (1977), p 69.
5. Conference papers Oct. 9–13 1911. National Union of Women Workers of GB
6. Kelly, S., 'A Sisterhood of Service', *Journal of the Society of Archivists* Vol.14 No 2, 1993.
7. See Gordon, *Women and the Labour Movement*.
8. Glasgow Trades Council, Minutes, June – December 1910
9. McIntyre, *Little Moscows, p89*
10. Neill, J., *Record and Reminiscences of Bonhill Parish* (1979), p 74.
11. Neill, *Record and Reminiscences,* p 81
12. Neill, *Record and Reminiscences,* p 81.
13. Agnew, J., *The Story of the Vale of Leven* (1975), pp 66–67
14. McIntyre *Little Moscows*, p83.
15. Robinson, A,. 'A Study of Women Workers in the Vale of Leven Cotton Finishing Industry' (unpublished Honours Dissertation, University of Strathclyde), 1994.
16. *Glasgow Herald,* 11 December 1911
17. UTR (V) ILP, National Library of Scotland, Acc 6088
18. Letter of 13th June 1913, from J.O. Ewing to Mr Carruthers of Burnbrae, Glasgow University Archive UGB 13 1/8.
19. *Forward,* January – February 1911.
20. *Forward,* 1 April 1911.
21. *Forward,* Jan – July 1911, see also Glasgow Trades Council Minutes 1911.
22. UTR (V) ILP, National Library of Scotland. Acc 6088.
23. *Lennox Herald,* 16 December 1911.
24. *Glasgow Herald, Forward & Lennox Herald,* November,1911.
25. *Glasgow Herald,* 5 December 1911.
26. *Lennox Herald,* 9 December 1911, *Glasgow Herald* 7 Dec 1911
27. *Lennox Herald,* 9 December 1911
28. *Glasgow Herald,* 12 – 21 December 1911

29. *Lennox Herald,* 16 December 1911

30. Such was the turnout for the meeting that an overflow meeting had to be held at the Fountain.

31. *Lennox Herald,* 16 December 1911

32. *Lennox Herald,* 16 December 1911

33. *Lennox Herald,* 16 December 1911

34. *Glasgow Herald,* 14 December 1911

35. Young, J., *The Rousing of the Scottish Working Class* (1977) comments made by William Stewart, veteran of the Glasgow ILP, p181.

36. *Glasgow Herald,* 14 December 1911

37. Minute Book of UTR Director's Meetings Nov.1911 to Feb. 1913. Meeting of 20th December 1911 – CLAM.M 75.

38. *Glasgow Herald,* 9 January & 9 February 1912.

39. McIntyre, *Little Moscows,* p 87.

40. Webb, S and B., *History of Trade Unionism 1666–1920.* (1920)

41. Research notes of Booth, P.J., 'The History of the National Union of Dyers, Bleachers and Textile Workers', 1980.

42. *Forward,* 20 January 1912

43. Hyman, R., *The Workers Union* (1971).

44. *Forward,* 16 December 1911

45. McIntyre, *Little Moscows* p 91

46. Porter, B., *Plots and Paranoia* (1992), p120.

47. *Glasgow Herald,* 26 August 1911

48. Gordon, E., *Women and the Labour Movement.*

CHAPTER 9

A Clash of Work Regimes: 'Americanisation' and the Strike at the Singer Sewing Machine Company, 1911

Glasgow Labour History Workshop[1]

Introduction

On Tuesday morning, 21 March 1911, twelve women cabinet polishers in the massive Singer sewing machine factory at Clydebank struck work over some reorganisation of their labour process which involved an increase in workloads, combined with a two shilling (10p) per week wage loss. Within days the vast majority of the 11,000 employees of the plant were out in sympathy and were to remain out, the factory at a standstill, for three weeks. Yet, Singer had no history of labour militancy like this. Indeed, in many respects it seemed an archetypal paternalist corporation with no obvious signs of strained industrial relations since the setting up of the company in Glasgow in the 1860's. This chapter investigates the causes and significance of the Singer strike. This is a worthwhile exercise, we believe, on several counts.

The strike at Singer was the largest single company strike in Scotland over the 1910–1914 – the years of the 'labour unrest'. Thus it provides an important case study informing the debate on the causes and consequences of this phenomenon. It is of significance in that it represents one of the first explicit confrontations between capital and labour resulting from attempts to graft American-inspired 'scientific management' practices onto the more indigenous working practices in Scotland. In this way the strike highlights a clash of work cultures. The dispute also encapsulates in microcosm some of the dynamic forces operating within the wider labour movement (including the prominent role of women workers in the struggles of the period and the growth of industrial unionism) and demonstrates the draconian labour relations strategies of one of the earliest multinational corporations in Scotland (mirroring the anti-unionism of most contemporary multi-nationals in Scotland). We will also argue that the strike at Singer in 1911 had broader ramifications for the germination and diffusion of the practice of the type of militant class action which was to be characteristic of the war years – thus making connections between this particular dispute and 'red Clydeside'.[2]

Background and causation

Singer was one of the world's earliest multinational manufacturing companies. From their American base, they expanded to Scotland, starting assembly of sewing machines at a small factory near John Street in Glasgow in 1867–8. With growing demand came expansion, firstly, into a larger plant in Bridgeton, before moving to the green field site at Kilbowie, Clydebank (population around 5,000), where construction started on a massive factory in 1882, capable of employing 3,500 and mass assembling 8,000 machines per week. Production began in 1884 and within a year numbers employed had grown to over 5,000, making it the largest sewing machine factory in the world. A good train link and relatively high wages encouraged many of the Bridgeton workers to commute to the Clydebank plant, and an additional 1,500 workers came from the Dumbarton and Vale of Leven area. By 1911, the works had expanded to employ over 12,000, around 3,000 of which were female. Within the plant there were 41 separate departments in which varying sizes of work teams undertook the myriad tasks of working the timber and metal, producing component parts and assembling the completed sewing machines, most of which were destined for export, the largest market being Russia.

From its origins, Singer was largely hostile to trade unionism. As Tom Bell, an activist during the 1911 strike recalled in his auto-biography: 'the firm refused to recognise any union, and those union men who were employed had to keep it quiet'.[3] Only a proportion of the very small minority of craft artisans in Singer (including the engineers, joiners and printers) were trade union members, a position apparently endured by the firm. A broader-based union was established at Singer in the late 1880s, but it had a very small membership and only survived for a few years. Amongst the majority of Singer workers, therefore, collective organisation failed to take root.

In the early years of the twentieth century, the Singer company began to experiment with new modes of managing and controlling labour. The initiative stemmed from America, where the ideas of Frederick Winslow Taylor had gained ground. Indeed, 'Taylorism' or 'scientific management' methods were spreading in large factories all over Europe and the USA at this time.[4] In Singer, Clydebank, the labour process was undergoing rapid reorganisation. Increasingly the work was broken up and fragmented into simpler, repetitive tasks, with the machines setting the pace. Whilst some new skills were created in this process, more than ever, mass production under 'Taylorism' was dehumanising and degrading the worker, who, in the interest of increasing profits, was seen as merely another element in the production process – as Taylor put it, the worker would be a 'trained gorilla'.[5] It was these conditions which helped to trigger the 1911 strike, the only major confrontation between capital and labour during the history of Singer U.K. from its inception in 1867 to after World War Two. The mass walkout and the rapid escalation of the strike suggests that the grievances within the plant were deep rooted.

Alienation with the imposition of a 'scientific management' work regime lay at the core of the 1911 strike at Singer. The socialist newspaper Forward, explained the conditions which led to the strike in these terms:

> . . . In many of these departments foremen stand with watches in their hands timing the men and girls so that the maximum amount of labour can be exacted from the operatives in return for the minimum wage. In one department especially, a foreman has been nicknamed 'Crippen' because of his timing propensities. The watch is seldom out of this individual's hand. Wages are not reduced collectively. In Singers' the wages of two or three are broken today; a few others tomorrow, and so on until all the workers have been reduced, and the game of SCIENTIFIC REDUCTION begins once more. . . .[6]

The specific effects of the extreme sub-division of labour under these new 'scientific management' methods was also commented upon by the Marxist revolutionary John MacLean:

> . . . The American Singers concern is Yankee from stem to stem. . . . There are 41 departments, and the various processes have been so divided and

sub-divided that I believe few outside the office staff will know exactly how many processes the wood, the iron and the steel have to go through before the machine is completed. Within recent years the sub-division of labour has been rapidly developed to an extreme, and new automatic machinery in many departments has displaced labour, or, at least, enabled the management to enormously increase the output without a very great absorption of fresh workers.[7]

This had important implications for the status and dispensibility of workers. As a result, one Singer worker commented, management could 'pick and choose as they liked'.[8]

The way the piece-rate and quality control systems were manipulated by Singer management served to compound discontent. Piece-work rates were set according to the pace of the most experienced, and thus faster, workers. One Singer worker claiming twenty years experience in several departments argued that they had no choice but to take direct action against 'the pernicious system of selecting the most expert workers for any given job and ruling the prices accordingly'.[9] Quality control was used by management to similar ends. During the inspection process, for example, a small proportion of a worker's output would be rejected as poor quality. The worker then toiled harder to replace the rejected pieces and make up lost piecework earnings. The foreman then claimed that the extra output was manageable by the worker and thus the higher rate of productivity was demanded on a permanent basis. At a later, opportune moment piece rates would be cut, often after a holiday period, or when trade was slack.

Additional evidence of the adverse working conditions at the Singer plant in Clydebank is provided by oral evidence. Bill Lang worked there between 1904 and 1911, five years of which were spent in the foundry as a coremaker and apprentice moulder.[10] Although the firm paid comparatively high wages, Bill recalled that conditions were 'terrible' from the workers' point of view and that managerial authority was sacrosanct: 'If you said a word to a gaffer . . . you just got chucked out'. This was buttressed by a policy of employing immigrant labour, directly recruited at the Broomielaw. Bill Lang also recalled, with some resentment, the presence of American 'efficiency engineers', sent over to examine the way work was performed and to make economies, thus placing pressure on wages and forcing on the pace of work. Spreading the system of payment by results, acute division of labour, and using the installation of modern machinery as justification for reducing piece rates and consequently forcing up productivity, were favoured managerial tactics. Moreover, according to Bill there was no guaranteed wage and favouritism existed in allocating the best paid jobs:

> . . . There wasnae good conditions in the foundry at all. It was all piecework – if you didnae make it, you didnae get it. I didnae like it. I didnae like the piecework because I didnae get the right jobs . . . I had a job one of the times and I could make ten shillings up to dinner time and then made my cores for the next day. But if you got bad work, you maybe got a pound [a week], maybe less. And if you were in the know, you got the good work. . . .[11]

Significantly, Bill Lang left Singer in 1911, a short while after the strike, because he felt Singer was exploiting his apprenticeship training period: 'I had some ambition', Bill commented, 'If I'd have stayed, I'd have only been able to work in Singers. In my mind was this. If I wanted to be a moulder I needed to get to some other place . . . so I served my last two years in Tullis'. His dissillusionment with the Singer corporation was deep-rooted: 'Singers had a bad name. . . . I myself thought as a boy that they should blow it up'. Bill Lang's experience and oral testimony thus provides graphic confirmation of the alienating effects of working in Singer under an American influenced scientific management regime. The recollections of other Singer workers, including David Bennett, the Raes and Margaret Ewing only serve to confirm such evidence.[12]

Against this background of general discontent caused by the imposition of novel American scientific management techniques on to a Scottish workforce it appears that the dispute in the polishing department was the straw that broke the camel's back, at least from the perspective of the workers. However, in order to understand why the camel's back breaks at this particular point in time we need to probe a little deeper and evaluate other factors, including the wider social, economic and political context in which the 1911 strike took place.

Economic factors

In the decades prior to the strike the capitalist economies of Europe and America had seen a significant trend towards the development of increasingly larger firms with a monopolistic orientation towards their markets. Increasingly, the largest of these firms turned towards imperialism – looking beyond their own countries to invest for profit. At the same time they devised detailed strategies to control their workforce and to maximize their productivity. Generally, this involved deskilling, speeding-up production and intensifying workloads – squeezing more out of the wage-for-effort exchange. Such policies could be used to hold down wages and, as in Singer, this seems to have contributed to a general downward trend in earnings.[13]

Spiralling price inflation worked to erode the real value of workers' earnings. A Board of Trade Inquiry published in 1913 estimated that between 1900 and 1912 real wages fell by as much as 10 percent. One commentator noted:

> . . . Necessaries that could be purchased in 1900 for £1 would now cost nearly 23 shillings. And these statistics take no account of reduction in quality that has frequently been the alternative to an increase in apparent price of necessaries in working class districts. Thus we may take it that the wages of the workers have, on the average, been reduced between two shillings and three shillings in the pound. . . .[14]

A Board of Trade survey of 23 articles of food consumed by 'the masses of the people' concluded similarly that between 1896 and 1910 retail prices had risen by some 20 percent. This placed massive pressure on working class budgets because before World War One over 60 per cent of total income was typically absorbed by expenditure on food.[15]

The years 1908 to 1910 were years of intense economic depression on Clydeside, as elsewhere in Britain, with massive rises in unemployment levels (to 60,000 in the winter 1908–9 in Glasgow alone), and a commensurate surge in levels of poverty and hardship.[16] John Rae (brother of the Clydebank suffragette and ILP councillor Jane Rae) recalled vividly this slump, when as a youth he witnessed Clydebank workers transformed into 'beggars on the streets' and when his father was forced to emigrate to New Zealand, where he found employment for several years.[17] Singer production figures indicate clearly that the firm shared in this downturn in trade. There was a marked fall in output at Kilbowie over 1907–10 (production levels being 13 percent lower in 1910, compared to 1907), after a long period of steadily rising output levels. This may well have had a significant bearing on the 1911 strike. Singer had a dominant market position in the business of selling sewing machines, but by no means a monopoly. The sales figures suggest that a profit squeeze, prompted by a more hostile market environment, lay behind managerial labour cost cutting strategies in the immediate pre-strike period.

When the economy improved markedly over 1910–11 Clydeside workers took the opportunity offered to take industrial action in an effort to claw back the erosion of their living standards in the mid-late 1900s and resist further wage cuts and work intensification. This turn of events can be seen clearly within Singer as well as more broadly across a number of industries in Britain. Wage rises were won across a wide spectrum of industrial labour in West Scotland over 1910–11, including carters, dock labourers and seamen. Such successes undoubtably encouraged the Singer workers to resist further wage cuts and to take direct action themselves to protect their living standards.

Changes in organised labour

At the same time, and partly as a consequence of the deteriorating social and industrial condition of workers, there was a growing awareness of the failures of the organised labour movement to protect and advance living standards. Trade unions were weak and frag-mented with over 1,300 separate organisations existing in Britain in the 1900s, recruiting around 2 million workers (1910), about one in every eight workers. Trade unions membership grew only very slowly in the 1890s and 1900s, and the loss of worker bargaining power is indicated clearly by a marked reduction in worker successes during strikes in this period. From the 1890s there was a clear trend amongst the existing unions to accept institutionalised collective bargaining with employers and their associations and to oppose militant direct action – what Tom Mann termed 'the true unionist policy of aggression'. Unions policed such agreements and often refused to support strikes which breached accepted 'procedure'. As the economy improved after the deep 1908–9 depression workers increasingly took unofficial action and often came to resent the restraints on their freedom of action which formal agreements between unions and employers imposed.

Frustrations also deepened with the apparent sterility of the Parliamentary Labour Party, which had achieved an electoral break-through in 1906, polling almost 6 percent of the total vote and obtaining 29 M.P.s. Many workers, perhaps unrealistically, had expected more from the Labour group, which had, above all else, been concerned to show their respectability, and to distance them-selves from their left wing – the revolutionary socialists. Lloyd George revealingly commented in 1912 that the 'socialists' in Parliament were 'the best policemen for the syndicalist'. Nevertheless, as Bob Holton has demonstrated, syndicalist ideas were spreading during the Edwardian period.[18] There was, therefore, a marked tendency over this period for workers to become disillusioned with their recognised, conventional organisations and hence they were much less likely to be guided and controlled effectively by them. In turn, they generated types of struggle and forms of organisation which were more appropriate to their changing environment and to their daily experience and struggles, and developed new ideas and beliefs about the way in which these struggles should be understood and conducted. The strength of this movement was augmented by a shift to relative prosperity in the Clydeside economy over 1910–14.

It is vitally important, we feel, to recognise the wider political, economic and industrial context because in 1911 the Singer concern and the Singer workforce were very much at the 'sharp end' of these historical developments. Firstly, Singer was a massive concentration of imperialist capital – indeed, it was one of the first multinational companies, with plants in Scotland, Germany, Russia and the USA. Secondly, Singer also had a highly developed and scientifically managed division of labour between and within its 41 departments. Thirdly, the only union representation in the plant was for skilled craft workers. Fourthly, at Singer, as throughout the labour unrest as a whole, we find this remarkable and spontaneous outburst of rank and file mili-tancy. However, the evidence also strongly suggests that a significant role in channelling and directing the radical challenge to Singer management over 1910–11 was played by a number of active industrial unionists, linked with two closely related organisations, the Socialist Labour Party and the Industrial Workers of Great Britain.

Industrial unionism at Singer

Pre-war Clydeside, dominated by large-scale heavy industry and a welter of trades and crafts in engineering and shipbuilding, proved to be receptive to the ideas of industrial unionism. In Singer, the presence of the industrial unionists was negligible prior to January 1910, when William Paul, one of the main theorists of the Socialist Labour Party (SLP), began a series of lunch-hour meetings at the Kilbowie plant. Growing attendance and interest in these meetings, together with encouraging sales of SLP literature, prompted the formation of the Sewing Machine Workers Industrial Union Group, with 18 people attending its inaugural meeting. The industrial unionists developed a wide base, including some support from local Independent Labour Party activists, and membership grew steadily to 150 by December 1910. There was a name change to the Sewing Machine Group of the IWGB (SWG-IWGB) and organising activities were cranked up:

> . . . Each department where IWGB members worked had its shop committee to whom every grievance occurring throughout the department was reported. Above this there was the General Committee of the Industrial Union Group comprising representatives of the Industrialists in all the departments. . . .[19]

There was a sound logic behind the form of organisation which was being adopted here because the sophisticated departmentalisation and fine sub-division of the labour process in Singer not only fragmented work, it divided the workers. The system of shop committees within the factory started to break down these barriers to solidarity. The slogan which the IWGB used to encapsulate this drive towards unity was simple but effective: 'An injury to one is an injury to all'. The slogan began to catch on and to show itself concretely in practice in the early months of 1911 when shop committees in a number of departments became embroiled in clashes with management.

The first of these confrontations occured at the beginning of February, 1911, when the foreman in no. 10 department increased the workload and reduced the prices of a 16 strong work squad. The workmen determinedly refused to accept this blatant work intensification and after being informed of this by the shop committee the foreman backed down. George Malcolm, Secretary of the SMG-IWGB, commented that, 'this is something that never happened before. Usually these breaks [piece rate wage cuts] had been taken lying down'.[20] An attempt by the same foreman several weeks later to reintroduce the wage cuts was met with a walk-out of 380 of the 400 strong department. On condition that the workers returned the following morning the wage cuts were once again abandoned.

A further dispute took place in the buffing department where, having already experienced speeding up of work 'almost to breaking point', some 16 men were told that they would receive one shilling more per 100 units as higher quality work was now required. On delivery of this higher quality, the one shilling rise was cut, whilst the same standard was demanded. In response, the shop committee began agitating for support for the squad affected and before long the whole department was expressing a willingness to strike. Faced with this possibility, the foreman reinstated the one shilling rise, declared it permanent and said that he regretted having to deprive them of a 'holiday'.

The scope of the workers' demands broadened. In mid-March the company's disciplinary measures were being challenged. In department 16, a 'policeman' had been the cause of various temporary suspensions being meted out. On Saturday 11 March, however, an indefinite suspension was placed on one worker. The rest of the department decided that no work would be done on the following Monday until this worker was reinstated. As a result, on the Monday morning the foreman gave orders for the man to be told to resume work on the Tuesday and also intimated that there would be no further suspensions resulting from the work of the 'policeman' in question.

Across these disputes we witness a growing militancy, first on the part of the single squad, and then on the part of the whole department. The shop committees refused to compromise and won. Precedents were being set which, in the context of an increasingly militant mood amongst the Singer workforce and across the economy, could only have raised workers' confidence in their own collective power. The Singer workers were effectively challenging and undermining the cost-cutting strategies of their management through collective organisation and action. This was clearly indicated by the snowball growth of the IWGB group through these disputes. From a membership of 18 in January 1910 it had grown to 150 in December 1910,

250 in February 1911, 850 in early March and 1,500 by mid-March 1911. As the group grew, the barriers to unity diminished:

> . . . The workers no longer suffered in individual ignorance of what was happening throughout the works. For the first time they shared their grievances through the medium of intercommunication supplied by the group and the knowledge it provided. . . .[21]

However, the meteoric growth of the IWGB group and the rapid, spontaneous ascendency of the workers concealed an underlying weakness. 90 percent of the 1,500 members of the SMG-IWGB were of less than three months standing, whilst almost 50 percent were of less than three weeks standing. Few would have experience of trade union organisation, never mind of running and sustaining a mass strike. Tom Bell reflected on this in his autobiography: 'We began to get more and more apprehensive of a factory strike. We were not yet ready to exercise firm control and discipline'.[22]

The strike and its aftermath

The dispute which arose quite spontaneously in the polishing department of the Singer plant at Kilbowie, Clydebank, in March 1911, triggered a strike which escalated rapidly to assume major proportions. To recap, the work squad of 15 female polishers was reduced to 12 by Singer's management, and piecerates cut. The workers refused to accept this attempt to intensify their labour and left work on 21 March 1911, being supported by 380 of the 400 workers in the department. The *Glasgow Herald* reported that the initial support for the polishers came from around 2,000 female workers who left work 'in feminine sympathy', whilst the Socialist Labour Party claimed the strike was confined on its first day to four departments with the largest IWGB membership.[23] Whatever, the second day saw the majority of the 11,000 strong workforce strike in sympathy with the polishers.

Worker solidarity characterised the strike for the first fortnight. A strike committee (of 150–190 representatives of the different departments) crystallised the workers' demands: an increase in piece-rate wages for those women affected by work reorganisation in the polishing room; and, significantly, the concession of union recognition and collective bargaining rights. The latter was seen as an essential step to ensure that concessions were permanent and workers should get a say in any future changes. Singer management simply interpreted this as an erosion of their inalienable prerogative to manage. This was the spectre of joint regulation of work in place of management's unilateral control. Elsewhere, across British manufacturing, employers were increasingly conceding collective bargaining rights and moving towards more corporatist approaches to labour relations.[24] Singer management wanted none of this. Rather, they remained committed to the 'American way': individuated bargaining between master and man and coercive anti-unionism. The strike was interpreted as the consequence of sinister outside forces. F.A. Park, the works manager commented: 'we are fighting a battle when we oppose the socialistic teaching which is at the bottom of this business'.[25] The company proceeded to smash the strike by closing the works, threatening widespread victimisation and strongly hinting that production would be transferred to their other plants across Europe and the USA. A postcard plebiscite was then organised by the company, each Singer employee being delivered a ballot card direct to their homes asking them to commit themselves to a return to work if more than half voted to do so. Amidst widespread claims of rigging an independent adjudicator counted 6,527 votes to return to work against 4,025 to continue the strike. That evening the strike committee conceded defeat and the dispute ended with an unconditional return to work on Monday 10 April.[26]

Within a few weeks of the termination of the strike, after a short honeymoon period, systematic victimisation of strike leaders and known members of the IWGB was taking place. Activists had been dismissed before and the Strike Committee must have known this could well be their fate. A series of lay-offs were initiated at weekly intervals, on the pretext of trade slackness. The IWGB claimed that such 'slackness' was 'manufactured' by Singer because the American plant in New Jersey was kept on overtime after the strike ended and was producing far above normal output levels. Moreover, some new workers had been taken on at Singer, Clydebank, after the strike.[27]

Estimates of the number of workers sacked and victimised in the aftermath of the conflict vary from 400 upwards to the 1,000 claimed in *The Socialist* in July 1911 by the Sewing Machine Group of the

IWGB. Those who lost their jobs included the whole of the Strike Committee; those members of the IWGB Shop Committees and General Committee that could be identified; Tom Bell, Arthur McManus, W.J. Douglas, Sam MacDonald and Jane Rae. All five members of the Committee in the shuttle department were sacked, despite three having over ten years service. Similarly, every known member of the Committee in the buffing department (where the activist Jane Rae was located) was dismissed. Other female workers were sacked, as Miss Brown of the National Federation of Women Workers testified at a Clydebank ILP meeting in June 1911.[28] Individuals were picked out and sacked by foremen who had identified workers in their shops at IWGB meetings or who presented workers with copies of IWGB application forms, asking if they endorsed the organisation. Affirmative replies got their cards. Victimisation had occurred at Singers before, but the April/May 1911 sackings, according to *Forward*, constituted 'victimisation on such a scale as we have never before had to face.[29] The issue was taken up nationally by the labour movement and a campaign to boycott Singer Company products was initiated by *Forward*. Complaints were also made in the House of Commons by Labour M.Ps George Barnes and Keir Hardie. Nothing, however, came of this.

Because many of the sacked strikers were also political activists this had a significant impact on radical socialist politics in Clydebank. By 13 May 1911, sackings included 60 ILP members, a number of SDF members and over 20 members of the Socialist Labour Party. The SLP were forced to give up their hall on Second Avenue and both the SLP and SDF branches became 'practically defunct' in Clydebank. As early as July 1911 there was a revealing small notice in the SLP paper, *The Socialist*: 'Would comrades of the Clydebank branch who have removed from the district kindly send their new addresses to the Secretary, R. Fleming, 58 Second Ave, Kilbowie Hill, Clydebank'. In the end of year Clydebank SLP branch report the same R. Fleming admitted:

. . . That the branch has been hard hit by the action of the Singer company would be folly to deny. . . . At the time of the strike we had 27 members, all, with the exception of five, employed in the Singer factory. They have been practically all cleared out and scattered almost all over the world. Some are still resident in the district, although they travel to various places to dispose of their labour power. When the reaction set in, as was inevitable after such an event as the Singer strike, some of our members lapsed into a sort of apathy. . . .[30]

The Glasgow SLP sent help in an attempt to revive the branch. Clark and Muir visited members still resident in Clydebank; special meetings were called; education classes restarted. All to no avail. The December 1911 Clydebank SLP branch report was the last to appear in *The Socialist* though it was not until February 1913 that the Clydebank SLP disappeared from the monthly published branch directory in the SLP journal.

Moreover, there is evidence to suggest that many other local firms, including John Brown and the Argyle Motor Works, refused to take any discharged Singers' workers on in 1911. This kind of procedure was customary amongst the more anti-unionist and unscrupulous capitalists and commonly practiced by members of the Engineering Employers' Federation and the Mineowners' associations.[31] Therefore, workers were forced not only out of Singer but also often out of the district seeking alternative employment. Bill Lang recalled how an acquaintance, MacKenzie (later Provost of Clydebank), became a baker and how a number of others who were victimised got into Co-operative Insurance.[32] Lack of data prevents us from estimating just how many of those victimised found themselves unemployed for a short or long spell, and, thus deprived of their livelihood, or from evaluating what problems this created for dependent families. However, over 1911–12 the economy was extremely buoyant and demand for labour was high. This probably helped the majority of those sacked by Singer to successfully obtain work elsewhere on the Clyde.

This forced dispersal of somewhere between 400 and 1,000 labour activists from the Singer corporation across the Clyde in the Spring and Summer of 1911 is an event of considerable importance in Clydeside industrial politics. The Glasgow Marxist Harry McShane testified in an oral interview in the mid-1960s that as a result of the victimisation after the Singer strike active industrial unionists cropped up all over the Clyde in different engineering shops.[33] Tom Bell (one of the Singer strikers) also asserted in his autobiography that ex-Singer workers played an important role in radical politics on the Clyde during the First World War: 'The war was to reveal in the Clyde Workers

Committee movement, shop stewards in factory after factory who had once been in Singer's'.[34]

Individuals have proven difficult, however, to identify, because we neither have a list of Singer strikers (no company records) nor those sacked (we only know the names of a handful), or a list of CWC members. Arthur McManus, however, provides a prominent example. McManus was an SLPer and one of the strike leaders at Singer in March–April 1911. After being sacked he worked at Barr and Strouds, the Albion Motor Works and the massive Weir engineering plant in Cathcart, building up a following for industrial unionism in each plant.[35] Significantly, these works were amongst the most militant during the First World War. McManus became convenor of shop stewards at Weir and a prominent leader of the CWC, being singled out with eight other CWC leaders for deportation from Glasgow in 1916. Other Singer workers involved in the 1911 strike were radicalised by their experience, including Fanny Abbott and Jane Rae, both of whom became much more active in the labour movement after the strike.[36]

Moreover, apart from the question of individuals, there was also an organic link between the Singer confrontation of 1911 and the CWC militancy. The CWC was in essence a federal industrial union, constituted of representatives of all firms involved in munition manufacture, irrespective of specific occupation or craft. It thus replicated the structures promulgated by the IWGB and initiated in practice in Singer in the shop committees and the elected Strike Committee. The militant use of the strike weapon, of direct action, by the CWC also owed much to the strategies previously formulated by the revolutionary industrial unionists on the Clyde – most notably, though not solely, in Singer – in the decade preceding World War One. The concept of breaking down craft sectionalism, of the sympathy strike – 'an injury to one is an injury to all' – evident in Singer in 1911, clearly set a precedent for the subsequent period of industrial militancy on Clydeside which continued through the war period and the immediate post-war years into the 1920s.

So, Singer succeeded in rooting out industrial militants from its workforce. This had a salutory effect. Trade unionism virtually collapsed amongst the majority of unskilled and semi-skilled men and women in Singer after the strike and only revived briefly during the

First World War, when the Workers' Union obtained a tenuous foothold. Such gains did not, however, survive the inter-war years of economic depression and mass unemployment on the Clyde. Ian MacDougall has shown how fifteen years after the 1911 confrontation Singer management repeated their brutal, coercive anti-unionist strategy by sacking and victimising numbers of Singer workers who participated in the General Strike of 1926.[37] The official explanation of these dismissals was 'plant reorganisation'. Acceptance and recognition of trade unionism by Singer management at Clydebank came only in the aftermath of World War Two.

Singer management had attempted to radically increase workloads and speed up productivity by introducing undiluted Taylorite American scientific management techniques. The attempt to graft such alien work methods on to a Scottish workforce had resulted in a massive confrontation, a well organised strike and over 4,000 workers registering their dissent to managerial policy in the plebiscite. Management was left with the problem of regaining control and discipline over its workforce and reproducing mass consent to the factory work regime. Part of the solution was coercive: weed out militant elements and remove forcibly the 'socialist cancer' from the shop floor. However, management was astute enough to realise that the use of the stick needed to be counterbalanced with the carrot.

Over the decade following 1911, the policy of Singer management became much more explicitly welfarist, with the firm establishing a plethora of institutionalised 'paternalist' schemes, including pensions schemes, sports clubs and facilities; sewing, music, elocution, dancing, arts and crafts classes; bands; drama groups; literary societies and even a 'Physical Culture Club'. Indeed, Singer after World War One gained a wide reputation for its sports and recreation facilities with the new Works Manager – the 1911 protagonist Hugh MacFarlane – especially keen to promote such activities. We would interpret such policies not as an expression of altruistic benevolence but rather as an alternative method of exerting social control over the workforce. This was an implicit attempt to induce loyalty to the firm and acquiescence to management, to counterbalance alienating conditions at the point of production and win ideological consent to modern capitalism. The SLP was aware of this general tendency and T.S. Mercer commented viciously on 'The Generous Employer' thus:

... Our contact with industrial strife has taught us that the more cunning of our masters today realise that a suavity of manner towards their workers, a pretended desire for their welfare and happiness, spurious offers to help us and reform us; that these and other proffers of counterfeit friendship from them to us, enable them to exploit us the more readily, blinds us to the class struggle, makes us meek and mild and contented till we become like well trained cows, running of our own accord to the milking shed and patiently waiting while our owners milk us, whereas an arrogant, bullying, intimidating master himself applies the match that starts the flame of revolt among the workers. . . .[38]

This is not to suggest that the weeding out process combined with a more welfarist strategy was entirely successful in stabilising industrial relations in Singer. Singer workers were involved, for example, in the Clydeside 40 hours strike, Jan–Feb 1919.[39] There was also considerable support within Singer for the General Strike in 1926. Nevertheless, what is significant is that these disputes in 1919 and 1926 were general, rather than specific to Singer. There is no evidence of any further major industrial relations confrontations emerging or of trade unionism gaining a more permanent foothold within Singer for more than thirty years after the 1911 strike. Margaret Ewing, a Singer worker who was sacked for smoking on the job, recalled that in the late 1930s 'the union' in Singer 'was a dirty word'.[40] It appears that the combination of sackings and victimisation of union and political activists, with a longer-term commitment to institutionalised welfarism by Singer management successfully maintained capitalist hegemony and control in the company. While militant working class action became more generalised throughout the Clydeside area during the First World War and the immediate post-war years, at Singer production was unaffected and industrial relations remained noticeably quiet. Singer management, it seems, had successfully excised what they might have seen as a malignant growth in their own factory, but at the cost of germinating and diffusing a broader and more dangerous growth throughout Clydeside more generally.

Conclusion

The strike at Singer in March–April 1911 represented a crisis for social relations within this particular corporation. Apparently consensual and deferential relationships that had previously kept the workforce quiescent were fractured by the alienating process of work intensification. This incubated deep resentments amongst the Singer workforce and mirrored what was happening across a number of industries in the late nineteenth and early twentieth centuries. What seems to have been particular to the Singer dispute, however, was the employers' experimentation with more impersonal 'scientific' modes of labour management, based upon the systematic time-study of the labour process. So many of the most advanced tendencies of capitalism were concentrated at the Kilbowie site – a large concentration of anti-trade unionist, multi-national capital, with a 'scientifically' managed labour process and with the most advanced technology.[41] Such developments were rare in Scotland and the UK before 1914.[42] The outcome was that worker resistance was very heavily suppressed and management successfully imposed their work regime in 1911.

Thus, it is important to be aware of the specificities of the Singer case, and so of the limits of applicability of the findings from a study of it. Here it is the relatively advanced nature of the Singer company which is most important. Capital, in Scotland, as elsewhere, was no monolithic entity. There was no homogeneous response to the challenge of labour, and prior to the First World War employers pursued a range of strategies.[43] While Scottish employers in general appear to have been very hostile to trade unions and to the idea of collective bargaining, few possessed the power of the multinational Singer corporation (notably its ability to transfer production to other locations) to ride roughshod over workers rights and aspirations. Perhaps more appropriate parallels can be found in the post-1945 foriegn-owned multinationals in electronics, oil and commercial shipbuilding in Scotland. Thus, at one level the confrontation at Singer in 1911 exemplifies the broader industrial relations crisis of 1910–14, but at another it reflected the future pattern of industrial relations within an economy increasingly dominated by faceless, profit-maximising, foreign-owned multinational corporations.

What merits reiteration, in conclusion, is that it was the spontaneous action of female operatives which initiated the strike. Until fairly recently, the role of women in industrial struggles has tended to be ignored or marginalised. Contrary to male labourist myths, the women workers in the 1911 Singer confrontation were neither weak, unreliable nor peripheral to working class struggle. Indeed, women played a critical and active role throughout the stoppage and were amongst those sacked and victimised in the aftermath of the strike. In Scotland, as the recent work of Eleanor Gordon has shown, female workers played an integral role in pre-war strikes and won a series of important victories.[44] This leads to another point: the confrontation itself was characterised by remarkable solidarity of the workforce – divisions based on occupation, skill, gender, religion and locality being submerged during the strike. The theory and practice of the industrial unionists seems to have played a quite significant role here. Together with the Socialist Labour Party they provided both the ideological and practical leadership necessary to harness the new assertiveness of the workforce to the task of building solidarity and sustaining a coherant challenge to the prerogative of management. They were also significant in contributing to the organisation and direction of the escalating struggle. Their sigificance is clearly demonstrated by the fact that their slogan, 'An injury to one is an injury to all' came to encapsulate the essence of the strikers most basic demand – collective bargaining rights.

Finally, we have argued that the strike at Singer in 1911 had important ramifications for the germination of class consciousness across Clydeside. In exporting their problem by the forced sacking and victimisation of hundreds of labour activists Singer successfully cleared their own stable. However, in so doing they cast forth a raft of committed and hardened activists who generalised their ideas and experiences of the organisation of militant rank-and-file trade union-ism far and wide within the metal working factories of Clydeside. Here there exists both tangible and organic links between the pre-war labour unrest and the classic era of 'Red Clydeside' during the First World War and immediate post-war years. In all likelihood a key formative factor in the approach of these activists to the authoritarianism of the state and capital during wartime would have been their experience of the inordinate authoritarianism of their employer in the pre-war era.[45]

NOTES

1. The research collective involved in this project comprised the following: I. Ballantyne; C. Collins; L. Forster; H. Maguiness; A. McIvor; H. Savage; L. Tuach.

2. For more detail on this strike see Glasgow Labour History Workshop, *The Singer Strike, Clydebank, 1911* (1989), pp. 1–85. Available from Clydebank District Library.

3. Bell, T., *Pioneering Days* (1941).

4. See Littler, C. R., *The Development of the Labour Process* (1982); Nelson, D., *Managers and Workers: Origins of the New Factory System in the United States, 1880–1920* (1975).

5. See Taylor, F.W., *Principles of Scientific Management* (1911). Braverman, H., *Labor and Monopoly Capital* (1974) provides the classic exposition of the degradation of work thesis. This has subsequently been much criticised for its oversimplicity.

6. *Forward*, 1 April, 1911. One Singer worker informed Forward that conditions in the factory had become so intolerable that 'it was either strike or suicide'.

7. *Justice*, 1 April 1911.

8. *Glasgow Herald*, 25 Mar 1911.

9. *Glasgow Herald*, 25 Mar 1911.

10. The following section is based on an oral interview with Bill Lang, 29 January 1988.

11. Interview, Bill Lang, 29 January 1988.

12. See the GLHW interviews with these respondents, archived in the local history department, Clydebank District Library.

13. There is much indirect evidence of this pressure upon wage rates at Singer in the 1900s. However, unfortunately we have been unable to locate any surviving company wage books to corroborate this.

14. *The Industrialist*, 1 Oct 1911.

15. *Justice*, 18 Feb, 1911.

16. See Treble, J.H., 'Unemployment in Glasgow, 1903–1910: Anatomy of a Crisis', *Scottish Labour History Society Journal*, no. 25, 1990, pp. 8–39.

17. Oral interview with John Rae, 13 May 1988.

18. Holton, B., *British Syndicalism*, 1900–1914 (1973).

19. *The Socialist*, July 1911.

20. *The Socialist*, April 1911.

21. *The Socialist*, July 1911.

22. Bell, *Pioneering Days*.

23. *Glasgow Herald*, 24 March 1911.

24. See Garside, W.R. and Gospel, H.F., 'Employers and Managers', in Wrigley C.J.(ed), *A History of British Industrial Relations, 1875–1914* (1982); McIvor, A.J., *Organised Capital* (1996).

25. *Glasgow Herald*, 4 April 1911.

26. *Glasgow Herald*, 6 and 7 April 1911.

27. David Bennett is one example, brought in to help supervise work in the needleflat (for details, see interview transcript and tape, deposited at the Clydebank District Library).)

28. *Clydebank and Renfrew Press*, 16 June 1911.

29. *Forward*, 13 May 1911.

30. *The Socialist*, Dec 1911.

31. See McIvor, A. and Paterson, H., 'Combating the Left', in Duncan, R. and McIvor, A. (eds), *Militant Workers*, (Edinburgh, 1992).

32. Bill Lang, oral interview (see above).

33. Cited in Vernon, H.R., 'The Socialist Labour Party and the Working Class Movement on the Clyde, 1903–21' (unpublished M.Phil thesis, Leeds University), p. 90.

34. Bell, *Pioneering Days*.

35. Vernon, *The Socialist Labour Party*, p. 128.

36. See Glasgow Labour History Workshop, *Singer Strike*, appendices, pp. 67–9; 79–81.

37. MacDougall, I., 'Some Aspects of the 1926 General Strike in Scotland', in MacDougall, I. (ed), *Essays in Scottish Labour History* (1978).

38. *The Socialist*, July 1912.

39. Area Report prepared for the Ministry of Munitions on 1 February 1919 [Public Record Office, London, File MUN 5/18]. We are grateful to John Foster for providing us with this reference].

40. Oral interview with M. Ewing, archived in the local history department, Clydebank District Library.

41. The epitome of developments so brilliantly caricatured in the Charlie Chaplin film, *Modern Times*, made in 1936.

42. Taylorite management ideology diffused quite significantly, however, during the interwar depression, aided by the collapse in trade union power as a consequence of mass unemployment. See Littler, *Development of the Labour Process*.

43. See Melling, J., 'Scottish Industrialists and the Changing Character of Class Relations in the Clyde Region, c1880–1918', in Dickson, T.(ed), *Capital and Class in Scotland*, (Edinburgh, 1982).

44. Gordon, E., *Women and the Labour Movement in Scotland, 1850–1914* (1991).

45. See chapter three by R. Devlin for some quantitative substantiation of employer hostility and authoritarianism in responding to strikes in pre-war Clydeside.

CHAPTER 10

Glasgow's Municipal Workers and Industrial Strife

Irene Maver

> ... some tramway managers were blamed for being a little too forceful on occasions. But how could they be otherwise? They had to be a little forceful. They had more critics than any of the other departments of the Corporation service. ...
>
> *James Dalrymple, Glasgow Corporation Tramways Manager, commenting on the 1911 tramways' strike.*[1]

For all that the public sector has been one of the few significant growth areas of Scottish trade unionism since the 1980s, its development during the early decades of the century has tended to be overshadowed by the dominance of groups in the industrial sphere, such as the miners, engineers and shipyard workers. This is understandable, given the indubitably industrial orientation of the West of Scotland economy; however, it is also puzzling, given that during the 1900s Glasgow boasted one of the most impressive municipal infrastructures in the United Kingdom, employing an establishment of some 15,000, a sizeable proportion of which was trade union organised. The conundrum can partly be explained by the unique bargaining position of municipal trade unions, which operated in an environment where wages were generally higher and more regular, and conditions considered to be model compared with private enterprise. Trade-union organisation – and the confrontationist approach to industrial relations – sat uneasily with the paternalism which had long been identified with Glasgow's city fathers; moreover, the civic tradition of the 'common good' was intended to bind the community, not fragment it. Leaders of organisations like the Municipal Employees' Association thus had to tread warily when it came to pursuing their members' interests, because of the moral leverage that town councillors could exert as duly elected representatives of the community.

Yet it should be stressed that while the circumstances of the workforce may have been qualitatively different from those in the industrial sector, there could still be a shared sense of grievance, not least about controversial issues revolving around the impact of new technology, changing work practices, and the role and influence of management. All of these were factors which contributed to the brief but bitter Glasgow tramways' strike of August 1911, which was deemed by contemporaries to be a shocking deviation from the hitherto harmonious labour relations prevailing on the Corporation. 'Strikes are in the air at present; they get infectious. That must be the reason for this outbreak', suggested one Glasgow journal, attempting – by means of the miasmic theory – to rationalise why the tramwaymen had become transformed into aggressive militants, emulating the style and tactics of London lightermen or Liverpool dockers.[2] The dogged stance of the Tramways Manager in refusing to capitulate to the workers' demands only reinforced perceptions that the heady mood of the moment had prompted such uncharacteristic behaviour.

However, this chapter will show that the municipal arena was much more complex than the conventional image suggested. The dispute was by no means the first example of direct action to be taken by a group of Corporation workers, and far from being spontaneous, the flashpoint of 1911 had been building up over months, if not years. The fact that it occurred in the midst of other manifestations of 'the great unrest' obscured these longer-term influences, and helped to absolve Glasgow Corporation from accusations that there was a less rosy side to the operation of its services than the municipal public relations machine liked to depict.

Trade unionism and Glasgow's municipal workforce

The expansion of municipal functions during the course of the nineteenth century inevitably required the recruitment of a substantial workforce in Glasgow, initially to provide for a range of environmental services (such as cleansing and lighting), latterly to ensure the smooth functioning of large-scale utilities (such as water and gas). The acquisition of prestigious undertakings, beginning with the Loch Katrine water supply in 1855, represented a symbol of civic purposefulness in a city notorious for its blighting social problems, and no expense was spared to make them a success. Yet despite their much-publicised pronouncements about the civic well-being, there was a strong streak of entrepreneurial canniness motivating the actions of town councillors. Prior to 1914 the Corporation was overwhelmingly dominated by businessmen, many of whom had built up fortunes in areas such as textiles, coal and shipping, and who readily understood the implications of cheap water and power supplies to Glasgow's economic success.[3] They believed that municipalisation promoted better business by providing the necessary financial underpinning to render services more efficient and cost-effective, and remove the unpredictable element of market-forces. Councillors were thus highly protective of their new utilities, ensuring a monopoly position by using the substantial assets of the Corporation to buy out rivals in the private sector, and insisting on rigorous standards of excellence, especially among the growing corps of workers who serviced all this.

While municipal powers were steadily consolidated from the 1850s, the last decade of the century proved to be one of the most crucial for the organisational development of Glasgow Corporation. In 1891 the addition of outlying suburban districts almost doubled the territory of the city, compelling the civic leadership to radically reappraise administrative arrangements. This, in turn, entailed a dramatic increase in staff numbers and responsibilities, with personnel matters becoming increasingly important for the efficient running of the Corporation. For example, a comprehensive superannuation scheme was first considered in 1893, not least to get rid of the more geriatric chief officials.[4] By force of circumstances, councillors were adopting a much more professional approach to management, and it was from this era that the civic bureaucracy began to burgeon. And, of course, the acquisition of the municipal electricity supply (in 1893) and tramways' system (in 1894) prompted a further reassessment of manpower resources, especially as the Glasgow Tramways and Omnibus Company refused to hand over its assets, horses or personnel to the Corporation, which had to start a wholly new service virtually from scratch.

The flux and change which characterised Glasgow Corporation during the 1890s meant that there was ambiguity in the civic leadership's attitude towards its growing workforce. One the one hand, councillors seemed anxious to cultivate amicable relations, but they were intent, also, to ensure the efficient operation of the municipal machine. The debate over the acquisition of the tramways graphically brought this out, with councillors blending moral and material interests in their single-minded quest to take over the system. Accordingly, while most did adhere to a genuine ideological belief in a municipally-owned transport service, the prospect of electric traction – and the need to maintain absolute control over the new power resource – was also a major determining factor. Councillors brooked no threat to their much-vaunted gas supply, and the surest means of self-protection was simply to buy out any prospective rival. Ironically, the appeal of technological innovation was not the main concern of councillors when they committed the Corporation to electricity, although what-ever the motivations, its advent was bound to make a substantial difference to work practices in areas like the tramways. However, the resistance of the private Tramways Company to the Corporation's predatory tendencies meant that councillors had to work harder to win round public support. As past masters in the art of constructing their own self-image, they consequently recruited allies to promote the cause of municipalisation – including the trade-union movement, which was growing in prestige and influence via the organisational activities of Glasgow Trades' Council.

The objectives of the Corporation and Trades' Council had not always coincided in seeking the demise of the private Company; economic interests had to a large extent guided the actions of councillors, while the Trades' Council was concerned about building a union base among the workforce. Yet there was a mutual identity of interests in seeing the back of the Company, which had become notorious for its lack of efficiency in servicing the outlying areas of Glasgow (much to the disdain of middle-class residents in the suburbs), and for the less than adequate working conditions for staff.[5] Against this dual onslaught, the Company was placed in an invidious position. The workers were quick to take advantage of their employers' insecurity and began to organise, with the help of Robert Chisholm Robertson, Secretary to the Forth and Clyde Valley Miners' Association, and miners' representative to Glasgow Trades' Council. In September 1889 a huge rally in favour of the workers' claims was held on Glasgow Green, and the *Glasgow Herald* enthusiastically reported that, 'for once Trades Unionism seems to have been altruistic'.[6] By the time the Corporation had formally approved its policy of municipalisation in 1891, the Trades' Council had already laid much of the groundwork for establishing a bargaining machinery in the new Tramways Department. As a result, Corporation representatives were scarcely in a position to turn against their erstwhile allies, and conceded conditions considerably in advance of the former system, including the regulation of working hours to ten a day, and a flat-rate 24s weekly wage.[7]

The favourable conditions for trade-union organisation were further boosted in 1896, when nine representatives – broadly designated as 'Labour' – were returned to the Corporation. This success had been stimulated by the far more equitable electoral conditions created by boundary expansion, as there had been no meaningful ward restructuring in Glasgow for fifty years. Taking their lead from the success of the London County Council Progressive programme, where socialists, Liberals and even some Unionists were attempting to create a model for industrial relations, Glasgow's new Labour councillors immediately committed themselves to policies for improving working conditions generally among the municipal workforce. This strategy included a campaign for fair contracts (to ensure that companies which tendered for Corporation work paid trade union rates); a minimum weekly wage of 21s for municipal employees, and a maximum working week of 48 hours.[8] Like their London counterparts, the Glaswegians could rely on support from outwith immediate Labour circles, with radically-inclined Liberal councillors particularly anxious that Corporation wages and conditions should set a precedent for workers in the private sector, and thus improve standards all round. Civic excellence therefore meant more than just the quality of services to ratepayers; it also ensured that the benefits of such services would be shared by the municipal workforce, as the direct employees of the community.

As the logical extension of this, Labour councillors also began to take an interest in municipal trade unionism. While membership had been growing in individual departments like the Tramways, there had been no meaningful co-ordinating movement within the Corporation as a whole, so that organisation remained localised and fragmented. There was an historic explanation for this, because of the piecemeal growth of the Corporation itself over the century. The limited legal remit of Scottish royal burghs like Glasgow had meant that utilities like gas and water initially operated as trusts on behalf of the Corporation, and were not completely integrated into the municipal infrastructure until 1895. Conditions thus varied substantially between the new departments, as did the relative strength of the collective bargaining machinery; a state of affairs which councillors and officials were reluctant to standardise, in the belief that power should be concentrated in smaller and more manageable units. The departmental focus also allowed officials considerable personal influence, given the freedom of action that councillors were prepared to delegate to them. From the trade-union perspective, this was construed as a divide and rule strategy, and towards the end of the 1890s efforts began to be made within the labour movement to help remedy the situation.

The catalyst was the mounting discontent among Gas Department employees over job security and the proliferation of short-term contracts, due to the cyclical nature of gas provision for heating and lighting. This in turn prompted a sustained effort by the Gas Workers' and General Labourers' Union of Great Britain and Ireland to establish a comprehensive base within Glasgow Corporation during 1899. The union was, of course, inextricably associated with Will Thorne, Eleanor Marx and the epic struggles for the Eight-Hour Day some ten years previously, and from this fiery baptism it had gone on to consolidate a reputation for militancy. Although its base remained firmly fixed in London, substantial membership gains began to be made beyond the metropolitan orbit, particularly during the relatively buoyant economic climate of the late 1890s. The union's high public profile was further boosted in 1898, when the borough of West Ham – in Greater London – became the United Kingdom's first Labour-controlled local authority.[9] Will Thorne, as Secretary to the Gas Workers' Union, was able to take a good deal of credit for the breakthrough, which reflected years of solid effort to promote the principle of labour representation on elected bodies.

Significantly, a Scottish District of the union was established in 1899 as part of a recruitment drive north of the border. This was the context which prompted the bid for recognition by Glasgow Corporation, and immediately compounded fears – vocally articulated in the press – that there was a sinister political subtext to the sudden flurry of activity. The dual position of Joseph Burgess as the union's acting District Secretary as well as Secretary to the city's Independent Labour Party only served to substantiate the questionable political connection.[10] The pro-Unionist *Glasgow Herald* was adamant that the city fathers should have no truck with an organisation, 'like this Union, whose principles are Socialistic and whose avowed objective is Collectivism'.[11] Notwithstanding the efforts of Labour representatives, the *Glasgow Herald's* remarks reflected the majority opinion on the Corporation. During a heated debate in January 1900, councillors spoke out against formal recognition of the Gas Workers' Union, and castigated Joseph Burgess as a professional agitator.[12] Not, it was added, that the Corporation would refuse to listen to the legitimate grievances of the workforce; however, the Gas Workers' Union was not the kind of organisation it was prepared to do business with.

The generally negative response of councillors to the gas workers' claims contrasted starkly with their espousal of the tramwaymen's cause during the early 1890s, and although expediency clearly had much to do with this turnaround, there were other factors too. Most crucially, the intrusion of the Labour Party into the municipal domain had complicated the political profile of the Corporation, and posed a challenge to the long-standing Liberal hegemony in municipal affairs. Indeed, by 1900 Liberalism was under assault from the right as well as left, with Unionism especially on the offensive, in keeping with the patriotic spirit of the South African War. While Labour representation was not numerically strong at the time, with a high point of eleven out of seventy-five elected representatives in 1899, the Party was nevertheless able to make a propaganda impact by promoting issues like fair contracts and housing reform; areas which the Liberals had to treat gingerly, for fear of raising the rates' bogey and alienating middle-class support.

All this had the effect of undermining the previous Liberal reputation for progressiveness, and placed its leaders in even more of a quandary as to precisely where the Party stood in the political spectrum. The debate over municipal trade unionism reflected this dilemma. There can be no doubt that the objectives of the Gas Workers' Union, with their conscious class orientation, were profoundly distasteful to Liberal-inclined representatives on Glasgow Corporation, whose own ideology repudiated class polarisation and identified with the harmoniously integrated society. There was also a very tangible political threat from the union, because of its key role in securing West Ham for

Labour in 1898. As far as Glasgow was concerned, therefore, the tramway workers represented a much safer kind of trade unionism, which was locally organised and had no grand claims to serve in the forefront of the class struggle. If trade union recognition was to be a fact of life on Glasgow Corporation – and it was desirable for Liberal credibility that this should be so – then the latter option was infinitely preferable to the civic leadership.

Even so, it did not need the Gas Workers' Union to encourage militancy among the municipal workforce when circumstances demanded direct action. In February 1902, over 1,200 members of the Cleansing Department went on strike for higher wages, after accusations that the Corporation was unduly prolonging discussions over their claim.[13] The strike immediately posed awkward public health problems, because of a smallpox outbreak in the city's East End, and local union representatives consciously used this as a bargaining lever against the employers. The cleansing workers were certainly in no mood to compromise, because of what they perceived as their particularly lowly municipal status and onerous responsibilities, which included night work, in order that public thoroughfares could be swept more easily when there was no busy traffic. Moreover, the stereotypical Glasgow 'scavenger' was deemed to be Irish, (at least, according to the jokes belaboured in *The Bailie*, a satirical weekly journal), so there was an added stigma attached to the job.[14] The solidarity of the workers, who steadfastly resolved not to move 'a shovel or brush' until their grievances were settled, prompted Cleansing Superintendent Donald McColl to advertise extensively for men to replace the strikers, thus precipitating what the *Glasgow Herald* described as 'disorderly street scenes', involving skirmishes with the police.[15] No serious damage was done, but the ugly turn of events, together with the rapidly deriorating fabric of the streets, brought together Trades' Council and Corporation representatives, who – after prolonged discussion – came to an agreement that was ultimately accepted by the workforce.

It was significant that the Cleansing Committee Convener at the time happened to be John Battersby, who had deep roots in trade unionism, having served as Secretary to the Scottish Typographical Association as well as President of Glasgow Trades' Council. Described by one contemporary publication as 'a Radical of the good old type', Battersby often made common cause with Labour councillors, and was deeply committed to progressing labour movement issues on the Corporation.[16] Yet he was also a prominent (if not uncritical) Liberal, and was personally and politically close to the then Lord Provost, Samuel Chisholm. The two seem to have acted quickly to nip the strike in the bud. Chisholm had already alienated an assortment of influential groups in the city because of controversial plans for housing and temperance reform, and some of his opponents were hoping to use the cleansing strike as a means of attacking supposed Liberal maladministration.[17] Intriguingly, too, Trades' Council delegates did not manifest wholehearted support for the workers' cause. Some considered the action to have been too precipitant, and one went so far as to accuse the men of selfishness, claiming that, 'Corporation employees as a class were not willing to give anything'.[18] Such pronouncements reflected continuing resentment over the perceived favoured status of public servants, who were deemed to be in a prime position to obtain the fruits of municipalisation. This related, above all, to more secure and regular employment compared with the rest of the labour force, which had proved to be an alienating factor in 1899 and 1900 during the abortive gas workers' dispute and would provoke a similar response in 1911 when the tramwaymen went on strike. Clearly, municipal workers were confronted with enormous difficulties in taking action to improve their conditions, given the added pressures that could be evoked from within the labour movement itself.

The tramways and the 'Model Municipality'

Despite the tensions which had arisen in the Gas and Cleansing Departments, plus mounting complaints from ratepayers about levels of public expenditure, Glasgow Corporation continued to project the image of benevolent civic government into the 1900s. 'We are even told that in America she is praised as the best managed 'municipal concern' on earth', enthused one contemporary publication, boldly adding that, 'the praise being no more that due brings no blushes to our cheeks'.[19] Glasgow's Tramways Department was perceived as the great jewel in this municipal crown, symbolising what was best in civic enterprise by combining efficiency with public service. Despite inauspicious beginnings in 1894, with virtually no property, plant or horses, the accounts stood at over £83,000 in credit after the first financial year, and were to go on to realise far larger surpluses.[20] The tramcars themselves represented the physical embodiment of ultra-efficiency; unsightly advertisements were banned, drivers were sprucely-uniformed, horses were well-groomed and shod. The electrification of the system by the summer of 1901 further demonstrated the civic commitment to state-of-the-art technology and cost-effectiveness, with overheads for electric traction being calculated at 2.35 pence per car mile less and the returns 2.57 pence greater than for horse haulage.[21]

Over time, the rapid success of Glasgow's tramways attracted admiring responses from all over the world. Commentators from the United States were particularly impressed, perceiving the Scottish city's example as one which combined efficiency and order according to sound business principles, albeit in the public rather than the private sector. In some quarters there was an almost millennarian passion for Glasgow's apparent ability to blend 'civic moral uplift with practical improvements', contrasting sharply with the tainted image of American municipal politics, which dated from the days of the notorious New York 'Boss' Tweed and his Tammany Hall acolytes.[22] To be sure, there were some jaundiced assessments of Glasgow Corporation, which – according to one anti-municipalist – was using the tramways, 'only for the purpose of putting money into the city treasury and for the purpose of "magnifying the office" of the municipal politician'.[23] Nevertheless, in 1905 the newly-elected mayor of Chicago went so far as to invite James Dalrymple, Glasgow's Tramways Manager, to come over on a consultancy basis to advise on the inauguration of a municipal service for the city. As a result of the visit, Glasgow featured prominently in the press throughout North America, and Dalrymple consolidated his reputation for being the global expert on tramway undertakings.

The seeming paradox of American support for municipal control can be explained by stressing that on both sides of the Atlantic during the 1900s, collectivist ideas and entrepreneurial activity were not necessarily regarded as incompatible. Lord Rosebery – the former Liberal Prime Minister, who had strong Glasgow connections – believed that government should be organised on a strict 'business footing', and that successful businessmen made the best politicians because they knew how to handle money and achieve maximum efficiency.[24] What applied in industry and commerce could equally apply to the state and, at a lesser level, the municipality. Rosebery's sentiments echoed the previously declared views of Glasgow Corporation that, 'the qualities which make a good Town Councillor are simply those which belong to the successful business man'.[25] The business dimension was also emphasised by F.C. Howe, an American who tried to reassure sceptical compatriots that municipalisation was not insidious form of socialism:

> . . . in its present stage of development municipal ownership is inspired by no ideal of a changed social order, and the movement is likely to continue to be one for improved service, for business thrift, for the relief of taxpayers from the burden of taxation and for increased revenue in the community. . . .[26]

In this context, it is revealing that James Dalrymple commented towards the end of his long career as Glasgow's Tramways Manager that there had been nothing wrong with his style of management, despite recurring criticisms that he had run the Department as if it were his own business enterprise.[27] An accountant to trade, Dalrymple represented the new breed of professional who had come to proliferate in the public service by the turn of the nineteenth century. He had risen quickly through the ranks of the Corporation, which he had joined as a teenager, and served in the Tramways Department from its inception. At age forty-four, he was still relatively young when he was appointed Manager in 1904, and his energy and ambition – together with a Scotch terrier sense of tenacity – soon made him one of Glasgow's best known municipal figures. (His imposing, bewhiskered features became something of a personal trademark.) Dalrymple's ideas of management were derived to a large extent from the American and German experience, where permanent paid officials were much more influential than their equivalents in the United Kingdom. As Dalrymple perceived it, municipal managers represented a stabilising factor in city government, and were thus aloof from the squalid squabbling of party politics. He made it a virtue never to exercise his vote in Corporation elections, as that would compromise his position as a public servant. He believed that the workforce should exercise similar restraint, and although he tolerated municipal trade unionism, he considered it to be unnecessary for the tramwaymen, as the city itself represented 'the best union they can have'.[28]

For all his claims of political neutrality, Dalrymple's background did demonstrate a certain ideological perspective which influenced his style of management. He made no secret of his 'interest in religious and temperance movements', and served as an elder in the United Free Church.[29] This decidedly moral outlook was shared with a number of leading town councillors, whose evangelical commitment had long underpinned Glasgow's policies of civic improvement. Dalrymple was especially devoted to the Volunteer Force, later the Territorial Army; an activity which represented the military dimension to public service, and was – as the movement's historian has put it – 'stamped with the seals of patriotism and respectibility'.[30]

And, certainly, military precision had come to characterise Dalrymple's running of the Tramways Department. It was an all-male preserve, where applicants had to undergo a rigorous medical examination before they could be taken on. The main areas for recruitment were rural districts beyond the city limits, presumably because Glaswegians were not considered to be robust enough for tramways' work. The bulk of employees were young, with ages ranging from the early twenties to mid-thirties. The smart green uniforms provided *gratis* to all motormen and conductors were, of course, a very visible symbol of the kind of discipline exercised within the Tramways Department. On the other hand, this was perceived as part of the generous benefits attached to the job, which also included a superannuation scheme (to be fully implemented from 1911), and an in-house Friendly Society, to provide against accident and sickness.[31]

The material inducements, together with the carefully controlled working environment, were intended to instil a sense of corporate belonging among the employees and ensure quality of service. The Tramways Department was a model of the kind of 'national efficiency' that Lord Rosebery and like-minded politicians were articulating at the time, in their quest to boost the imperial status of the United Kingdom, and fend off industrial and military rivals, most notably Germany. Dalrymple's obsession with the health and physical appearance of the workforce illustrated such contemporary concerns, although there was also a streak of old-fashioned paternalism in his approach to municipal management. Yet whatever his complex motivating influences, Dalrymple's message was clear to the tramwaymen. Their wages and conditions were already considerably in advance of private industry, and – as he explained in 1909 – any further improvements would be 'unfair to tradesmen who have served a long apprenticeship at a low wage'.[32] From this it can be seen that underlying the Corporation's outwardly paternalistic attitude, there was a determination not to allow the workforce to take the initiative in making demands for improved conditions of service. The tramwaymen thus had little room for manoeuvre in terms of bargaining; the employers set the standards, and could play on public sympathy if the workers ungratefully attempted to bite the hand that fed them.

It should be added that Dalrymple, for all his formidable sense of self-mission, did not operate in isolation. He had an intricate network of connections both at home and overseas, and was a dominating figure in the Municipal Tramways' Association, founded in 1902 to co-ordinate management strategy among the various United Kingdom local authorities. The organisation reflected the growth in the number of municipal transport undertakings from the 1890s, and the rapid technological changes that were confronting the industry. However, it was not simply a forum for debate, but also served as a united front against the anti-municipal movement. Private interests, notably in the electricity supply industry, resented the apparent ease with which Corporations like Glasgow had been able to construct their civic infrastructure, and squeeze out competition. It rankled particularly that electric traction had opened up greater opportunities for the consolidation of the transport network, yet the municipalities seemed to exercise virtual monopoly control.[33] Unease was expressed, too, about the collective strength of municipal employees, who – it was alleged – were becoming too politicised under Labour Party influence. In 1905, one former Glasgow Lord Provost conceded the dangers of this by stating:

> . . . As the city grows, the army of employees grows, and there have been indications at times that they may wield a power in the direction of the city government which is not altogether for the best interests of the municipality. . . .[34]

Thus, if Dalrymple's Association was in the business of defending municipal transport, it was scarcely likely to present hostages to fortune by appearing to be unduly solicitous to the demands of the workforce.

Roots and development of municipal trade unionism

Notwithstanding the short shrift received by the Gas Workers' Union from the Corporation in 1900, the municipal workforce had eventually been able to make meaningful headway in terms of organisation. In 1903, Labour representative William Forsyth pushed successfully for the principle of trade union recognition at departmental level, and one year later a national union – the Municipal Employees' Association – took on the task of recruitment within the Corporation.[35]

The MEA had been founded in 1894, and organised initially among London County Council manual workers, although it subsequently absorbed several locally-based municipal unions, including Glasgow. Like the Gas Workers' Union, the MEA's roots were metropolitan, although its tactics and style differed considerably, and proved to be controversial within the wider labour movement. By a curious irony, given the high profile of industrial unionism during the 1900s, leaders of the general unions accused the MEA of consciously creaming off municipal workers and their all-important membership contributions, thus dividing loyalties and leaving workers in the private sector at a disadvantage. Such was the strength of feeling that the Trades' Union Congress took a policy decision in 1906 against exclusive public sector unions, which forced the MEA to disaffiliate both from Congress and the Labour Party some two years later. Yet despite the problems over its status, which were compounded by a damaging leadership struggle and split in 1907, the MEA steadily strengthened its membership base, and recouped its losses sufficiently to represent over 13,000 workers nationally by 1910.

Scotland proved to be particularly fruitful territory, providing a fifth of the total membership of 50,000 by the end of the First World War, much of it centred on Glasgow. For many years the Scottish Secretary was Alexander Turner, who directed his considerable organisational energies towards building up the MEA's Glasgow base. A young, earnest and ambitious man, Turner was no stranger to municipal affairs, having worked in the Corporation's Gas Department before taking on his full-time MEA commitment. Significantly, he was also prominent in the leadership of Glasgow Trades' Council, to the extent that in 1908 he was appointed from that organisation to the Parliamentary Committee of the Scottish Trades' Union Congress, forerunner to the STUC General Council. While the MEA did not have the same ambiguous status in Scotland as elsewhere in the United Kingdom, it is revealing that Turner was able to have considerably more freedom via his Trades' Council activities than his southern counterparts. Politically he had started out as an enthusiastic Liberal, but 'grew weary of its abundant promises and poor results', and joined the ILP.[36] Such were his electoral aspirations that he contested the Townhead seat on the Corporation in 1908, albeit unsuccessfully, at a time when the Labour profile was beginning to re-emerge forcefully in the municipal arena. Of course, by so doing he helped to fuel further fears that the Corporation workforce was exercising undue influence over the direction of civic affairs.

Undoubtedly, Labour's improved electoral showing during the late 1900s was an important factor in shaping a trade union consciousness among Corporation workers, and here Glasgow Trades' Council was the pivotal connection. For a while the Party's perfomance at the polls had been decidedly sluggish, due to a combination of internal disunity and anti-socialist pressure, and the representational base had all but been obliterated. However, fortunes altered towards the end of 1908, in the midst of a serious economic recession in the city. Despite almost twenty per cent of the workforce jobless, the official response to the crisis had been muted, with initiatives like the Lord Provost's Relief Fund perceived as grossly ineffective. The public reaction reflected a burning sense of frustration, with violent protests outside the City Chambers serving as an unwelcome reminder to town councillors of their inability to cope adequately with the crisis. The labour movement was compelled to co-ordinate joint action under the aegis of an Unemployed Workers' Committee, with much of the direction being given by Trades' Council leaders.[37] As a consequence, several activists – including Alexander Turner – consolidated their reputation, and went on to stand for municipal office. Thereafter, representation steadily increased from a solitary Labour councillor in 1908, in the person of James Alston, to seven after the 1910 municipal elections, including the veteran Trades' Council Secretary, George Carson.

With Labour prospects opening out once again on the Corporation, the MEA became emboldened in its negotiating strategy. The union was already in a position of relative strength, because it recruited across-the-board in the larger departments; unlike many municipal authorities south of the border, where membership could often be divided among individual unions, such as the Gas Workers or the Amalgamated Association of Tramwaymen and Vehicle Workers. One effect was to provide greater membership cohesiveness in the Scottish city, and a more united approach towards the civic management, which from 1906 seemed to be yielding results. Under MEA pressure, councillors agreed to set up a formal Service Conditions Committee, to examine the state of wages and conditions in all departments. This was an important concession towards a central bargaining machinery, although – as with most of its industrial relations initiatives during the 1900s – the Corporation's remit promised more than it fulfilled. By early 1911 one *Forward* correspondent was remarking that nothing of any real significance had been forthcoming from the Committee, despite repeated MEA representations:

> . . . For five years application after application was remitted to this 'Conditions of Service' Committee and the result patiently and loyally awaited by the men. It could not be expected that the men would patiently tolerate such treatment; indeed, they would be less than men if they did not show resentment at such a result. . . .[38]

This restlessness was evident in several Corporation departments, notably Cleansing, but the most burning sense of grievance was manifested by the tramwaymen. Among the many pending applications that had been submitted to the Committee was one seeking shorter hours and longer paid holidays for conductors and motormen. There was no corresponding demand for a wage increase; only an improvement over the existing requirement to work a 54 hour week, with five days' paid leave. In January 1909, councillor James Alston informed *Forward* readers of the background to the claim, and the strong feeling among the workforce that the rigorous standards demanded for recruitment deserved appropriate recompense:

> . . . The department and the public are justified in demanding only the best nerves, the best intelligence, and the most perfect bodily health and eyesight and hearing. At the same time, the public is bound under the

circumstances to see that the conditions and working hours of the men are the best that can possibly be given. . . .[39]

Such improvements included the introduction of the eight-hour day, which had long been a labour movement objective. Alston went on to suggest that if changes were not made within the Tramways Department, then the substantial public investment in the undertaking would be dissipated, as the health of the workforce would inevitably suffer due to the onerous nature of the job. This was the argument which consistently formed the core of the claim, and was to the fore when it was formally resubmitted after discussions between Alexander Turner and Labour councillors in May 1910. Specifically, the MEA was seeking a 48 hour week, plus fourteen days' holiday.

However, the demands underpinning the claim were not unique to the Glasgow tramwaymen, despite the extraordinary circumstances of their employment. They also reflected the general reaction of many workers in the 1900s against what they perceived as excessive employer pressure to speed-up and intensify production.[40] In 1909 *Forward* had gone so far as to publish a series of articles on 'The Machine Monster', which probed the threat posed by automation and increased industrial competition from overseas.[41] These changes to the work environment had a bearing on the public as well as the private sector. With ratepayers demanding cheaper services and anti-municipalists on the look out for any sign of mismanagement, pressure was constantly being exerted to produce results. This was especially so in Glasgow, which had carefully cultivated its reputation as 'the Mecca of the tramway world', and thus had a good deal to prove. However, the tramwaymen believed that their welfare was suffering because of the intensification of the work-load, and the rapid development of transport technology since the 1890s.

Most crucially, electric traction had fundamentally altered the nature of the job, not least because of the substantially extended mileage covered by the tramways' network since 1901. As James Alston put it in 1909, 'since the change from horse haulage . . . the average speed has been increased from 5.75 miles per hour to 7.93'.[42] Although an hour had been lopped off the working day because of the advent of electrification, this was considered scant compensation for the demands to cover vaster areas at higher speed, which – the MEA alleged – was causing the men to work 'at a very high tension', and contributed to the brisk turnover of personnel in the department. Moreover, although the men were contracted to work nine hours a day 'on the car', this was invariably spread over a far longer period, averaging out at twelve hours a day. In a phrase replete with Dalrymplian overtones, the MEA suggested that increased holidays would allow the men 'to leave the city and renew their physical efficiency', particularly as so many originated from outside Glasgow, and were seeking more time to return to their roots.[43] While wages were not at issue, the MEA pointed out that the basic weekly rate was still 24s, although the flat-rate principle had long been abandoned and a grading structure was in force, up to a maximum of 34s, including bonuses.

The MEA's emphasis on the health and welfare dimension was not unique to Glasgow, as a similar claim had been put forward in Manchester by the Association of Tramwaymen and Vehicle Workers – and rejected, after Board of Trade arbitration in 1911.[44] The labour movement objective of the 48 hour week underlay these demands; a prospect which the Municipal Tramways' Association did not relish, and had resolved to stand firm against. James Dalrymple was therefore acting out of broader loyalties when he made his detailed rebuttal of the Glasgow tramwaymen's claim. Using Friendly Society statistics, he demonstrated that stress was not to the fore among the ailments which prompted absences, notwithstanding that the incidence of colds, 'flu and throat infections begged several questions which he failed to address. He claimed that any request for extra unpaid leave would be 'freely granted', despite the evidence of his own figures, which revealed that the number of paid holidays permitted by Glasgow Corporation was on average less than elsewhere.[45]

However, Dalrymple managed to persuade councillors to reject the claim, despite the support of a few sympathetic members for the MEA. Most were swayed by the argument that shorter hours involved financial complexities, not least the need to employ 200 extra staff to cover for the decrease in the working week. It was cheaper and logistically easier for councillors to increase wages, which they duly did, thus undermining the spirit of the original claim. In an attempt to divide the workforce and deflect public sympathy away from their case, an extra 1s a week was imposed on the wages of all conductors and motormen with more than two years' service, as from June 1911. This manoeuvre, which councillors claimed to be conciliatory, only strengthened the resolve of the tramway workers to demonstrate unity against the employers' intransigence.

Matters were not helped by the fact that financially the Tramways Department had never been in better shape. In the financial year 1895–96, profits had been sufficient to allow £9,000 to be transferred to the Corporation Common Good fund, for the benefit of Glasgow's citizens; in the year 1910–11, the amount transferred was £68,698.[46] There was much self-congratulation among Corporation representives, especially during a year when the city's public profile was much to the fore, with the imposingly titled Scottish Exhibition of Natural History, Art and Industry being staged in Kelvingrove Park. It seemed highly ironic to the tramway workers that their department was popularly perceived as Glasgow's municipal crock of gold, yet their own contribution in creating the Corporation's profits was blatantly disregarded. To compound the resentment, councillors seemed to be particularly free with public money in awarding sizeable pay increases to assorted chief officials. For instance, in a foretaste of the 'top people's' pay scandals of the 1990s, the General Manager of the Gas Department was given a rise of £100 over his existing salary of £1,000. Amidst stormy scenes in the City Chambers during June 1911, Labour councillors protested at what they called the 'greasing of the Big Fellows'.[47] This was to no avail in preventing the increases, but it scored good propaganda points in favour of the tramwaymen's cause.

By August 1911 the tramwaymen had gone some way towards compromise by moderating their claim to a working week of 51 hours, plus seven days' holiday. However, this was rejected, and the MEA resolved to ballot its membership. The workers were in buoyant mood and aimed to show solidarity, particularly as there had recently been a successful tramways' strike in Leeds and there were rumblings of discontent elsewhere.[48] They even went so far as to censure the MEA for dilatory tactics, although Alexander Turner continued to stress the responsible nature of the union and its distaste for industrial action. He also believed that the workforce was not ready to undertake a major confrontation with the Corporation, and win. Turner was in a position to have some inside information from Labour members of the Tramways Committee, like his great friend Hugh Lyon of the Carters' Union, and doubtless understood that James Dalrymple was not a man to be messed with. Perhaps, too, he was anxious to protect his own position, given that he was strongly placed to be returned as a councillor in the forthcoming November elections. There may even have been tension between Turner's forthright political stance and the more circumspect image of the MEA nationally, which tested his personal loyalties. Whatever the imponderables in terms of the MEA and its leadership, Turner seemed strangely reluctant to endorse the over-whelming decision of his union members when they voted by 1,667 to 171 in favour of the strike, out of a total of 2,739 conductors and motormen. As if disclaiming any responsibility for what had happened, and what was likely to happen, he stated to the men at a mass meeting on the eve of the strike:

> . . . You have been spoiling for a fight for over three months. I have done my best to get a settlement without any cessation of work. All means are now exhausted, and I say to you it is up to you to do what you have been threatening to do. . . .[49]

The tramways' strike and its aftermath

The strike commenced on Saturday, 12th August, with picket lines placed in all the city tramway depots and an ominous presence of police on standby. The press gave extensive column inches to the unusual Glasgow street scenes, with the 'tramless city' serving as a cautionary metaphor for what happened when channels of communications broke down. Initially there was an almost carnivalesque atmosphere on the picket lines, which was heightened by the presence of strikers' friends and families. One *Daily Record* headline read, 'FEMALE DEMON-STRATORS WORSE THAN MEN', in an allusion to an incident involving a pugnacious young mother at Langside depot.[50] This, of course, only added to the sense that the strike had somehow inverted normality, and – with industrial miltancy evident elsewhere in the United Kingdom – that it was all part of an inexplicable outbreak of summer madness. The employers were certainly not prepared to show weakness, and James Dalrymple and the Tramways Convener, William F. Russell, took speedy steps to recruit replacement workers to service the tramcars. The strike-breakers were ferried to the depots in taxi-cabs and bitter scenes ensued, including sabotage, in order to prevent the cars from taking to the streets. As the press reported, handles were wrenched from controls, trolley lines cut, while 'abusive and threatening language' was used against the tramwaymen on duty.[51] This was by no means surprising behaviour during a strike, but – as was shown by the sensationalist newspaper coverage, and the horrified public reaction – it was an extraordinary development. Given the hitherto exemplary reputation of the Corporation workforce, Glasgow's public image was deemed to be seriously tarnished.

Tactically the strike was a disaster. The 'battered and windowless' tramcars proved to be a chastening sight to Glaswegians, and councillors played upon this negative image. Their controversial decision to place the resolution of the strike entirely in the hands of the Tramways Manager meant that Dalrymple had considerable freedom of action. Nor was the Tramways Convener a conciliating influence, as was John Battersby during the Cleansing Department strike of 1902. William F. Russell was a wealthy coal owner with little sympathy for trade unionism; he also happened to be President of the Scottish Unionist Association. Dalrymple and Russell easily split the workforce by using lower paid staff to fill in for more senior staff, who seemed much more resolute in their determination to adhere to the strike call. Ironically, the very conditions that the workforce had been trying to improve turned out to be their downfall, given the flood of applications to fill the striking men's jobs. Numerous strikers were deemed to have broken their contracts, and were not re-employed. *Forward* later pointed out that the strike would have been rendered more effective by the simple expedient of stopping the electricity supply at source – that is, by closing down the generators at Pinkston, one of the largest traction stations in Europe.[52] However, this was an option the MEA did not use. There seemed to be a lack of sophistication about the entire episode, which contrasted starkly with the cool efficiency of the Tramways Manager, and the dispute fizzled out after three days.

The impact of other industrial disputes during 1911 had clearly defined the tactics used by James Dalrymple in his successful challenge to the demands of the tramwaymen, particularly the use of police and the importation of strike-breakers. Significantly, however, both had been a feature of the cleansing dispute in 1902, so nothing fundamentally new had taken place in Corporation strategy during 1911. Yet the response of the police to the tramwaymen was undoubtedly more vigorous, and it was wryly remarked in *Forward* that, 'Workers intending to strike in future should provide their pickets with more than glib tongues; otherwise heads cracked by police truncheons will be the rule'.[53] The public perception of the 1911 strike was also far more acute. The press had not given the same extensive coverage to the four-day cleansing dispute in 1902, although then there were other preoccupations, most notably the South African War and Liberal Party splits over imperial strategy. However, the 'industrial turmoil' during the summer of 1911 was the headline-grabber, perceived as part of a national malaise, the political and economic causes of which were hotly-debated. The motivations of the tramwaymen were thus magnified to a scale which belied their fairly modest claim for improved conditions, and provoked the Corporation – in the person of the Tramways Manager – into a showdown.

The nature of management within the Tramways Department is a crucial factor in understanding the causes of the 1911 dispute. On the one hand, paternalism had long been a feature of the civic ethos in Glasgow, with councillors anxious to demonstrate that they were taking the interests of the workforce to heart, in keeping with their 'model' image as employers. Yet as far as consultation was concerned, this had not necessarily been a two-way process, and employee input could often be minimal. The dismissive response to trade union recognition in 1900 was evidence that councillors could be highly selective in their dealings with worker representatives. And, despite the efforts of Labour councillors, attitudes hardened even further during the 1900s, as the Corporation sought to outdo the private sector in its quest to achieve results. Accordingly, by 1911 the old paternalism was no longer tenable in the more competitive municipal environment. This trend was by no means unique to Glasgow, as employer intransigence in the face of growing trade union assertiveness was a feature of the Leeds Corporation strike of 1913, where hard-line tactics were similarly adopted, and with very similar results.[54] However, north of the border the problem had been compounded by the very personal dimension to the dispute. The perceived 'autocratic' demeanour of the Tramway's Manager was bitterly resented by the workforce; indeed, it is tempting to suggest that the widespread vandalism against Dalrymple's beloved tramcars was somehow retribution against him. From this perspective, the 1911 strike represented a momentary release of tension; a reaction against the perfectionist, quasi-military style of management that had come to prevail in the department.

The growing power of the Tramways Manager, and the equivocal response of councillors to his handling of the dispute, reflected a further change in attitude since 1902, when the cleansing strike had been settled as a result of direct intervention by civic representatives. Such equivocation was construed in 1911 as a failure of nerve; an accusation also directed against the Liberal Government, especially by groups like the ILP. This sense of disenchantment had been glaringly exposed during the difficult winter of 1908–09, and despite improved economic prospects thereafter, the seeming insensitivity of the authorities to the crisis was not forgotten. Accordingly, numerous professedly progressive Liberal councillors on the Corporation were deemed to have revealed their true colours by sanctioning anti-union exploits during the 1911 tramways' strike. For many Glaswegians, Labour began to present a positive political alternative, particularly as it was constructing a much more effective organisational base than hitherto. A centralised Glasgow Labour Party was created in March 1912, which was able to promote issues like housing as part of a comprehensive municipal strategy, and made a great propaganda impact with John Wheatley's famous £8 cottages' scheme. Significantly, the substantial surplus from the Corporation tramway profits was to be the source of funding for Wheatley's proposed model municipal housing programme.[55] From 1911, representation was steadily consolidated, and the Labour group on the Corporation came to comprise eighteen members by the outbreak of the First World War. Such a development had obvious ramifications for the progress of municipal trade unionism in Glasgow, especially as the Labour Party began to pose a serious challenge for control of the Corporation after 1918. Significantly, it was this changing political climate which eventually brought down James Dalrymple, who was eventually pressurised into resigning in 1926, after claims from councillors that he had come to resemble 'Glasgow's Mussolini' in his dictatorial approach to industrial relations.[56]

NOTES

I am most grateful to Hamish Fraser of Strathclyde University for his scrutiny of an earlier draft of this chapter, and helpful suggestions for its revision.

1. Quoted in the *Glasgow Herald*, 28th September 1911. The comment was made during an after-dinner speech at the annual conference of the Municipal Tramways' Association.

2. *The Bailie*, 16th August 1911.

3. For the background, see Irene Maver, 'Politics and power in the Scottish city: Glasgow Town Council in the nineteenth century', in Devine, T.M., (ed.), *Scottish Elites* (1994), pp. 98-130.

4. Strathclyde Regional Archives [SRA] D-TC 14.1.26, 'Report on grading of offices and old age pensions', in *Minutes of Special Committee on Council Work, 1892-95*, pp. 126-130.

5. Glasgow Trades' Council, *Annual Report, 1888-89*, pp. 9-12. See also Fraser, W. H., 'Municipal socialism and social policy', in Morris, R.J. & Rodger, R. (eds.), *The Victorian City: A Reader in British Urban History, 1820-1914*, (1993), pp. 266-7, and his 'Labour and the changing city', in Gordon, G. (ed.), *Perspectives of the Scottish City*, (1985), pp. 166-7.

6. *Glasgow Herald*, 23rd September 1889.

7. SRA C2.1.11, 'Report by General Manager re-hours and wages of motormen and conductors', in *Corporation of Glasgow, Reports, &c, 1910-11*, p. 841.

8. Fraser, 'Labour and the changing city', p. 169.

9. Thompson, P., *Socialists, Liberals and Labour: the Struggle for London, 1885-1914* (1967), pp. 132-34.

10. Burgess's early career is discussed in Howell, D., *British Workers and the Independent Labour Party, 1888-1906*, (1983), pp. 286-7. He came to Glasgow from Leeds in 1899, and served as a town councillor between 1902 and 1905. For the background to the Gas Workers' Union, see Hobsbawm, E.J., 'British gas workers, 1873-1914', in *Labouring Men: Studies in the History of Labour* (1964), pp. 158-78.

11. *Glasgow Herald*, 8th December 1899.

12. *Glasgow Herald*, 19th January 1900.

13. *Glasgow Herald*, 25th February 1902.

14. *The Bailie*, 26th February and 5th March 1902.

15. *Glasgow Herald*, 25th and 27th February 1902.

16. *The Bailie*, 4th May 1904.

17. For the background to Chisholm and his relationship with the labour movement, see Sweeney, I. [aka Maver], 'Local party politics and the temperance crusade; Glasgow 1890-1902', *Journal of the Scottish Labour History Society*, 27, (1992), pp. 44-63. Battersby and Chisholm were close not only because of their politics, but their shared commitment to the temperance movement and adherence to the United Presbyterian Church.

18. Quoted in the *Glasgow Herald*, 27th February 1902.

19. Muir, J.H., *Glasgow in 1901*, (Glasgow, 1901), p. 47.

20. Bell, Sir J. and Paton, J. *Glasgow: Its Municipal Organisation and Administration* (1896), p. 302.

21. Muir, *Glasgow in 1901*, p. 57.

22. Aspinwall, B., *Portable Utopia: Glasgow and the United States, 1820-1920* (1984), p. 152; see also his, 'Glasgow trams and American politics, 1894-1914', *Scottish Historical Review*, LVI, (1977), pp. 64-84.

23. Meyer, H.R., *Municipal Ownership in Great Britain*, (1906), p. 99.

24. Searle, G.R., *The Quest for National Efficiency: A Study in British Politics and British Political Thought, 1899-1914* (1971), pp. 86-92.

25. Bell and Paton, *Glasgow*, p. xxii.

26. Quoted in Aspinwall, *Portable Utopia*, p. 155.

27. Oakley, C.A., *The Last Tram* (1962), p. 79. For further biographical background, see *The Bailie*, 19th October 1904, 23rd August 1911 and 1st September 1915; Eyre-Todd, G., *Who's Who in Glasgow in 1909: A Biographical Dictionary of 500 Living Glasgow Citizens* (1909), pp. 56-7; and Dalrymple's obituary in the *Glasgow Herald* and *Daily Record*, 2nd July 1934.

28. The quote appears in a feature, 'Glasgow' written by Howe, F.C., *for Scribner's Magazine* in 1906. This has been reproduced in Berry, S., and Whyte, H., (eds.), *Glasgow Observed*, (1987). See p. 184.

29. *The Bailie*, 19th October 1904.

30. Cunningham, H., *The Volunteer Force: A Social and Political History, 1859-1908* (1975), p. 155.

31. The tramwaymen's conditions are described by Dalrymple in detail in SRA C2.1.11, 'Report by General Manager re-hours and wages of motormen and conductors', pp. 837-63, and SRA C2.1.6, 'Chicago Street Railways', in *Corporation of Glasgow, Reports, &c., 1905-06*, pp. 727-50.

32. Glasgow Corporation, *Our Tramways* (1909), p. 11.

33. Fraser, W. H., 'From civic gospel to municipal socialism', in Derek Fraser (ed.), *Cities, Class and Communication: Essays in Honour of Asa Briggs* (1990), pp. 72-4.

34. Quoted in Meyer, *Municipal Ownership*, p. 310. The speaker was Sir John Ure Primrose.

35. Glasgow Trades' Council, *Annual Report, 1902-03*, p. 16. For the MEA's origins, see Clegg, H.A., *General Union: A Study of the National Union of General and Municipal Workers* (1954), pp. 16-7, and Clegg, H.A., Fox, A., and Thompson, A.F., *A History of British Trade Unions since 1889: Volume 1, 1889-1910* (1964), pp. 86-87 and 449-50. The MEA amalgamated with the General and Municipal Workers' Union in 1924.

36. *Forward*, 9th October 1909. For further biographical information, see *The Bailie*, 27th February 1918, and Turner's obituary in the *Glasgow Herald*, 12th July 1923.

37. *Forward*, 23rd January 1909. See also Tuckett, A., *The Scottish Trades Union Congress: the First Eighty Years* (1986) p. 86. For an analysis of the unemployment crisis, see Treble, J.H.,'Unemployment in Glasgow, 1903-1910; anatomy of a crisis', *Journal of the Scottish Labour History Society*, 25 (1990), pp. 8-39.

38. *Forward*, 22nd April 1911.

39. *Forward*, 16th January 1909.

40. Glasgow Labour History Workshop, 'Roots of Red Clydeside: the labour unrest in west Scotland, 1910-14', in Duncan, R. and McIvor, A. (eds.), *Militant Workers: Labour and Class Conflict on the Clyde, 1910-1950* (1992), p. 89-95.

41. See *Forward*, 16th January to 13th February 1909.

42. *Forward*, 16th January 1909. The number of lines open for traffic in Glasgow increased from 88 in 1900 to 196 in 1911. See Glasgow Corporation, *Municipal Glasgow: Its Evolution and Enterprises* (1914), p. 76.

43. SRA C2.1.11, 'Report by General Manager', p. 856.

44. SRA C2.1.11, 'Report by General Manager', pp. 850-1.

45. SRA C2.1.11, 'Report by General Manager', p. 840.

46. SRA D-TC 7.26.2, *Glasgow Corporation Tramways: Abstract Statement of Income and Expenditure, for Year from 1st June 1910 to 31st May 1911*, p. 13.

47. *Forward*, 10th June 1911.

48. *Forward*, 19th August and 16th September 1911.
49. Quoted in the *Glasgow Herald*, 12th August 1911.
50. *Daily Record*, 14th August 1911.
51. For a collection of *Glasgow Herald* press cuttings on the strike, see SRA D-TC 14.1.40, *Miscellaneous Prints*, pp. 100-114.
52. *Forward*, 19th August 1911.
53. *Forward*, 19th August 1911.
54. Williams, J.E., 'The Leeds Corporation strike in 1913', in Briggs, A., and Saville, J., (eds.), *Essays in Labour History, 1886-1923*, (1971), pp. 70-95.
55. Wheatley, J., *Eight-Pound Cottages for Glasgow Citizens* (1913), pp. 6-8.
56. The subsequent career of James Dalrymple merits much more detailed discussion than this account can provide. Suffice it to say, his combative response to the role of tramway workers during the 1926 General Strike lay behind his resignation. See the *Glasgow Herald*, 9th July 1926. Dalrymple died of a stroke, aged 74, on his way to attend the annual conference of the Municipal Tramways' Association. Intriguingly, Alex Turner also died suddenly in 1923, aged 43. He had achieved high office as a Glasgow town councillor, and en route severed his connection with the Labour Group. Notwithstanding his shift to the right, the MEA continued to recruit steadily among Corporation workers.

CHAPTER 11

'From Industrial Unrest to Industrial Debacle'?: the Labour Left and Industrial Militancy, 1910–1914

James J. Smyth

Introduction

Labour history in the years immediately prior to the First World War is dominated by two major issues: the labour unrest, and the political fortunes of the Labour Party. As regards the labour unrest there is considerable debate as to how politically motivated this massive strike wave was, what was the influence of syndicalism, and whether or not this unrest was evidence of a deeper (even a revolutionary) class consciousness.[1] As regards the Labour Party, the major issue of debate is how far Labour had gone in displacing the Liberal Party as the political voice of the industrial working class.[2] What is perhaps surprising is how little these two questions impinge on each other in the historical literature. The purpose of this essay is to examine the electoral fortunes of Labour on Clydeside during a period which witnessed unprecedented industrial mobilisation and militancy among the working class and to consider what, if any, relationship existed between the political and industrial struggles.

Glasgow ought to be a fruitful area for a study of this relationship since in Scotland the Lib-Lab pact did not operate and in the years prior to the war Labour's electoral performance in Glasgow, as judged by its performance in the municipal polls, was on an upward curve.[3] Also, as the recent researches by the Glasgow Labour History Workshop has shown, the industrial unrest did not peak in 1912 but, at least on Clydeside, was growing in intensity during 1914.[4] Joan Smith has argued that it was at this point that the ILP established its effective leadership of the Labour movement in Glasgow, a position which was strengthened by the subsequent strike wave.[5] With a considerable and increasingly politicised labour movement (some 30,000 marched on May Day in Glasgow), with growing Labour representation on the Town Council, and continuing industrial unrest, this period seems to offer plenty of evidence that Labour was the coming political power. But, if the 'roots of Red Clydeside' are to be found here, just how deep had those roots struck? While attempting to analyse Labour's political strength at the local level, it is necessary also to pay attention to the national picture; the labour movement on Clydeside did tend to go its own way but it was not immune to national developments and debates.

Disappointment with the parliamentary labour party

A critical issue for all socialists, but most especially the members of the ILP, was the performance in Parliament of the Labour Party. For most activists the lack of dynamism exhibited by the Labour MPs was, at worst, disgraceful and, at best, deeply disappointing. The extent of this disappointment is partly explained by the tremendous, almost millenarian, hopes that accompanied Labour's success in 1906 when 29 MPs were returned. If the nature and extent of the Gladstone-MacDonald pact had been wider known there may not have been the same enthusiasm among the grassroots, but the fact of this enthusiasm is undeniable and should be emphasised in any account of the period. To quote John Paton writing some thirty years later but then an ordinary member of the ILP in Glasgow:

> . . . It was a period of rapid growth for Socialism. The arrival of the first Labour Party in Parliament after the General Election of 1906 had given us a great impetus which had not yet spent itself. A new political power of unknown potentialities had arisen. The imagination of the workers had been stirred. There was an immense interest in the new party and a great hope. . . .[6]

Perhaps of more significance are the contemporary comments of Joseph Duncan, a union secretary in Aberdeen, soon to become the ILP's Scottish organiser and very much on the pragmatic MacDonald wing of the Party. In a private letter to his fiancée, Duncan expressed his own hopes:

> . . . And so the Revolution is started at last. I have been living in a state of suppressed excitement all the week. The labour men have been romping home merrily until now one begins to wonder where it is all going to end. I expect by the finish we shall have 30 independent labour men in. . . . We shall arrive. We shall do things. The old country will get shaken to its very centre. . . .

Moreover, Duncan was also positive about Scotland's relatively poor performance (only two MPs returned) since these were won directly against the Liberals and so counted for much more.

> . . . in Scotland we have not a clear fight anywhere. In every constituency we have to fight both Liberal & Tory. Although this makes harder fighting it is much more satisfactory. When we get our own men in it means that they go in on our own votes. It declares the open war. It guarantees our independence. It is the clear trumpet call of the revolution. . . .[7]

This intoxication did not last long. Within a couple of years Ben Tillett had produced his emphatically titled pamphlet, *Is the Parliamentary Labour Party a Failure?* Tillett's rhetorical question was answered in the affirmative by increasing numbers of ILP members. One of these was John Paton who saw, 'more and more clearly the Labour Party in Parliament appeared as merely the wing of the Liberal Party.' Paton admitted that 'hopes had been pitched too high' and that now there was a more realistic understanding of the possibilities (or lack of them). However, 'as the weary months dragged on, disappointment for many of us deepened to disgust.'[8] The success of Victor Grayson in winning the Colne Valley by-election in July 1907 in the face of both Liberal and Tory opposition provided a beacon of hope for the left. Here was evidence that truly *independent* labour representation could be achieved. Moreover, Grayson's performance in parliament which culminated in his expulsion in October 1908 was welcomed, in spite of misgivings about Grayson's character, as showing a fighting spirit so absent in the majority of Labour MPs.[9] Opposition to the policy of avoiding three-cornered contests emerged at both the ILP and Labour Party conferences but in the 1910 general elections the arrangement with the Liberals was continued with.

For a significant number of ILP activists this was too much and they were attracted to the growing movement for Socialist Unity instead of the Labour alliance. For instance in October 1910 the Busby ILP

242

branch seceded giving as its reason: 'Weak stand of L.P. in Parl. & forsaken the R[ight] to W[ork] Bill.' In January 1911 the Bonnybridge branch seceded stating, 'Policy of Labour Party' as the reason.[10] Such dissatisfaction culminated in the creation of the British Socialist Party (BSP) which was promoted by Robert Blatchford and the *Clarion*, and Victor Grayson. The Social Democratic Party (SDP), also decided to join but without sufficient new members of its own or secessions from the ILP, the BSP became pretty much controlled by the older SDP leaders such as Hyndman and Quelch. Only two ILP branches in Scotland (Forfar and Inverness) appear to have gone directly into the BSP,[11] with most secessions being of individual members. Harry McShane, then a member of the Kingston ILP, has described how he and two colleagues attempted to get the whole branch to shift allegiance to the BSP and when this failed the three simply joined the new party.[12]

In this account McShane leaves a tantalising glimpse of what the BSP might have been before the SDP joined and effectively took it over. Seeing this new group as distinct from both the ILP and the SDP, McShane comments, 'We began to get in between the two and to preach class struggle, revolution, and extra-parliamentary activity without being anti-parliamentarian.' He contrasts this to the revolutionary bombast of the SDP leadership which, in actual practice, Harry McShane took to mean, 'if you can't vote right then you can't strike right. Now what does that mean? For the SDP there was never any way except the purely parliamentary way.'[13] The important point here is that whatever differences in ideology may have existed between the ILP on the one hand and the SDP/BSP on the other, in terms of political strategy there was little to distinguish their approaches to political activity. This explains why a number of individuals found it possible to be members of both organisations and why most ILP members stuck with the Labour Party approach and the alliance with the (non-socialist) trade unions. The Socialist Labour Party (SLP) did have a distinctive approach through its concentration on industrial unionism but its anti-political stand limited its wider impact; the SLP refused even to participate in the unemployment agitation of 1908, whereas both the ILP and the SDP took active roles.[14]

It was the agitation over unemployment which galvanised the Glasgow labour movement out of despondency and helped lay the foundations for future political advances. Ten years previously Glasgow had provided a benchmark for Labour municipal success through the grouping known as the Stalwarts which included not only the ILP and the trades council but also the co-operators and the Irish nationalists. However, the component parts had gradually left until only the ILP remained, and Labour representation on the Town Council went into an almost terminal decline. The November poll of 1908 actually proved to be Labour's worst ever performance when all eight of its candidates were defeated. However by 1909 the Trades Council had established an Election Committee and, with one seat gained, Labour representation began a steady, if at first unspectacular, improvement.[15]

Labour's local success

Local politics proved to be one of the brightest spots for Labour both in terms of organisation and votes. In the years before the war Labour Parties were at last constituted for London and Glasgow and municipal election results on a national scale showed constant progress.[16] In Glasgow it was the ILP Federation and the Trades Council which together promoted the formation of the Glasgow Labour Party. Protracted wrangling over the constitution meant that the Party was not fully constituted until May 1912. The secretary of the new Party, Ben Shaw, provided a report for the first annual meeting in April 1913 which listed all the Party's elected representatives. This included George Barnes, the MP for Blackfriars and Hutchesontown, and there were party representatives on nine Town Councils, Parish Councils and School Boards. The most significant were the twelve members of Glasgow Town Council. All of this represented considerable improvement on the situation of a few years before, yet Shaw still wrote in his report that, 'The Party recognises that it has still to justify its existence . . .'[17]

The Glasgow Labour Party was a different type of organisation from the Workers' Election Committee which had been the organising body behind the Stalwarts in the 1890s. The composite elements of the WEC – the ILP, the trades council, the Co-operators and the Irish National-ists – were collectively referred to as the 'forces of the Democracy'.[18] This alliance made Glasgow a model of successful working class representation but, as we have mentioned above, the alliance had broken down and by 1908 Labour representation in Glasgow was in a state of crisis. With the formation of the Glasgow Labour Party neither the Co-operators nor the Irish were to play a part. As eventually constituted in 1912 the Glasgow Labour Party comprised: Glasgow Trades Council, Glasgow Federation ILP, Women's Labour League, Glasgow Fabian Society and the Labour Representation Committees of Bridgeton, Blackfriars and Hutchesontown, Camlachie, Central, College, St Rollox, Tradeston, Govan, and Partick. This was a much more cohesive Labour grouping and could operate as a 'controlling body', where the old WEC had been a 'composite body'.[19]

At one level this was a sign of Labour's own strength – the crucial pivot being the ILP and the Trades Council – which witnessed an increased municipal representation. However, the absence of the Co-operators could be seen as a sign of Labour's continuing weakness. Like the SDP the Co-operators had been invited and sent delegates to the first meetings of the committee which had been set up to draft a constitution for the new Labour Party. The SDP withdrew in December 1911 which was almost certainly expected and was unlikely to have caused many regrets.[20] But the withdrawal of the Co-operators was much more serious as they were a potential source of voters and an important contributor of funds, particularly important in the absence of any large affiliated trade unions.[21] When the Co-operators joined the WEC in the 1890s it was because they were suffering a sharp attack from private traders hostile to the success of the growing co-operative movement, retail and wholesale. It was the Co-operative Defence Association which took part in the preliminary discussions of the Glasgow Labour Party but there was at this time insufficient pressure to encourage them to take the actual step of joining the new party.

The Co-operative Defence Association balked at the name Labour Party and wanted the new organisation to be called the Progressive Party, 'as other bodies than those eligible for affiliation to the Labour Party could be admitted.' It also complained that the LRCs had too large a representation.[22] As much as Labour wanted the Co-operators in it was impossible to countenance any title other than Labour Party. To do so would have been to take a step backwards into old Lib-Labism.[23] However, the position of the Co-operators, many of whose prominent members were also prominent local Liberals, indicates the continuing strength of Liberal loyalties within the Glasgow working class. It is significant that the political programme of the Glasgow Labour Party while focusing almost exclusively on the provision of municipal services, stretching from housing all the way to bread and milk, also included the taxation of land values.[24]

The Glasgow ILP, in a series of articles in *Forward* in 1906 and 1907, had intellectually demolished the 'single tax' or 'land tax' position which had been popularised by John Ferguson of the United Irish League and was integral to the approach of the Stalwarts.[25] However, in 1911 it still felt it incumbent to include the demand in the Labour Party programme. With Lloyd George's budget of 1909 introducing the principle of taxing land values and his continuing attack on the landed interest, especially with land taxation being increasingly pushed by the Liberals as the means to finance social reforms, Labour found it impossible to discard a policy which had become something of an article of faith. The continuing resonance of the land issue operated to the benefit of the Liberals, something which ILP activists were only too well aware of.[26] Including the land tax in the party programme could also be a way of appealing to the Liberal-inclined co-operators. Yet, this and the decision by the Co-operative Defence Association not to join the Glasgow Labour Party shows how far Labour still had to go in winning working class support away from the Liberals.

Socialist responses to the labour unrest

As the extent of the labour unrest became apparent – i.e. that this was something more than just a random number of strikes – so it was welcomed by almost all sections of the labour and socialist movement. Even the right wing of the left wing, if we can identify the national leadership of the ILP in that contradictory way, were supportive, initially. The *Socialist Review*, founded by Ramsay MacDonald and edited by Bruce Glasier, commented in the latter part of 1911, 'We hail with unalloyed satisfaction the uprising of Labour on the industrial field. . . .'[27] The level of unrest was of a scale and scope previously unknown in this generation. 'Let us understand first of all that it was *unrest*. It was not merely a demand for a programme. It was deeper than that. It was revolutionary and was that kind of upheaval which comes like a flood released from hidden depths.'[28] At this stage the ILP leadership saw in the strike wave a means of galvanising the Labour Party in Parliament. The argument, as expressed in the *Socialist Review*, was that in the last few years trade unionism had become quiescent and this had concentrated expectations upon the Labour MPs. Quite simply too much had been expected of the forty or so MPs, 'to realise at once the new heaven and the new earth'.[29] A more active trade unionism would be more apprecia-tive of the efforts made by the Parliamentary Party but also it would help the Party by making it impossible for labour issues to be continually ignored: Industrial and political efforts were the complement of each other. W.C. Anderson put the argument as follows:

> . . . As a matter of fact, the hands of the Party in Parliament are greatly strengthened by these direct and far-reaching evidences of industrial unrest. . . . Industrial action cannot possibly supersede political action. . . . But industrial action can speed up political action, whose pulse is ever inclined to beat weak and slow. A militant Trade Union movement, guided by sensible but thoroughly alert leaders . . . would provide a magnificent driving force in Parliament, and backed up by a growing Labour Party, would result in substantial economic gains. . . .[30]

This positive association between the industrial and the political was further cemented with the 'magnificent' results of the municipal elections in that year which were seen, at least partly, as due to the industrial unrest.[31] However, as the unrest continued into 1912 and the miners' strike took hold, the attitude of the *Socialist Review* began to change. At no time had MacDonald or any of the ILP leadership been sympathetic to syndicalism and the notion of the revolutionary general strike – MacDonald categorised syndicalism as an 'absurdity' and one of the 'vipers' nestling within the bosom of the labour movement.[32] Nor had they ever questioned the self-evident supremacy of the political struggle over the industrial. But, as the strike wave continued there was less and less mention of the 'complementarity' between industrial and political struggles and more and more overt criticism of the strikes and strikers. Victories won by direct action would be short lived and 'pyrrhic'. Objection was made to the 'Jacobin' or 'rabble spirit' which 'cuts off the supply of Parliamentary leaders and encourages the disintegration of Parliamentary forces.'[33] Sympathy strikes and national strikes were castigated both for 'coercing' the community and also for failing to achieve their ends:

... The miners' strike has, in fact revealed as no previous industrial struggle has done the tremendous hurtfulness of strikes to the strikers themselves as well as to the community, and the futility of "direct action" when directed against the monopoly power of capitalism while that power remains entrenched behind the needs of the community and the political forces of the State. . . .[34]

Warning was made against the 'strike fetish' and with the London transport workers strike in the summer of 1912 patience had worn very thin, 'What is termed the "Labour Unrest" shows perilous signs of degenerating into a Labour debacle.'[35] There was now no direct association made between industrial action and electoral success. Rather it was pointed out at a series of three-cornered by-elections where Labour came bottom in every one (including mining constituencies) that the strike wave had no effect in raising class consciousness.[36] While it is hardly surprising to find that Ramsay MacDonald held such views it is important to emphasise just how prevalent such views, or variants of them, were within the socialist movement.

Within the BSP leadership there was a superior attitude which at times verged on being dismissive of industrial action. Some prominent members such as Will Thorne who was also a Labour MP did take a positive approach. Thorne explained the unrest principally as due to the rise in the cost of living but also due to the increased speeding up of the work process and provoked, in part, by the sharp contrast between rich and poor, which workers were increasingly being made aware of. Thorne appreciated the discontent felt by the rank and file with their leaders and identified a younger generation of activists who were forcing the pace for union amalgamations and greater consolidation.[37] However, the editorial line taken in the BSP's journal, as expressed by Harry Quelch among others, saw no great significance in the strike wave. In 1911 when it was in the nature of a 'revolt', then there was cause for congratulation. But, commenting on the workers' defeat in the cotton lock-out in early 1912, 'It has added another to the countless lessons we have had of the dubious efficiency, not to say futility, of what is called industrial action unsupported by political effort. It is idle for the workers to strike against their masters while they continue to vote these same masters into power.'[38] At no point would anyone argue that workers should not organise themselves industrially or take strike action when they saw fit, but there is a clear sense of detachment from the trade unions and the continuing labour unrest. Quelch writing on the coal strike raised the matter of the 'national' or 'community' interest and, unlike say MacDonald, took a class position and showed how this interest always operated against the workers. But, at the same time, he denied there was any political element to the strike, it was purely an economic concern with wages.[39] Indeed Quelch was at pains to dismiss the notion that there was any 'revolutionary' aspect to the labour unrest. 'The revolutionist', Quelch wrote, knows . . .

> . . . that when the British working class . . . really want the revolution, and are prepared to strike or fight for it, they will at any rate have the sense to vote for instead of against it. In the meantime, he can only smile sceptically at the frothy talk of inner revolutionary meaning of foolish outbursts of impotent violence. . . .[40]

Sentiments like this were completely opposed to the perspective summed up in John Maclean's famous remark about being 'in the rapids of revolution.'[41] Maclean was at this time, in the words of David Howell, 'a model social democrat'.[42] Like the vast majority of members of the BSP, and ILP for that matter, Maclean saw the political struggle as having priority – it would only be through a conscious political mobilisation that socialism would be achieved. However, Maclean was quite different to a Hyndman or a Quelch in his approach to industrial issues. There was nothing ambivalent or superior in Maclean's analysis of the potential significance of the labour unrest. Writing at almost exactly the same moment as Quelch was writing on the miners' strike in 1912, Maclean's perceptions of events were quite different, 'Never were the masses so pugnacious . . . never before were they so class conscious . . . No doubt we would like to see them fight for something substantial; but to get them to fight the masters at all is a God's blessing in this realm.' Moreover, the experience of such strikes had a greater impact than constant socialist propaganda. 'Fighting leads to new facts, these to our new theory, and thence to revolution.'[43]

This seems closer to what Harry McShane had hoped the original BSP would be and Joan Smith has commented that by the end of 1913 Maclean was seeking 'ways of reconciling industrial and political action.'[44] In fact Maclean's position on this can best be understood through his continuous concern over the nature of what a socialist party ought to be and his debate against the leadership of the SDP/BSP. In the pre-war years Maclean was a well-known member of the BSP in Scotland and relatively well-known south of the border but he was not the national figure he would become during the war. Maclean was not in a position to have much influence on party policy, especially as on a whole series of issues he was deeply antagonistic to the established leadership. These included the critical issue of militarism and rearmament but the most recurring point of conflict was over the question of party organisation. In alliance with the Russian socialist exile Peter Petroff, Maclean was attempting to make the SDP/BSP a more coherent and more disciplined political body. This included reorganisation of the executive committee, party control of the party press (rather than the personal control exerted by Hyndman and fellow shareholders), and a common party programme for elections. Maclean first raised the issue of the poor state of party organisation in an article in 1910 where he argued that, 'Every year we should organise our forces to press forward resolutions at co-operative, trade union and other working-class congresses or conferences.'[45] This was an issue Petroff also wrote on and which he raised at the party conference. In 1913 Petroff moved a resolution declaring that, 'the proper function of the British Socialist party is to lead the working class in its *economic* and political struggle', and which contained within it an instruction to the executive, 'to organise the trade union members of the BSP for systematic work and Socialist propaganda inside the trade unions.' In another debate at the same conference Petroff also argued, 'It was useless to wait for the majority to become Socialists before anything was done. They would not become Socialists unless something was done.'[46]

Maclean's position was not simply a response to the labour unrest but reflected a deeper concern with party organisation and strategy which was influenced by the example of the Russian Social Democratic Labour Party (RSDLP). At its 1907 congress held in London the RSDLP had laid down the principle of political agitation within the trade unions and it is clear that Petroff acted as a conduit for such ideas to Maclean.[47] Without exaggerating the influence Maclean had at the time it is of interest, in terms of the labour unrest, to see that Maclean and Petroff at least had an approach to industrial activity which sought to encompass it within the political activity of a socialist party. What is of more significance, however, is that almost no-one else on the left shared such a perspective. In effect the dichotomy of politics on the one hand and industrial issues on the other was continued.

Increasingly the left in Glasgow distanced itself from the anti political stance of syndicalism but it did not, unlike the leaderships of the ILP and BSP, grow detached from or hostile to the actions of strikers themselves. *Forward* continued to report positively on the labour unrest (as did Maclean in *Justice*) and large numbers of ILP members were active participants in strikes and in organising unskilled workers into trade unions. In fact it was the ILP which was much more consistently and successfully active in the trade union field, rather than the self-proclaimed champion of industrial unionism, the Socialist Labour Party (SLP).[48] But, for all that, the political strategy of the ILP did not alter – the focus remained exclusively on electoral politics, on building up labour representation in Parliament and the municipality. At a time of unprecedented industrial unrest and with greater numbers of workers becoming organised (many of whom had been regarded as beyond organisation) there was no real change in strategy or approach.

Labour's limited progress

That there was no direct correlation between increasing strike activity and electoral support for Labour is quite clear. Even Maclean had to admit in 1913 that Scottish workers were, 'still seething like lions industrially, but lying like lambs politically.'[49] In the five parliamentary by-elections fought by Labour in Scotland between 1910 and 1914, its candidates came bottom in every contest. The same fate befell Labour candidates in England over the same period but in Scotland Labour was winning a smaller share of the poll.[50] In municipal elections Labour did considerably better with 1911 and 1913 being particularly good years; in the latter year Labour made four net gains in Glasgow.[51] In 1914 (the last local election until 1919) Labour made one net gain which gave it an all-time high of nineteen representatives on the town council.[52] Evidence of Labour's political strength in Glasgow is, therefore, ambivalent. Moreover, what growth in popular support Labour did enjoy at this time was not directly due to the labour unrest. The one issue above all others which lay behind Labour's local success was housing.

251

After the local elections in 1909, when Labour in Glasgow managed to stop the rot and actually win a seat, *Forward* commented, 'For the present, Municipal Socialism is in the lean and dry stage. It stands in need of new ideas and a new inspiration.'[53] The new inspiration was to be found in the housing issue, not in industrial or trade union issues. In housing, in particular the policy of workmen's cottages promoted by John Wheatley, Labour developed a distinctive and popular issue. The significance of the housing issue to Labour's electoral and organisational development has been well documented and needs no reiteration here.[54] One indication of how important it had become, at least to party activists, is indicated by the local elections of 1913 where the two council seats Labour lost were those of the two sitting Labour councillors who opposed the cottages scheme.[55] At the heart of Labour's local political strategy was the notion of increased municipalisation, a gradual extension of the services controlled and provided by the local state for its citizens. It was an approach geared to consumerist issues: provision of houses, banks, laundries, coal, milk, bread, and controlling the drink trade. Given Glasgow's already highly advanced level of municipal provision such a programme appeared firmly within the realm of practical politics. The absence of industrial issues – apart from fair wages clauses and minimum wages for council employees – may simply reflect the difficulty of incorporating such issues into an electoral programme. The BSP does not appear to have contested local elections on Clydeside with a radically different programme; Maclean regarded Wheatley's approach to housing basically as being the same as his own and the BSP used Wheatley's 'cottages' pamphlet in its own campaign in Pollockshaws in the 1913 municipal contest.[56]

Undoubtedly, the Labour Party and the trade unions were stronger in 1914 than they had been in 1910. For the trade unions this is clearly shown in membership figures as new members flooded into the societies. Total union membership in Britain grew from c. 2.5 million in 1909 to 4.1 million in 1913; a *rate* of expansion which was greater than the further growth that would take place during the First World War and immediately after.[57] The British trade unions re-established their position as the largest trade union movement in the world. Moreover, this growth was all along the line. Existing societies, both skilled and unskilled, expanded and previously unorganised workers, including female workers, developed new organisational strength. Much of the industrial unrest involved unskilled workers pushing for union recognition and collective bargaining.[58] With the passing of the Trade Union Act of 1913 which replaced the Osborne judgement, the way was open for this trade union strength to flow into the Labour Party, and a series of ballots of union members were in favour of establishing political funds.[59]

However, if there is some degree of agreement among historians that the Labour Party was stronger in 1914 than in 1910, the important question of how much stronger remains. On one side there is McKibbin who argues that Labour was very much stronger and was preparing to ditch its electoral alliance with the Liberals by fighting on a much wider front at the forthcoming general election which would have been held in late 1914 or early 1915; perhaps as many as 150 or even 170 candidates compared to the 78 put forward at the last election in December 1910.[60] Arguing against this is Tanner who sees the most likely scenario as a continuation of the Progressive Alliance with Labour remaining the junior partner, contesting the election with the same number of candidates, more or less, as in 1910.[61] In this perspective Labour had improved its position, in both elections and in party organisation, but not sufficiently for it to be a serious rival to the Liberal Party. In spite of grass roots hostility to and frustration with the link to the Liberals, it was unlikely that Labour would have countenanced challenging the Liberals across the board. Even in Scotland, where the electoral pact forged by Mac-Donald and Gladstone in 1903 had never operated, there is evidence that Labour and the Liberals were considering an arrangement over candidates for an election in 1914 or 1915.[62]

Certainly, by 1914 Labour was much stronger in Glasgow politically than it had been four years previously. The Glasgow Labour Party was established and it operated as a more cohesive political force with a common policy to be adhered to by its candidates and representatives.[63] This new disciplined approach seemed to have brought results and Labour had more councillors in the city chambers than ever before. Proportionately, though, Labour representation was no higher than it had been under the Stalwarts in the 1890s.[64] This observation suggests that there was nothing inevitable about Labour's electoral progress; what gains had been made could be lost.

Labour's success was encouraging but hardly spectacular; winning actual control of the town council remained far beyond its grasp. Moreover, it was unlikely that the gains in municipal elections could be repeated in the parliamentary arena. Any all-out war between Labour and Liberals may have damaged the latter but it could have obliterated Labour as a parliamentary party. For Labour to progress further – to become a governing party at either national or local level – there would need to be a more fundamental shift in political loyalties.

Such a shift did occur eventually but did so under the impact of the First World War. Consideration of the war and immediate post war years is beyond our concerns here but it is interesting that Cronin sees the years from 1914 to 1920 when 'economic problems became political' and when industrial militancy 'went hand in hand with the transformation of working class political consciousness.'[65] If, in this period labour unrest went hand in hand with the rise of Labour, by implication there was no such connection between 1910 and 1914.

Conclusion

As illustrated above, a considerable body of labour and socialist opinion quickly turned against the unrest once it was clear that it was not going to be easily channelled into established political routes. Even among the left wing of the ILP there was little attention given to the unrest.[66] John Wheatley, the principal architect of Labour's new strategy in Glasgow, seems to have been completely unaffected by the industrial unrest. One of the principal features of the unrest was the involvement of women workers in both strikes and union organisation yet, as Eleanor Gordon has argued, the labour movement found it difficult to respond to women as workers and thus, failed 'to recognise them as a potential political constituency.'[67] This argument could, in fact, be extended to include considerable numbers of unskilled male workers.

Labour operated with a clear but exclusive picture of what its natural political constituency was and it most certainly did not include the poor. Time and again leading socialist and labour figures expressed the view that the poor were repositories of support for reaction. As Keir Hardie put it, 'It is the slum vote that the socialist candidate fears most.'[68] David Howell has commented on the 'fear of the masses' felt by ILP spokesmen and its 'almost neurotic anxiety about disorder on the left.'[69] Individual members may have had quite different views but such a predominant attitude among its leadership must have left the ILP ambivalent, to say the least, on how to respond to the mass upheaval of the pre-war years. According to the *Socialist Review*, 'What sterling virtue there was in the real middle class is now found in the better-paid and more regularly employed working class – just that stratum from which we get our most substantial Socialist support.'[70] This comment was made in an article on the labour unrest and shows little or no appreciation of the masses of new workers, semi-skilled and unskilled, male and female, who were exhibiting their willingness both to strike and to establish permanent organisations.

The argument being presented here is that there was no direct transference of industrial militancy into political class consciousness. However, this is not to say that no relationship existed between industrial and political struggles; the involvement of activists in both areas of activity proves a clear link.[71] However, most activists operated within a dual framework whereby there were industrial issues that were the preserve of the trade unions and there were political issues which were the proper sphere of Labour and its constituent organisations. The Glasgow Labour Party discussed housing endlessly in the years before the war but never once considered the labour unrest as an issue. In addition to this Labour was dominated by a view of where its political support was (and should be) located – the respectable working man – which left it poorly equipped to respond to the upsurge in militancy and organisation of workers (male and female) who did not fit into the mould.

Objectively, Labour was strengthened in the long run by the rise in membership of the trade unions which was a direct consequence of the unrest. But in the short run the unrest did not promote a major transference of political loyalties. That there was no clear electoral shift towards Labour, either on Clydeside or nationally, indicates the continuing popularity of Liberalism and the Liberal Party. But, Labour's own inability to respond to and accommodate the unrest within a political strategy is part of the equation also.

NOTES

1. Clegg, H.A., *A History of British Trade Unions since 1889, Vol. II 1911–1933* (Brighton, 1985); Pelling, H., *A History of British Trade Unionism* (1984); Hinton, J., *Labour and Socialism* (Oxford, 1983); Cronin, J. E., *Industrial Conflict in Modern Britain* (1979); Holton, B., *British Syndicalism* (1976).

2. The two most extensive treatments of this issue are McKibbin, R.I., *The Evolution of the Labour Party 1910–1924* (1986) who argues in favour of Labour displacing the Liberals, and Tanner, D., *Political Change and the Labour Party 1900–1918* (Cambridge, 1990) who argues in favour of the continuation of the Progressive alliance.

3. Smyth, J., 'Labour and Socialism in Glasgow 1880–1914: the electoral challenge prior to democracy' (unpublished Ph.D. thesis, University of Edinburgh) 1987, pp. 127, 141.

4. Glasgow Labour History Workshop, 'Roots of Red Clydeside: the Labour Unrest in West Scotland, 1910–14', in Duncan, R. & McIvor, A. (eds) *Militant Workers: Labour and Class Conflict on the Clyde 1900–1950* (Edinburgh, 1992), pp 84–6.

5. Smith, J., 'Taking the leadership of the labour movement: the ILP in Glasgow, 1906–1914', in McKinlay, A. & Morris, R.J.(eds) *The ILP on Clydeside 1893–1932: from foundation to disintegration* (Manchester, 1991) pp. 65–71.

6. Paton, J., *Proletarian Pilgrimage: An Autobiography* (1935), p. 199.

7. Joseph Duncan letters, NLS Acc. 5490. 21 Jan 1906.

8. Paton, *Proletarian Pilgrimage*, p. 208.

9. Paton, *Proletarian Pilgrimage*, p. 208; McKibbin, *The Evolution of the Labour Party*, pp. 49–50.

10. ILP Archive, Harvester Microform collection, Series 2 pt. 1, NAC minutes and related records, Card 49, Item 53, 'Register of lapsed and seceding branches, March 1910–28 Feb 1911.

11. Hutchison, I.G.C., *A Political History of Scotland 1832 – 1914* (Edinburgh, 1986), p.247.

12. McShane, H., and Smith, J., *No Mean Fighter* (1978), p38

13. McShane & Smith, *No Mean Fighter*, pp 38–9.

14. Smith, 'Taking the leadership'.

15. Smyth, 'Labour and Socialism in Glasgow 1880–1914' (thesis), pp. 126–7.

16. McKibbin, *Evolution of the Labour Party*, pp 84–5.

17. Glasgow Labour Party, minutes, 'Report for Annual Meeting', B.A. Shaw, 22 April 1913.

18. This issue is dealt with in detail in Smyth, 'Labour and Socialism in Glasgow 1880–1914', chapter 2; see also Smyth, J., 'The ILP in Glasgow, 1888–1906: the struggle for identity', in McKinlay & Morris, *The ILP on Clydeside*.

19. Labour Party, 13th. Annual Conference, Glasgow 1914, Souvenir, (Glasgow Labour party), p. 38.

20. GLP, minutes, 21 Dec 1911.

21. The co-operators were to contribute 20 per cent of the Party's central finances. GLP, minutes, 30 June 1911.

22. The basis of representation was to be five delegates from the Co-operative Defence Association, three each from the trades council, the ILP and the SDP, and two each from the Fabians, the Women's Labour League, Govan trades council, and each LRC. The women's committee of the SDP was refused affiliation. GLP, minutes, 13 June 1911.

23. McKibbin, *The Evolution of the Labour Party*, pp. 30–1.

24. GLP, minutes, single page, typed dated 26 June 1918, by Edith M. Hughes (secretary) and Wm. Shaw (chairman) giving a brief history of the Glasgow Labour Party.

25. Smith, J., 'Labour Tradition in Glasgow and Liverpool', *History Workshop*, XVIII (Spring 1984), p. 35; also Smith, 'Taking the leadership' p. 63.

26. On this see Hutchison, *Political History*, pp.242–5.

27. *Socialist Review*, Sep. 1911.

28. *Socialist Review*, Oct. 1911.

29. *Socialist Review*, May 1911.

30. Anderson, W.C., 'The Significance of the Labour Unrest', *Socialist Review* Oct. 1911.

31. *Socialist Review*, Dec. 1911.

32. *Socialist Review*, Oct. 1911.

33. *Socialist Review*, Feb. 1912.

34. *Socialist Review*, May 1912.

35. *Socialist Review*, July 1912.

36. *Socialist Review*, Aug and Sep. 1912.

37. *The British Socialist*, Vol. 2, No. 1, 15 Jan 1913.

38. *The British Socialist*, Vol. 1, No. 2, 15 Feb. 1912.

39. *The British Socialist*, Vol. 1, No. 3, 15 March 1912.

40. *The British Socialist*, Vol. 1, No. 4, 14 April 1912.

41. Milton, N. (ed), *John Maclean: In the Rapids of Revolution* (1978) p. 62. 'The times we are living in are so stirring and full of change that it is not impossible to believe that we are living in the rapids of revolution.' Speech to Renfrewshire Co-operative Conference, 25 Nov. 1911.

42. Howell, D., *A Lost Left: three studies in socialism and nationalism* (Manchester, 1986), pp161–171.

43. *Justice*, 24 Feb. 1912. Quoted in Howell, *A Lost Left*, p. 162.

44. Smith, 'Taking the leadership' p. 79.

45. *The SDP News*, Dec. 1910. The whole matter of Maclean's close political relationship with Petroff and the latter's influence on Maclean' thinking is explored in, Rodgers, R., & Smyth, J. 'Peter Petroff and the Socialist Movement in Britain 1907–1918', in Slatter, J., (ed) *From the Other Shore: Russian Political Emigrants in Britain, 1880–1917* (1984).

46. BSP, Conference Report 1913. My emphasis.

47. Rodgers & Smyth, 'Peter Petroff' p. 102. It should be pointed out that other authors have denied Petroff had any influence on Maclean at this time, Ripley, B.J., & McHugh, J., *John Maclean* (Manchester, 1989), p. 30.

48. Smith, 'Taking the leadership' p. 75; Gordon, E., *Women and the Labour Movement in Scotland 1850–1914* (Oxford, 1991), pp 258–9.

49. Quoted in Howell, *A Lost Left*, p. 162.

50. Hutchison, *Political History*, pp. 257–9.

51. *Glasgow Herald*, 5 Nov. 1913.

52. *Glasgow Herald*, 4 Nov. 1914.

53. *Forward*, 13 Nov. 1909.

54. The most thorough treatment is Melling, J., *Rent Strikes* (Edinburgh, 1983).

55. *Forward*, 8 Nov. 1913. As a result local activists did not canvass for their candidates.

56. GLP, minutes, 24 Oct. 1913; Ripley & McHugh, *John Maclean*, pp 67–8.

57. Hunt, E.H., *British Labour History 1815–1914* (1985),p. 295; McKibbin, *Evolution of the Labour Party*, p. 86.

58. Glasgow Labour History Workshop, 'Roots of Red Clydeside' p. 81.

59. Clegg, *History*, p. 223.

60. McKibbin, *Evolution of the Labour Party*, p. 76.

61. Tanner, *Political Change*, p. 336.

62. Hutchison, *Political History*, p. 265.

63. GLP, minutes, 24 May 1913.

64. Smyth, 'Labour and Socialism in Glasgow 1880–1914' (thesis), p 141.

65. Cronin, *Industrial Conflict*, pp 53, 109.

66. This is borne out negatively in a recent biography of Wheatley which makes no mention of the labour unrest, presumably because it made no impact upon Wheatley. Wood, I.S., *John Wheatley* (Manchester, 1990)

67. Gordon, E., *Women and Labour Movement*, pp 283–4.

68. J. Keir Hardie, *From Serfdom to Socialism* (1924) quoted in Morgan, K.O., *Keir Hardie: Radical and Socialist* (1975) p. 208.

69. Howell, D., *British Workers and the Independent Labour Party 1888–1906* (Manchester, 1983)p. 334.

70. *Socialist Review*, Oct. 1911.

71. Smith, 'Taking the leadership, p. 70; see also Gordon, *Women and Labour Movement*, p 259.

Index

Aberdeen 52, 241
Abbott, Fanny 207
Ackland, Alan 185
Agriculture 7, 8, 22
Agricultural Labourers' Union 8
Allen, William 159, 172
Alston, James 228, 229
Amalgamated Association of Tramway-
   men and Vehicle Workers 229
Amalgamated Society of Dyers 49
Amalgamated Society of Engineers 20,
   98- 101, 103
Anarcho-syndicalism 8, 185
Anderson, W.C. 247
Anderson, W.F. 137
Apprentices strike,
engineering and shipbuilding 29-30
Arbitration Boards 52, 76-77
   see also Board of Trade
Ardrossan and Saltcoats Herald 36
Ardrossan Harbour Company,
use of strike-breakers 31, 49, 146
Ardrossan harbour strike 24, 31 36, 146
Argyll Motor Company, Alexandria 25,
   59, 206
Askwith, George (Board of Trade) 35,
   59, 139, 155, 160, 185
Asquith, Herbert Henry 156
Association of the Chambers of Com-
   merce 2, 35
Association of Foremen Engineers 93,
   103
Ayr 136

Balfour, Arthur James 155

Barnes, George 205, 244
Battersby, John 221, 234
Bayne and Duckett's, Glasgow 29
Belfast 139
Bell, Tom 21, 194, 203, 205, 206
Biggar, J.M. 126
Bird, John 159
Blanchford, John 243
Blackleg labour
   use of 10, 11, 30-31, 49
   Scottish/UK statistical comparisons
      31, 49,
   see also strike-breaking
Blacklisting 13, 48-50
Board of Trade,
   Labour Department 11, 61, 161
   Reports on Strikes and Lockouts 23-
      24, 72, 75, 76, 78, 139, 164,
      178, 185
   Strike statistics, problems with 25, 83
   Directories of Industrial Associations
      46
   Arbitration services, 121, 232
   Real wages survey 198
Boilermakers' Union 52, 94, 96-7,
Bo'ness 148
British labour historiography 1910-14
   2-15
British Locomotive Works,
company housing 56
British Socialist Party 5, 243, 249-50,
   251, 252
Bridgeton 194
Building industry 4, 8, 22, 52, 53, 71,
   80

259